𝄆: The Music of Our Lives

: THE MUSIC OF OUR LIVES

Kathleen Marie Higgins

TEMPLE UNIVERSITY PRESS
Philadelphia

Temple University Press, Philadelphia 19122
Copyright ©1991 by Temple University.
All rights reserved
Published 1991
Printed in the United States of America

The paper used in this publication meets the minimum
requirements of American National Standard for
Information Sciences—Permanence of Paper for
Printed Library Materials, ANSI Z39.48-1984 ⊗

Library of Congress Cataloging-in-Publication Data

Higgins, Kathleen Marie.
    The music of our lives / Kathleen Marie Higgins.
        p.   cm.
    Includes bibliographical references.
    ISBN 0-87722-756-X
    1. Music—Moral and ethical aspects.   2. Music—
Philosophy and aesthetics.   I. Title.
ML3920.H5   1991
781.1'7—dc20   90-34259

For my parents,
Kathryn and Eugene Higgins,
who taught me to seek harmony

Music do I hear?
Ha, ha! Keep time. How sour sweet music is
When time is broke and no proportion kept!
So is it in the music of men's lives. . . .

—Shakespeare,
Richard II, act 5, scene 5

Contents

Acknowledgments : xi

Introduction : 1

1. Music "in Itself": Its Development and Status : 10

2. The Many Faces of Form : 47

3. Music and Emotions: The History : 81

4. Music and Emotions: Theories, Problems, and
   Suggestions : 99

5. The Ethical Aspects of Music: Music as Influence
   and Educator : 138

6. The Ethical Aspects of Music: Music as Metaphor,
   Symbol, and Model : 164

7. How Music Can Assist Philosophical Ethics : 191

Notes : 207

Bibliography : 235

Index : 245

ǁ : Acknowledgments

Many people have influenced my understanding and thought about music. My father, Eugene A. Higgins, and my brother, Timothy P. Higgins, have no doubt had the most sustained impact on what I hear when I listen to music. But others have also had a marked influence on my ability to listen and perform. My professors of music at the University of Missouri–Kansas City developed my understanding of music and musical thought as well as my ability to analyze and articulate musical details. Of these, James Evans and Marjorie Ounsworth had the strongest influence on my musical understanding and my ability to make music, and Marion Petersen and LeRoy Pogemiller contributed most to the development of my analytical skills and framework. I also owe much, on all of these fronts, to my counterpoint teacher, John L. Swanay, who taught music as a kind of flying. John expanded my musical horizons with his conversation and his record collection. Perhaps more than anyone else, he made me appreciate music as spiritual and magical.

Other friends, too, have added insight and delight to my musical experience. In particular, Richard C. McKim and Garret D. Sokoloff have turned me on to some of the greatest music I know and have often given me new insights into what a particular piece of music is about. Others whose conversation over the years has enhanced my musical life include Jenene Allison, Lynne Beaty, Frances Berenson, Mary Bodine, J. Byron Butts, Peter Czipott, James P. Davis, Peter Derksen, Dionisio Escobedo, Wanda Farah, Janice Frey, Ron Grant, Nettie Hornbuckle, Kevin Kissinger, Christopher Middleton, Nicholas Partridge, Stephen Phillips, Diana Raffman, David Ring, Jorge Valadez, and Sanford Weimer, M.D. In particular, I wish to thank Paula Fulks and Douglas Buhrer, who not only have exchanged music and ideas with me for many years, but have also been willing to accommodate my various musical enthusiasms.

Many people, from various fields, have helped me to develop the ideas involved in this specific project. My dissertation adviser, Karsten Harries, has shaped my aesthetic thinking in innumerable ways, which are no doubt reflected throughout this book. Sarah Canright has been an inveterate compatriot in aesthetic discussion, and much of my treatment of art's relationship to life has been strongly influenced by our conversations. Steven Feld and Stephen M. Slawek have been tremendously generous in helping me learn about non-Western music. Patricia Muoio is responsible for turning my attention to the importance of time in ethics and philosophy generally. Among others (besides those mentioned above) whose conversation and presentations have furthered my work on music and ethics are Philip Alperson, Elliott Antokoletz, John Benoit, Frances Berenson, Timothy Brace, Christopher Brooks, Donna Buchanan, Victor Caston, Renée Cox, Stephen Davies, Aaron Fox, Cynthia Freeland, Roger Gathmann, Mary Gilbert, Lydia Goehr, Roger Graybill, Douglass Green, Lars Gustafsson, Jean Gabbert Harrell, Eileen Heaney, Jay Hullett, Jo Ellen Jacobs, Peter Kivy, Robert Krunden, Jerrold Levinson, Robert McDermott, Louis Mackey, Bernd Magnus, Joseph Margolis, Alexander Nehamas, Susannah Page, Rita Vonn Prater, Jenefer Robinson, Sandi Salstrom, Janet Sepasi, Anita Silvers, Francis Sparshott, Michael Tanner, Laurence Thomas, Alan Tormey, Leo Treitler, Bruce Vermazen, Kendall Walton, Susan Walton, Paul Woodruff, Julian Young, those who attended the Conference on Philosophy and the Human Future (sponsored by the Rockefeller Foundation and the Esalen Institute) at Cambridge University in August 1989, and the students in my various aesthetics courses and my humanities course on music.

The analysis in Chapter 2, in particular, was assisted by comments from a number of audiences to whom I presented certain sections of it. Among the individuals and audiences that I wish to thank in this connection are Tom Moody, John Passmore, Thomas K. Seung, and the audiences at California State University–San Bernardino, Simon Fraser University, the University of Auckland, the University of Texas at Austin, and the Australasian Association of Philosophy meeting in Perth, May 1988.

Projects like book-writing rarely reach completion without the background support of many people. My editor, Jane Cullen, has been continually helpful and encouraging. Although each has been mentioned in other contexts, I wish especially to thank Jenene Allison, Douglas Buhrer, Sarah Canright, and Paula Fulks for "being there" through the whole long course of this project. Peter Czipott, too, has been not only morally but editorially supportive. I am deeply grateful for his detailed comments on every chapter.

My family, besides tolerating years of my piano-playing at unusual hours, has been both an inspiration for this project and a source of stability. I would therefore like to take this opportunity to thank the various individuals who compose it: Eugene and Kathryn Higgins, Timothy P. Higgins, Colleen Cook, Jeanine Felten, Maureen Higgins, and James Higgins. Finally, I wish to thank Robert C. Solomon, essentially for everything.

‖: The Music of Our Lives

1 : Introduction

"Benevolence is akin to music," Confucius tells us; Plato claims that "musical training is a more potent instrument than any other, because rhythm and harmony find their way into the inward places of the soul, on which they mightily fasten, imparting grace, and making the soul of him who is rightly educated graceful, or of him who is ill-educated ungraceful."[1] The pervasive influence of music, and its intimate connection with our ethical outlook, has been a matter of cross-cultural comment for millennia. The world's philosophical traditions have often treated music as a central tool for the promotion of harmonious living for both society and the individual.

But this idea seems foreign to most contemporary Americans. When I've mentioned my interest in writing a book on music and ethics, more than one acquaintance has asked, "Do you mean the controversy between Frank Zappa and Tipper Gore?" For most Americans, "rock lyrics gone wrong" is the paradigm case of music having an ethical impact. Only occasionally does one hear of the ethical impact of music apart from lyrics, and then usually as a complaint. Allan Bloom's controversial *Closing of the American Mind* devotes an entire chapter to lambasting the depravity of rock music, which in his view has "one appeal only, a barbaric appeal, to sexual desire."[2] His vitriolic attack on a whole species of music lacks even the qualified tolerance that Nikita Khrushchev voiced when he conceded, "We are not against all jazz music. . . . But there is music which makes one feel like vomiting, and causes colic in one's stomach."[3] Bloom at least "remembers" music serving a positive ethical function, although he despairs of its operation in a society that dances to rock 'n' roll.

Bloom is right in thinking that music can provide "cultivation of the soul" and express humanity's "noblest activities . . . while providing a pleasure extending from the lowest bodily to the highest spiritual" aspects of the human being.[4] But he is wrong to withhold this praise from any but our tradition's classical repertoire. In this, he makes a common and pernicious rhetorical move. Bloom praises the glories of a fictitious past when everyday folks (at least the well-to-do) found spiritual sustenance in classical music (which in Bloom's usage comprises the output of a single continent over twice as many centuries). But this praise demeans our actual musical lives, in which most of us hear music almost continuously and have unprecedented resources for experiencing the wealth of music produced throughout the world and the course of our own history.

Bloom's move is pernicious because it reinforces the poverty that *does* characterize our everyday musical experience, while failing to acknowledge that it is a poverty of riches. Music is so pervasive in our environment that many of us are startled by silence; but we often feel its presence as an intrusion. For most of us, our everyday encounters with music are neither "encounters" nor "experience" in any meaningful sense. No wonder, then, that the thought of "spiritual experience" or "ethical edification" from music seems as foreign to us as Bloom's lament suggests.

The irony is that musical experience is more available than ever before. Developments in recording technology have done more than produce stars and millionaires. Recorded music can give us experiential access to an incredible range of music, a range spanning centuries and the world's cultures. While serious questions remain regarding the appropriate way to approach the music of other cultures, we have the unprecedented opportunity to *experience* it. But for the most part—with exciting exceptions like "Afro-Pop"—we take little advantage of this possibility, either as institutions or as individuals. We hear more music than our ancestors in any other era of history, and yet our sense of music's contribution to life is singularly impoverished.

In this book, I have written about musical experience from the standpoint of philosophy. This field reinforces and is imprisoned by this same tendency to demean our everyday lives. Philosophy encourages aesthetic and musical insensitivity. In doing so, philosophy itself becomes "unmusical" and "anesthetic."

As a society we regard our everyday lives as virtually immune to transformative aesthetic experience, as John Dewey complained in *Art as Experience*. Dewey blamed this on Americans' tendency to put "art" on a distant pedestal. If what he says is true with respect to all art—and I think it is—his complaint is particularly apt with respect to music. Philosophy in America, moreover, has contributed to the problem by reinforcing the divorce between "objects worthy of its consideration" and the everyday world. To be sure, philosophical discussion may not have wide-ranging cultural impact on American musical habits, but that in itself is a manifestation of the dissociation between musical aesthetics and everyday life.

Contemporary American philosophy has little place for music, let alone for the music of everyday life. Musical aesthetics is a marginal phenomenon within aesthetics, and the whole field of aesthetics is treated as a "fringe" of philosophical concern. I suspect that, in response to this marginalization, aestheticians frequently adopt more "impressive" stylistic models from other, "technical" areas of philosophy, describing the arts in overly serious and somber dissections, with as many gestures toward precision as possible. Although most willingly admit that aesthetics cannot aspire to "more precision than it admits of," in Aristotle's phrase,[5] recent writers have assumed that it admits of a remarkable degree of precision—distorting, I argue, both the arts and aesthetic sensibility.

In musical aesthetics, such endeavors have a built-in scaffold. Western musical notation is designed to provide precise indications of pitch and rhythm. Thus, musical aestheticians have frequently set to work on the musical score, ignoring or even denying the importance of the performer and, for that matter, the listener. Nelson Goodman, for instance, considers the score the sine qua non of the musical work, so much so that if one departs in the slightest detail from the written score, one has not, on his analysis, performed the work.[6]

The problem with this is that the score just isn't the music. Not that most philosophers are likely to say that it *is*. Francis Sparshott calls it a "recipe" that provides an "opportunity" for the experiences of musical performance and listening.[7] And few besides Goodman would consider it "the truth, the whole truth" about a musical work. But the score receives undue attention. And as a consequence, the sphere of discussion becomes quite narrow. Improvisation, for example, is treated as aberrant, even though this characterization describes most of the world's music. And nonnotated features of musical experience—the vital character of performance as well as the where, the when, and the circumstances of listening—are rarely discussed.

Conservatism, ethnocentrism, and divorce from experience characterize the now established philosophical approach to music. They result from what is seen as a requirement of philosophical procedure: restriction of one's topic to yield precise results. But such restrictive analysis involves deliberate disregard for the points of connection that one phenomenon may have with another. If the idea of discussing music's connection with ethics sounds bizarre to today's philosophical audience, this is partially due to a methodological obsession with keeping subject matters distinct and isolating music not only from morals and social philosophy but even from its performance and enjoyment.

American philosophical thought, I believe, has lost a great deal through its obsession with topical distinctions. One such loss is the disappearance of music's ethical dimension from philosophical discussion. In this book I want to resurrect this ancient but still relevant concern. Our loss of sensitivity to the ethical dimensions of music coincides with a cultural tendency to treat music as a "background" phenomenon or a mere means to reinforce other messages. (I recently received an advertisement for a tape boasting "Subliminal Weight Loss with Pachelbel's Canon.") But what gets ignored are aspects of musical value that would be plentifully available if they were both noticed and nurtured. Music's capacity to engage our intellectual, emotional, and physical natures simultaneously, its suitability for promoting social cohesion, its reflection of practical and ideal modes of human social interaction, its ability to stimulate reflections regarding our basic values—consider the role of music in churches—all these are basic features of musical experience. Yet these are lost to philosophical attention when "music" is defined as "a musical score" and aesthetics becomes a technical enterprise.

In order to demonstrate and diagnose what has been lost, I begin by tracing the history of philosophy's willful amnesia. In Chapter 1, I contrast the narrowness of the term *music* in the discussion of most philosophers with the wide range of musical phenomena that ethnomusicologists have brought to our attention. To account for this discrepancy, I trace the history of music's gradual "objectification" in Western thought, that is, the process by which "music" came to be thought of less as an immediate experience and more as an entity that transcends space and endures beyond its own performance. The extreme expression of this development can be found among the philosophical proponents of musical "Platonism," who contend that music is an ideal entity, only imperfectly embodied in this world. In Platonism, the divorce between music and its real-life contexts becomes absolute.

One reason for this divorce has been the aesthetic fixation with form. In Chapter 2, I consider the philosophical arguments that launched aesthetics (in particular, *musical* aesthetics) on its formalist course. I examine Immanuel Kant's formalist aesthetic and Eduard Hanslick's defense of musical autonomy with an eye to their depiction of music and their concern with musical form. Despite Kant's own difficulty in fitting music into his aesthetic scheme, his analysis retains both an appreciation of experience and a recognition of the resonance that we often sense between the aesthetic and the moral realms. Hanslick, by contrast, emphasizes "objective" structure over experience (even experience of structure); and in defending music's status as fully "intellectual," he sets out to refute the ancient adage that music has good effects on "morals." Hanslick's version of formalism is thus considerably more inimical than Kant's to a recognition of music as ethical. And

Hanslick's analysis has had much greater impact on musical aesthetics. Yet I demonstrate that even such emphatic focus on form in musical aesthetics is more compatible with recognizing music's ethical character than Hanslick was willing to acknowledge.

In Chapters 3 and 4, I argue against formalist reduction in musical aesthetics, and insist on the reinstatement of one of the factors that Kant and Hanslick explicitly remove from its purview: music's emotional features. After briefly sketching the development of thought on music's relation to emotion in Chapter 3, I show in Chapter 4 that it parallels the history of Western thought about the relationship of music and ethics before Hanslick. When the field of musical aesthetics embraced a Hanslickean focus on structure and eliminated all consideration of context and emotion, it found little room left for an association of music and ethics. Recent defenses of music's connection with emotion tend to tie emotion to structure, and thus to miss the ethical features of musical experience that stem from contextual factors. But an appreciation of such factors is essential to an accurate account of what listeners value in musical experience. Recognition of nonstructural features of music (including many relating to context) would redirect aesthetic attention to the "ethical" features of music that I cited above.

In Chapter 5, I show how the nonstructural components of musical experience suggest reasons for believing that music has an "ethical aspect." Music's affective character, which involves intersubjective empathy and often shared delight, makes listeners socially aware of their intimate connection with others—and does so in a context in which social and individual existence are not at odds. Engaging in satisfying shared experience heightens our receptivity and emotional sensitivity. Music's motivation of listeners to appreciate the range of affective experience (and often its nuances) without the situational pressures that would lead them to decisive action (and to taking emotional sides) also enhances sensitivity to the motivations and emotional perspectives of other human beings. By so developing our potential to understand others, music serves a role of decided ethical significance. Aesthetic recognition of the importance and the extent of the emotional texture of musical experience should, therefore, lead to an appreciation of these "ethical" effects.

Recognition of the physiological bases of musical experience would also pave the way for renewed recognition of music's role in "harmonizing" our powers—physical, emotional, and intellectual. Music enlists the entire "self." "The good life," the ultimate aspiration of ethics, requires the balanced and harmonious operation of these basic aspects of our beings. By providing experiences of exactly such operation *and* by demonstrating the satisfaction that it affords, music develops our capacity for good living and encourages our conviction that life can be harmonious and satisfying.

I argue here that a narrow, structurally based formalism has been largely responsible for the disappearance of the ethical dimension from philosophical accounts of music. But if "form" is understood more broadly—in terms of symbols and not just as mathematical structure—form itself can be seen as a basis for connection between music and ethical life. In Chapter 6, therefore, I consider the symbolic roles that music has served in various societies. Music, I argue, can stimulate the ethical imagination by presenting fluid "forms" reminiscent of fundamental patterns in human experience. Ethnomusicologists have indicated music's "modeling" of basic ideas for social organization and interaction. Philosophers and critics have noted music's capacity to parallel the satisfactory resolution of tension in our organic and practical lives. Outside the Western tradition, Indian musical aesthetics is built upon the idea of using music as a basis for detached reflection and insight into emotional and spiritual experience. To trivialize the association between music, emotional context, and social relations is to trivialize basic features of our listening response to musical form. Of course, associations provoked by music range from the humanly universal to the solipsistic; and any philosophical approach to musical association must recognize and take account of such broad variations. But to ignore such associations—or to use them as an excuse for avoiding consideration of affect altogether—is to sever from philosophical attention a basic way in which music can stimulate and guide reflection on the patterns of temporal and practical living.

In Chapter 7, I suggest that music can assist reflection in philosophical ethics as well. The field of philosophical ethics has been dominated by an obsession with questions of moral conflict and with special instances of the moral dilemma, that crisis-ridden moment in which moral decision is required. By focusing on such moments of crisis, usually analyzed with little attention to context or the circumstances or personalities of the agents, ethics has underemphasized the dynamic but nondramatic character of ethical life as actually lived. The recent emphasis on game theory in ethics testifies to moral philosophy's lack of concern with either complexity or temporality in our ethical experience. Ethical choice is treated as a "game" in which clean choices can be made and judged as "right" or "wrong" without concern for the particular persons or contexts, except so far as these can be described in terms of "utility preferences" and "risk aversion." Not surprisingly, such abstraction in ethical theory discourages, and implies the irrelevance of attending to, the connection of ethics with music and musical ways of thinking.

The recent philosophical countermove toward "virtue ethics" testifies to the need felt by some philosophers to integrate consideration of the on-going, continuous character of our behavior into models for ethical thinking. Music, I argue, can assist in this important effort. Music presents textured, temporally extended developments of complex patterns in process; and most of the music of our classical tradition is constructed on the principle of developing satisfying resolutions from complicated tensions. Such patterns, I suggest, can serve to stimulate thought regarding the successful resolu-tion of tensions—as opposed to decision theory's overly rational solutions to narrowly defined problems—in ethical contexts as well.

Minimally, music can assist the development of ethical models. Music typically presents visions of coherent, ultimately satisfying arrangements of discrete elements in continuously changing tension. I suggest the jazz solo as an example of a musical model for ethics with respect to the interaction of individual and group, or minority and majority populations in a com-munity. The model of harmony and counterpoint here provides us with a far more appealing resolution to our most serious social problems than the usual statistic-mongering, policymaking, and politicking.

But beyond this, attention to musical experience can suggest a better central model for ethics than the moral dilemma. The traditional emphasis on the moral dilemma in ethical thought is symptomatic of a perspective that seeks atemporal, abstract "solutions" to ethical problems while paying virtually no attention to the practical, transitional considerations involved in implementing them. In addition, mainstream ethics has largely ignored the possibility of organizing the temporal structure of one's life in such a way that its tensions do not become "moral dilemmas." Music reveals the possibility of coherent and dynamic conceptions of our ethical situation as involving problems in transition and tensions that need not necessarily be considered problems. Music, I submit, is a better model for human life.

The happy human life is my concern in ethics. My aim is to investigate ways in which music might make life happier. Mainstream philosophical ethics tends to restrict its concerns rather narrowly, to peculiarly "moral" dilem-mas and their resolution. By contrast, I construe the term *ethics* broadly. Ethics, as I understand it, is concerned with thought-mediated human be-havior. The range of behavior involved extends from action chosen as a result of detailed deliberation to habitual, even "mechanical" behavior, but in all human behavior, thought or attitude plays some causal role. Ethics uses reflective consciousness to influence our behavior. Ethics is also the practice of self-consciously cultivating attitudes and habits, including habits of thought.

But ethics is essentially social. The very term stems from the Greek word *ethos,* which means custom or character. Decisions and actions occur in a societal context, which determines much about their human significance. The possibility of harmonious living within a community is an essentially ethical concern. Ethics inquires into what makes a human life valuable from the point of view of the person who lives it and desirable from the point of view of the community in which the person lives and interacts with others. What I do *not* mean by "ethics" is some set of purely rational moral rules that may or may not be conducive to happiness and that transcend all particular persons, their contexts, and their emotions.

The focal choices of life and the major decisions that settle moral dilemmas are important matters of ethical interest. But so are a host of less conspicuous matters, including how one balances the diverse demands one faces in everyday life as an adult. Relevant to ethics are the range of details and the implicit models that comprise one's way of living and interacting with others. Music, I argue, illuminates some of those details and provides some valuable models.

Over the course of my discussion, I inevitably reveal several of my own ethical biases. I am not concerned, however, to advance a particular ethical position. I am approaching "ethics" here as an inquiry into living well and getting along with others, and I want to ask how music can further this reflection, both for sensitive human agents and for philosophers.

My use of the term *music* also deserves comment. I use the term to refer to a general category. As I observe in Chapter 1, "music" means different things to different people, and different senses of the paradigm case can yield radically different conclusions about what matters in music. The presumption of those who focus on the classics of either the Western or the Indian tradition is that detachment is the appropriate stance of the listener, while those who think of rock 'n' roll when they hear the word *music* are likely to consider detachment a sign that the music is poor.

My reason for using the category term *music* is that I mean to address possibilities available in our musical experiences taken collectively. I do not suppose that an individual's musical experience in modern American culture is likely to be homogeneous or of even quality. But I do mean to suggest that reflection on our musical experiences (even some of our worst ones) can be of value to our ethical lives. Because I am concerned with the average American's musical life, I focus on the experience of listeners. I am convinced that more active, practical experiences with music—performance, composition, improvisation, and amateur music-making—can similarly benefit ethics, but I focus on the more widespread phenomenon of listening. My point is that the typical American musical life, as already constituted, is potentially valuable to ethics.

These claims do not entail that every human encounter with music has a positive effect on ethics, or even that every such encounter is desirable in some respect. I am assuming that the typical American's life includes at least some musical experiences that he or she values, and that the reasons for this are relevant to life outside the experience of music.

I am convinced, in addition, that openness to a broad range of musical possibilities is of value to developing ethically valuable capacities, such as openness to other human beings in general. But my basic case does not depend on the breadth or narrowness of particular listeners' musical exposure. The general features of musical experience that I depend on—such as the implicit sociability of musical experience, the multiple aspects of the listener that are simultaneously addressed, the susceptibility of "humanly organized sound"[8] to symbolic interpretation, and its suitability to provoke analogical thought—are common to experiences of music of virtually all types and for everyone.

Admittedly, my discussion is located in a context—specifically, the context of American listening experience. I do not presume to discuss the nature of what every musical listener in the world gets out of music. Instead, I focus on the range of musical experience available within my own society. But—and I think this is important—the range of music available to Americans is incredibly large. Recording technology has made music from around the world available for American consumption. Our *own* musical experience involves the music of other societies (and the "fusion" productions of diverse cultural interactions) as well as that of many popular traditions, in addition to Western classical music.

This diversity is another reason I talk about "musical experience" generally. I am interested in the diversity of musics available to us, and the diverse contributions that they might make to our lives. Insofar as some musics give more prominence to particular inherent potentials of sound for experience, and insofar as some of these potentials provide the basis for a comparison with certain features of ethical life, consideration of the range of our experience is essential to my effort. Music is a means of exploring the wealth of our ethical world.

1 ‖: Music "in Itself": Its Development and Status

Music is a product of the behavior of human groups, whether formal or informal: it is humanly organized sound.
—John Blacking, *How Musical Is Man?*

Music . . . is sound understood in response.
—Roger Scruton, "Analytic Philosophy and the Meaning of Music"

"Music," as commonly used, may refer to sound, a piece of paper, an abstract formal concept, a collective behavior of society, or a single coordinated pattern of neurochemical impulses in the brain. It can be a product or a process. . . . For now let "music" signify anything that is normally called "music." —Lewis Rowell, *Thinking about Music*

What Is Music?

Music, to most of us, would seem to be an unproblematic term. We know it when we hear it, and that seems sufficient for most purposes. But the persuasiveness of the claim that music bears a relationship to ethics depends on what is meant by *music.* And when a definition is demanded, the term turns out to be anything but clear. In setting out to discuss music, we must immediately confront the problem: what is music and what is it not?

How can we define music? The compositions of Bach, Beethoven, and Brahms certainly count as music. Presumably, the works of the Beatles and the Rolling Stones do, too. But does everything that the Sex Pistols, or even Lou Reed, have recorded count as music? And what about John Cage's notorious "4′ 33″," a "composition" that consists of four minutes, thirty-three seconds of silence? Can silence count as music? Does the term *music* imply a certain level of quality? Is it appropriate for someone to say of trivial background music, "That isn't really music"? Does music have to be produced by human beings? Is birdsong music? Is the howling of wolves? What about whalesong, or music produced by machines?

Bruno Nettl observes that even music dictionaries published in the West usually "avoid the definition of music in its most fundamental sense." As he points out, the second edition of Willi Apel's *Harvard Dictionary of Music* discusses the etymological history of the term, but "without specifically attempting a definition." Paradoxically, the more recent *New Harvard Dictionary of Music*, edited by Don Randel, does not include the term at all. Music encyclopedias tend to be a bit more helpful, but their characterizations of music remain vague. They tend, says Nettl, to "suggest that music is made up of tones, that it has emotional impact, and also that it is an art, in the sense that it is something people *do,* as well as a science, that is, something about which they think in a systematic, disciplined fashion."[1] *The Macmillan Encyclopedia of Music and Musicians*, for instance, defines music as

(1) in the general sense, the art of tonal expression registered through the sense of hearing; (2) the science of combining tones to create melody in combination with harmony and rhythm; (3) the written or printed copy of a musical composition; (4) the performance of a musical composition.[2]

On this definition, interestingly, the term *music* is more basically used to refer to a score (3) than to a performance (4), a matter to which we return below.

Webster's emphasizes some of the same features that Nettl observes in music encyclopedias, although the later definitions include many other phenomena as well (such as birdsong):

1. the art and science of combining vocal or instrumental sounds or tones in varying melody, harmony, rhythm, and timbre, especially so as to form structurally complete and emotionally expressive compositions.   2. the sounds or tones so arranged, or the arrangement of these.   3. any rhythmic sequence of pleasing sounds, as of birds, water, etc.   4. (a) a musical composition; especially the written or printed score of this; (b) such compositions collectively; as the *music* of Brahms.   5. ability to respond to or take pleasure in music; as, he has no *music* in his soul.   6. a group of musical performers. (Rare or Obs.)   7. liveliness in speech or action; excitement. (Colloq.)[3]

The cluster of tones, emotion, art, and science thus recurs in the nontechnical definition of *Webster's*. But Nettl is quick to point out that, although it represents a consensus, this cluster is culture-bound. "There are societies and musics where these criteria make no sense at all."[4] When the range of music's cultural contexts is taken into account, the term *music* resists a clear, universally applicable definition.

The Evidence of Ethnomusicology

The idea that music consists of definite tonal structures, for instance, would make little sense to members of the Basongye tribe of the Congo. The Basongye do not conceive of musical intervals as absolute distances; some of our distinct intervals are not distinguished in their musical practice. They treat major and minor seconds more or less interchangeably, for instance, and the same is true for major and minor thirds.[5]

The idea that music has emotional impact, although common to a number of cultures, is far from universal. The Navajo consider the impact of music to be medicinal, not emotional. Music is good if it cures the patient, bad if it does not.[6]

The Western idea that music is an object of aesthetic contemplation is not extended to all sorts of music in the West (even when this term is taken to apply only to Europe and most of North America). Jazz is an obvious example of music that most Westerners take to be participatory. Another is rock 'n' roll (in that appropriate response involves at least moving to the beat). Rock is not primarily seen as a phenomenon for contemplation (hence the oddity of rock magazines, which Frank Zappa describes as interviews with those who can't talk by those who can't write for those who can't read). Neither are hymns in church or the songs performed at sing-alongs.

If we look farther across the world, we find that music has a wide variety of functions. Alan Merriam notes ten such functions (including "symbolic representation of other things, ideas, and behaviors" and "enforcing conformity to social norms"), only one of which is directly linked to aesthetic value; and he is hesitant to claim that all cultures consider music to be an object of aesthetic enjoyment. He concludes that while many societies may view music as an object of aesthetic enjoyment in our Western sense, it is clear that some do not. The literature of ethnomusicology, moreover, is replete with examples of societies that do not share another assumption Westerners often make about art: that good art is a product of special talent, not common to everyone. In many societies, the ability to make music is considered a universal human capacity.[7]

Nettl's use of the plural term *musics* suggests a difficulty in our task of defining *music* that may not have occurred to many of us. We tend to think of music as all of a piece, even as "the universal language," but the evidence of ethnomusicology suggests that music is not a single, natural kind. Even if the use of musical instruments seems to be common around the world, the significance of their use may vary considerably. As Sparshott puts it, "Who is to say that all pipings belong together, much less that all pipings belong with all drummings?"[8]

An account of music's ethical character must address this difficulty. Indeed, the ethical dimension of music for many cultures depends on a paradigm of music different from the one we are accustomed to in the West. And the West's recent disinterest in music's ethical dimension is related to its own conception of music. How we construe the term *music* determines our ability to see it as ethically relevant.

The Western classical tradition is unique in taking the paradigm of music to be a musical *work* that endures over time, and whose existence is established once it is notated, whether or not it is ever performed. This tendency of the Western classical tradition, developed over the past several centuries, allows us to think of music unproblematically as a natural kind. In Jan Broeckx's words, we identify "the concept of 'music' with the totality of all actual and conceivable musical works—and nothing but that."[9] This move to identify "music" as a set of works of music may sound innocuous, but we will see in the course of this chapter how it has assisted the creation of serious gaps in our understanding of music, not only the music of other cultures, but that of our own culture as well.

Even on first inspection, the characterization of "music" in terms of "works of music" is obviously faulty, or at least incomplete, for it does not apply to all music. The music of the world does not all conform to the Western model of the "separate, identifiable, coherent, intentionally developed and individually composed" work. Even a significant percentage of Western music fails to match this description. Broeckx cites four major categories of music that resist it:

A) Musical products, lacking a preconceived, written composition: e.g.: Improvisations and Tape-Music (= sonorous compositions, directly planned and realized on tape); B) Musical products of non-individual authorship (or products the authorship of which is either uncertain or of which the impact on the ultimate, sonorous result is indeterminable: Multi-individual and Collective products in Avant-garde Music, in Jazz-Music and in Folk-Music; Quotation-Music and Traditional liturgical Repertories (e.g. Gregorian Chants); C) Musical products of non-autonomous function and character: Film-Music and some types of Incidental Music; D) Musical products without fixed beginning and termination, with indetermined course and variable extent and with heterogenous contents: Full Aleatory Music and Background-Sounds.[10]

The Quest for a Common Denominator

We could resign ourselves, in our quest for a definition of music, to a set of disjunctive characterizations, each of which describes music as conceived by a particular culture or group of cultures. But the applicability of Broeckx's categories to many instances of music in our own culture suggests that there may not be a single conception of music reigning even within a given culture at a given time. And clearly different conceptions of music reign within a culture at different times. Full aleatory (that is, "random") music may be acknowledged as music by most serious present-day musicians in the West, but it would not have been considered music by the musically literate contemporaries of Beethoven.

That a single conception of music may not be common even to the members of a single society is further supported by the range of cultural characterizations of music studied by ethnomusicologists. Many cultures do not have a term equivalent to our term *music*. Our term describes a wide collection of phenomena; and while other cultures might have similar phenomena, they often categorize these phenomena differently than we do. Nettl observes, for instance, that the Iranian singing of the Koran is not considered music by Iranians. The phenomenon primarily identified by the term most similar to our *music* (*mūsīqī*) is instrumental music. The distinction grounds an important difference in status. The singing of the Koran is a valued religious practice, while *musiqi* is "in certain ways an undesirable and even sinful activity" that must, as a concept, "be kept separate from religion." Philip Gbeho similarly notes that African Gold Coast "music" is understood to include "drumming, dancing, and singing," which are "all the same thing, and must not be separated." The Navajo have no word for music at all, while the Blackfoot use their term for "dance" to include music used for dancing (but no other music).[11]

But is there really no common denominator among the various phenomena in the world that we might describe as "music"? Perhaps we are seeking too much detail in our definition and ignoring obvious basics. Charles Culver suggests a candidate for a common denominator when he observes that we in the West tend to distinguish musical from nonmusical sounds on the basis of acoustic criteria. Music involves "sounds with regular and periodic vibrations."[12]

But this fails as a universal criterion. Scraping sounds are considered musical in some cultures if they are so designated by context. Merriam observes that this is true for certain African tribes, and Steven Feld notes that scraping sounds are frequently an element in women's work songs among the Kaluli tribe of Papua, New Guinea. The Japanese folk music of the Ainu people of Hokkaido Island includes a form called *upopo* ("sitting song"), which is "noted for its polyphonic texture produced by imitative group singing and the beating of chest lids (*hokai*) by the singers." Haydn's "Toy Symphony" is a Western example in which traditionally "unmusical" sounds are employed. And countless others can be found in recent Western popular music (for example, Kate Bush's use of whalesong in her song "Moving").[13]

Nettl observes that the phenomena that we colloquially include in our category "music" are rather arbitrarily chosen: "Birds sing, we say, but not donkeys and dogs. . . . The sound of a machine is not music unless it is produced in a concert with a program that lists its 'composer' and with an audience which applauds (or at least boos)."[14] Many theorists would disagree that our description of birds "singing" is evidence that we believe birds to be making music. Moreover, Westerners typically consider music to be something produced by human beings, and, indeed, this might be considered essential to a definition of music. (Computer music poses a problem for this criterion, but presumably it could be described as ultimately a human product, albeit a highly mediated one, in that humans have constructed the computer's compositional program.) John Blacking does loosely define music as "humanly organized sound."

But the demand that music be made by human beings is not universal. The nightingale's songs are considered musical models by classical Iranian musicians. And the Kaluli tribe of Papua New Guinea interprets forest sounds as musical in an even stronger sense. The Kaluli themselves make duets with birds, cicadas, and other forest sounds; and they often sing when near a waterfall, for they consider the waterfall to be a desirable musical accompaniment. When Plato's Socrates in the *Phaedrus* tells the story of the cicadas being granted the Muses' favor because of their constant singing, we might consider this to be metaphorical "singing." But contemporary American philosopher Charles Hartshorne considers many animals to be literally "music-making," among these not only songbirds but also the gibbon ape and the humpback whale. And Hartshorne does not use the term *music* metaphorically in this context. He argues that some species of songbirds have "a primitive aesthetic musical sense" that is not only biologically useful but motivated by "an innate capacity to enjoy the making and hearing of musical songs," and that "the song of birds . . . has (in many cases at least) a definite musically analyzable structure."[15]

Regarding a definition of music, Nettl concludes, "If music can be defined, it cannot easily be circumscribed, its boundaries are unclear."[16] As recordings of the world's range of music become increasingly available to us in the

West, this conclusion seems unavoidable. A strict definition of music can be maintained only at the price of excluding many phenomena that one could and might want to call "music." More perniciously, as I argue in the latter half of this chapter, philosophical adherence to a rigid definition of music in terms of "musical works" has led many philosophers to counterintuitive misunderstandings about the nature of music as a phenomenon in human experience.

Nevertheless, we need a working description of our subject matter. I use the word *music* as a category term identifying a broad and open-ended range of intentionally produced auditory phenomena. Although Western classical music occupies an important part of this range, popular music, non-Western music, and even what is often dismissed as "background music" are also among the phenomena I mean to examine.

Within this general characterization my purpose is to examine the kinds of relationships that music has and can have with the rest of human experience and to consider the ways in which music can serve as an imaginative point of departure for thought about extramusical life. The amorphous boundaries of "music" that Nettl observes are, for my purposes, desirable. I aim to defend the desirability of conceiving of music much more broadly than philosophical aesthetics typically has done, and of recognizing that the significance of music depends on the context in which it is experienced.

The Importance of Musical Context: A Preliminary Defense

Although often theoretically neglected, one of the most important features of music is experiential context. Most musical experience throughout history and across cultures has been imbedded in extramusical experience—indeed it is unimaginable without it—and the extramusical has had decisive impact on the meaning of music for the listener. Until recently, music in the West and elsewhere was almost always associated with community events that excited, entertained, or at least involved other senses besides the auditory. Traditionally, music has usually been employed in connection with civic, religious, or social events that contribute significantly to the way it is understood.

The contrasting ideal of the distraction-free concert hall as the appropriate context for listening to music is a recent ideal even in the West. The idea of listening to music for its own sake and deliberately minimizing other stimuli would have been unintelligible to pre-Baroque musicians and listeners. And even since the Baroque period, when the large concert hall was developed, music has been employed in many other contexts, contexts that contribute significantly to the listeners' experience *of the music,* even if one is narrowly concerned with the sense the listener makes of what he or she hears.

Religious employment of music in the West, for instance, still plays a significant role in the musical lives of many people. The religious context contributes to and even defines the meaning that the music has and is intended to have. Consider the different audience experiences at a heavy metal rock concert and at a Christian rally where "heavenly metal" is played. ("Heavenly metal" is a form of rock that resembles heavy metal but has Christian lyrics.) And when we look beyond our own very specialized and ethereal employment of music in the concert hall, we find that music divorced from context is a foreign idea to most people in the world and even in our society. American popular musics tend to have their own performance settings, be they nightclubs, dances, public streets, hotels, empty warehouses, or suburban garages. The setting has much to do with what one looks for in the musical experience. The fact that the automobile is such a standard setting for musical experience for many of us allows us to ignore the situated character of our encounters with music.

If only to avoid rightful charges of elitism and ethnocentrism, philosophical aesthetics should address the nature of musical experience as it occurs for most people, that is, within a context that contributes significantly to its import. Instead, the field has recently occupied itself excessively with musical structure, and notatable structure at that. This obsessive focus on structure has preempted any consideration of music's possible relationship to ethics. But as soon as context is considered, music's central position within a cultural ethos is evident.

One overwhelming reason musical aesthetics should attend to context has to do with the *value* of music. One of the most important and most obvious cross-cultural values of music is its power to induce social cohesion. Music brings people together, and the way in which it brings people together often impresses them as profound. Music is often said to "move one deeply" or to "stir one to the depths."[17] Although other experiences might be similarly described, music is exceptional in affording such powerfully personal experiences to many people at the same time. The most striking feature of experiencing great music is often one's sharing it with others. And this sense of sharing is one of the things that people value most in hearing music. (One might object that many people enjoy isolated listening, a fact attested to by the popularity of the Walkman. But this is the aberrant case of musical experience. I am convinced that its frequency in our society reveals a cultural loss of intersubjective musical contexts that speak to our spiritual needs.)

A disastrous consequence of the common tendency in recent musical aesthetics to ignore context in favor of structure has been that the field has lost sight of music's intersubjective experiential character. Admittedly, attention to structure involves focus on publically observable features of music; thus the emphasis on such features in recent musical aesthetics cannot be criticized for ignoring *all* intersubjectively observable features. But these features are more "objective" than "intersubjective," in the sense that they can be conceived as definitive of an "object," understood apart from any subject actually experiencing it. The experiential dimension of listening is deemphasized or entirely ignored in the structural accounts that many recent aestheticians consider definitive of musical works.

The experiential dimension of music includes such matters as expectations regarding the work's style and its role in the larger context of one's daily life, models (sometimes metaphorical or analogical) used in apprehending and following the course of a work of music, and emotional and behavioral responses to the music's "objective" features. Such experiential aspects are what I mean to highlight in my "contextual" approach to music. Expectations, models, and responses *are* contextual features, for they can be observed and considered only when one locates musical structures within a context of human expectation that is conditioned by societal belief, thought, and practice. As I argue at a later point, these are also the bases of music's legitimate claim to have an impact on ethical life.

This "contextual" dimension is properly called "intersubjective." It can be appreciated, or even recognized, only when the musical "object" (however understood) is situated in the context of a community of subjects who experience it in a fashion informed by common beliefs and expectations. Greater attention to context would thus involve greater attention to music's social nature. And attention to music's social nature, I believe, is indispensable to an account of why music is so important in human life.

A Working Definition of Music

While I reject the goal of finding a precise and limiting definition of music, I see some value in certain definitions that have been proposed, as long as they are understood as rough characterizations of use for certain purposes. The various definitions at the head of this chapter, for instance, all indicate some important feature of the range of phenomena I mean to discuss. The open-endedness of Lewis Rowell's definition resonates with my purposes of considering music as an imaginative catalyst, and of exploring the ways in which this role can assist ethical reflection. "Anything that is normally called 'music'" may be stimulating to the imagination, as may any sound productions that are not necessarily called "music" by their producers. Therefore I do not peremptorily exclude anything called "music" from consideration. However, I want to focus on music that also concurs with Blacking's and Roger Scruton's respective characterizations as "humanly organized sound" and "sound understood in response."[18] Both of these definitions call attention to the social and cultural matrices from which specific musics emerge.

I consider a cross-section of musical phenomena, though perhaps not a particularly balanced one. To the extent that I am discussing the understanding listener's experience of and response to music, I sometimes focus on musical examples that have been greatly admired by many or noteworthy in engaging audiences, particularly in positive ways. No doubt booing, hissing, and walking out on a performance are distinct responses of their own; but because I am largely concerned with the range of positive contributions that music can make to our experience, I believe it legitimate to emphasize its outstanding achievements. However, I use other examples that may seem remarkably banal, even offensive, to some readers. I see no reason the value of a particular instance of music as an occasion for reflection must reflect the aesthetic value that one might place on it.

Primarily, however, I emphasize valued experiences of listening, allowing the reader to insert his or her own examples. This may result in some degree of idealization of musical experience. But this consequence is justified in the same way that any account of "aesthetic experience" is justified. "Aesthetic experience" has often been described as blissful, ecstatic, and absorbing, so much so that one might feel hard put to think of many of one's actual experiences, realistically recalled, as "aesthetic experiences" at all. In actuality, our aesthetic experiences are diluted by distractions of all sorts, including (in the performing arts, at least) that caused by mediocrity or incompetence in performance.

I believe that we are, nonetheless, justified in idealized accounts of aesthetic experience. These accounts describe what is important and treasured in our experiences of "aesthetic" phenomena (however defined), despite the fact that few of these experiences may strike us as near-perfect. Similarly, while our musical experiences (which are often "aesthetic" experiences as well) may not actually be as focused or full as we might wish, discussing them in terms of what they may optimally provide is useful. At the very least, such a treatment has the potential to encourage us to be more receptive toward the emphasized features of music in our future musical experiences.

As a consequence of my interest in the production and experience of music in a wide range of human contexts, I emphasize the auditory character of music. I also take as primary the perspective of the "understanding" listener (the listener who finds particular instances of music intelligible, at least to some threshold degree, within their particular contexts). Because I am mainly interested in music as performed and experienced, as opposed to music as an abstract object, I consider "music as performed" paradigmatic, rather than "music as composed." Surprising as it may seem, this emphasis on performed music as the paradigm case goes against the grain of many of the most prominent aesthetic theories of music of the past hundred and fifty years.

Music in Itself: Hanslick's Intellectual Legacy

The emphasis on music as heard marks a rebellion— I would like to think a populist rebellion—against the dominant view in nineteenth- and twentieth-century Western musical aesthetics, which treats performance as inessential to what music is. The musical formalism that has come to dominate musical aesthetics since Hanslick's *On the Musically Beautiful* (1854) sees music's essential aspect as a stable structure that can be notated in a score. It is the score, not the performance, and certainly not the listening, that represents the reality of music. Hanslick is forthright in denying that performance is essential to a work of music: "philosophically speaking, the composed piece, regardless of whether it is performed or not, is the completed artwork."[19]

Formalism can be defined in various ways. The term *form*, on which "formalism" is based, admits of a broad range of meanings, each of which may be useful for some purposes. In attacking the dominance of formalism in musical aesthetics, I do not mean to deny that "form," in the sense of "recognizable organization," is fundamental to music of virtually any description. I do not know how one could even begin to describe musical experience without some such concept in mind. The "formalism" I am rejecting is the range of views that take the essential aspect of music to be structure independent of performance.

I want to consider the historical developments that contributed to the rise of this view and also the ontological position that is their most extreme modern descendant: musical Platonism. In the next chapter (as well as those succeeding it), I concentrate on "aesthetic formalism," the view that form is the only essential focus of aesthetic appreciation of music. While musical Platonism and aesthetic formalism answer very different questions about music ("What is music?" and "What is the proper focus of aesthetic appreciation of music?" respectively), their common tendency to view music as a formal structure makes them heir to a common intellectual lineage, one that I see as damaging to our ability to appreciate music fully.

Formalism has come to dominate the field of musical aesthetics since the middle of the last century. That actual performance has come to be seen as dispensable to a conception of music is suggested in Jerrold Levinson's essay "What a Musical Work Is." According to Levinson, the consensus view holds the musical work (the object of focus in current philosophical discussions of music) to be a kind of abstract object, specifically "a structural type or kind."[20] The work is specified by means of structural elements that are "fixed," typically in a score. Any performance of a work must correspond (with more or less accuracy) to these structural features. To the extent that performance offers us more than the structure, it gives us something in addition to (and inessential to) the properties of the musical work as such.

The Objectification of the Musical Work

How has Western thought come to see music as a set of "abstract structural kinds"? Rowell offers a clue when he observes that the history of Western music can be analyzed as a history of music's gradual objectification.[21] That is, music has increasingly come to be viewed as an object in itself, enduring over time and independent of any particular performance. One of the primary developments that have assisted the objectification of music is the evolution of musical notation.

Although the ancient Greeks had a kind of letter notation to designate pitches, their music was essentially improvisatory. A step toward the objectification of music was made by the Christian church, beginning with Pope Gregory I (A.D. 590–604). Gregory and the popes who succeeded him attempted to standardize the diverse liturgical chants that had grown up in the Christian world into a uniform musical practice. This effort resulted in the development of a standardized notation. The earliest notation for liturgical chant indicated melodic contour, although duration was not very precisely indicated.

Over time, musical notation became increasingly elaborate. The addition of a line to the diagrammatic notations for melodic contour in the eleventh century added more precision to what was communicated, and gradually this addition led to the development of the multilined musical staff. In the thirteenth century precisely assigned rhythmic values were added to the notation. These developments in notation assisted the shift in Western music from an improvisatory performance tradition to a tradition based on composition.[22] In addition, they enabled composers to indicate complicated musical structures to performers, a possibility that was rapidly exploited.

The development of musical printing in the Renaissance promoted both an emphasis on composition and the objectification of music. With musical printing, the composer gained greater control over the performances of his music. Musical printing also enhanced another trend that resulted from expanded notational resources: the tendency for the composer's and the performer's roles to be distinct, enacted by different individuals. As a result of the invention of musical printing, multiple copies of scores were easily produced and disseminated. Thus, the making of music became increasingly associated with musical *works,* which could be performed repeatedly, by different musicians, and in different locations. The musical work, in turn, was increasingly viewed as a construction that a composer established once and for all, without assistance from a performer.[23] And as the score itself became more prominent in its own right, it came to be considered an artwork itself, quite apart from its being performed.

As the Renaissance gave way to the Baroque, another trend assisted the growing prominence of the idea that "music" primarily referred to structurally designated musical works. Compositional practice began to favor harmonic over contrapuntal organization, and this change required an increasingly structural vision of a given musical composition as a whole. Contrapuntal music of the Renaissance involved the independent movement of several melodic lines. Although great efforts were made to minimize dissonance between voices, no emphasis was placed on the specific progression of chords. Baroque music retained a contrapuntal conception of distinct melodic voices blending with one another. But the freedom of these voices was constrained by a new ideal: the chords resulting from the movements of melodic lines themselves were to move in accordance with musically coherent chord progressions.[24] Simultaneous musical tones were thus comprehended as a single structural unit, and successive musical events were understood in terms of logical progressions from one term to another.

The Baroque's transformed conception of dissonance also reflected this increased tendency to think of music in terms of structural units. The Renaissance ideal was that intervallic distances between simultaneous voices should be perfect consonances (unisons, fourths, fifths, and octaves) at all structurally important junctures, including virtually every beginning of the metrical beat. Even imperfect consonances were considered relatively dissonant. And dissonances were tolerated only in relatively inconspicuous positions (for example, when used as "passing tones," which arise in the context of two consonances that were approached by stepwise motion, or in strictly defined ornamental roles).[25]

By contrast, the Baroque ideal not only tolerated dissonances—it manipulated them. Indeed, dissonances were "liberated" precisely because the harmonically structured music of the Baroque could give them positive structural functions. Dissonances could motivate harmonic movement. Chords that included dissonant intervals were experienced as demanding resolution, in the form of a chord without (or with less extreme) dissonance. With composition now comprehended much more in terms of harmonic teleology than formerly, dissonance could be seen as a means to an end. The increased use of dissonance in Baroque music thus reflected the development of the idea that musical compositions were unified structures, with every part subordinate to the structure as a whole.

Theoretical advances underscored the move toward harmonic organization and directed the attention of those attempting to understand music both to structural features and to the structural expanse of the work as a whole. Jean-Philippe Rameau's many theoretical innovations were based on the science of acoustics. Among these were the development of such concepts as chord inversions and acoustically based chord progressions. Rameau's discovery of chord inversions was the discovery that a chord consisting of three tones—let us say C, E, and G—would retain its identity to the ear regardless of which tone were the lowest and which the highest. Thus, the triad C–E–G (moving, left to right, from lowest tone to highest, with "C" here referring to middle C) is in an important sense *the same chord* as the chord E–G–C (where E and G remain the same tones as before, but C is the C above middle C) and also the same chord as the chord G–C–E (where G remains the same tone as before, but C is the C above middle C and E is two whole tones above that). This insight is exploited in many ways in both classical and popular music after Rameau; the practice of "singing harmony" for community songs and hymns is a common practical employment of this principle.

Despite the common identity of a chord through its inversions, one of the tones is fundamental and is called the "root" of the chord. Chord progression depends on the relationships of the roots of successive chords. Although any chord can follow any other in principle, certain successions are more satisfying to the ear. The reason for this satisfaction, as Rameau explained it, is that the motion from one root to another is distinctly perceived. Successions in which this is the case are called "progressions," and these can be "strong" or "weak" depending on the particular intervallic distances between roots of adjacent chords. Rameau systematically analyzed the relative strength and weakness of various progressions based on acoustic theory. Taken up in practice by composers, Rameau's account indicated which chords were more and less likely to succeed others and to what effect (for example, to create a cadence or to further the opening of a phrase). These developments and others assisted composers' efforts to build and unify their works around organized structural principles.[26]

The tempered tuning system, another innovation of the Baroque era, also helped to entrench the idea of the musical work as a structure made up of structurally comprehended components. It did so by facilitating modulation from key to key, thus enabling the composer to write works with discrete sections in different keys. The motivation behind a new tuning system stemmed from an observed problem with tuning on an acoustically pure basis. Accustomed as we are to the piano, many of us may casually think of G-sharp and A-flat as referring to the same tone when we see them in contexts like hymnals. Tones such as these, which can be described in terms of either their flat or their sharp relationship to other tones (the G or the A that stands a halftone away in this case) are termed "enharmonic equivalents," and the two names ("G-sharp" and "A-flat") are termed "different enharmonic spellings." In natural acoustics, however, G-sharp and A-flat are slightly different tones. This means that the tone that is the third tone of the E-major (G-sharp) scale is not acoustically the same as the fourth tone of the E-flat-major scale (A-flat). This discrepancy created practical problems. *The New Harvard Dictionary* summarizes the situation as follows:

> The chromatic scale can be expressed as a linear series of 12 fifths bounded by the pitch class A-flat and its enharmonic equivalent, G-sharp: A-flat, E-flat, B-flat, F, C, G, D, A, E, B, F-sharp, C-sharp, G-sharp. If these fifths are kept acoustically pure . . . , then enharmonic pitch classes such as A-flat and G-sharp will differ. . . . This enharmonic discrepancy is a practical disadvantage when, for example, an organist, transposing in order to match (say) the range of some singers, must use the out-of-tune G-sharp–E-flat as a proxy for the true fifth A-flat–E-flat. The remedy for this is temperament, which dilutes the acoustic discrepancy by distributing it among several intervals.[27]

The tempering system tuned on a basis slightly altered from natural acoustics, with the result that all keys were "satisfactorily in tune" but not necessarily modified by identical amounts.[28] By facilitating modulation, the

Baroque tempering system encouraged the harmonic organization of musical works. Besides facilitating clear sectional differentiation by means of key changes, tempering expanded the range of possibilities available within the constraints of harmonic organization. Increased focus on modulation also directed listeners' attention to harmonic organization, for modulations depend on the tones of all voices being heard in a new key, and this requires attention to the way in which the voices function together.

By the eighteenth century, music was understood in terms of "pieces of music," and these, in turn, had come to be thought of in terms of structure. Even those theories that retained the earlier emphasis on music's relation to emotion had come to focus on specific structural elements. The *Affektenlehre,* the German version of this theory, linked feelings to specific tonal patterns, which were thought to produce motions in the "vital spirits" of the human being.[29]

Earlier theories of the connection between music and emotion tended to acknowledge the importance of the performance situation in generating emotion and to focus on the most general aspects of a piece of music (scale pattern and rhythmic character) as the determinants of emotional association. The *Affektenlehre,* by contrast, held that musical formulas *in and of themselves* had affective power over human beings. Richard Wagner, in the next century, would integrate this idea of affectively powerful musical formulas into his basic compositional strategy. He argued that leitmotifs (musical themes and figures associated with specific characters, ideas, or things in the drama) could be structurally employed to convey impressions of inner and unconscious emotional life. Attention to structural detail had become so dominant over the preceding centuries that even Wagner, the primary romantic spokesman against musical formalism, embedded it in his fundamental principles of composition.

Formalism in Musical Aesthetics

The idea that a musical work is more essentially a structure than a performance was given its most powerful philosophical impetus by the aesthetics of the eighteenth-century philosopher Immanuel Kant. Kant argued that form and form alone was relevant to aesthetic judgment. Among those features of music relegated to irrelevance were its sensuous character and the context in which it appeared. Because Kant himself found the sensuous character of music to be more impressive than its formal nature, he had difficulty applying his analysis to music. And (like both the Platonic and the Islamic traditions) he also distrusted the sensuous element (and sensuality in general) and therefore endeavored to limit its aesthetic and philosophical significance.

Despite his own skepticism regarding music, the enormous influence of Kant's general aesthetic formalism extended to the person most responsible for the rise of musical aesthetic formalism, Eduard Hanslick. Hanslick developed a formalist account of music as a foundation for criticizing the popular view that music has an emotional meaning. Music, as Hanslick defines it, is "tonally moving forms." In other words, music consists of tones that are combined in transitory rhythmic and harmonic relations, and these alone give music its meaning and account for its beauty.[30]

Tonal relations are precise, unaffected by subjective differences among listeners, and this fact struck Hanslick as particularly important. Part of his motivation was his belief that musical aesthetics could be made "scientific," grounded in necessary laws. The problem he saw in emotional accounts of music's meaning was that no such necessary connection between music and definite emotions could be established.[31] Form, however, could be analyzed with a mathematical kind of precision. Arguing that the beauty of a musical work is a direct consequence of its formal features, Hanslick sought to show that musical beauty itself could be provided with a "scientific" explanation.

One of Hanslick's claims is critical for later musical aesthetics. While not denying that many people do enjoy other things besides musical form in listening to music, Hanslick insists that properly *aesthetic* appreciation focuses on form, and form alone. He contrasts "aesthetic enjoyment," which involves appreciation of formal "musical ideas," with "pathological" enjoyment. "Pathological," as Hanslick uses the term, does not mean diseased; instead, in keeping with its etymological link to "feeling," it refers to sensuous enjoyment. The term has as negative a connotation in Hanslick's usage as in ours, however. He disparages pathological appreciation of music as involving mere "sensation and reverie."[32]

By contrast, Hanslick applauds aesthetic appreciation, which requires intellectual sophistication. Pathological appreciation, in his view, is unworthy of the designation "aesthetic." For those who appreciate music pathologically, he notes sarcastically, "a fine cigar of a piquant delicacy or a warm bath produces the same effect as a symphony."[33]

Hanslick thus makes "aesthetic" an honorific designation for musical appreciation of the right sort. He has an obviously intellectualist notion of what this appropriate appreciation consists of, for he links it to the intellectual grasp of musical elements and their relations. More recent musical aestheticians have similarly tended to limit "aesthetic appreciation" to intellectual appreciation of form, similarly acknowledging that people can and do get other satisfactions from music.[34] Given this highbrow narrowing of the notions of "music" and "aesthetic," it is not surprising that the focus of musical aesthetics has been largely restricted to classical music of the Baroque and after, with almost complete neglect of pop, jazz, and the music of most other cultures.

Hanslick took it for granted that aesthetic appreciation of music occurs primarily when one perceives music as a listener. He was concerned primarily with *how* people listened. Thus, he acknowledged in this minimal sense the importance of musical *experience*, but he stressed sound's role as the *medium* through which form is perceived (not as something of comparable importance to form). Moreover, by insisting that form and logical structure are the proper concerns of musical aesthetics, Hanslick paved the way for later thinkers to take the score, rather than the performance, as the primary mode of access to a musical work. Hanslick is thus largely responsible for the extreme notion, current in musical aesthetics, that for those sufficiently trained, it is reading the score, rather than listening to an oftentimes flawed performance, that is the ideal source of aesthetic appreciation.

The move toward formalism in aesthetics involved several concomitant moves away from traditional ideas about music. As the musical work came to be seen increasingly as a formal structure, the familiar association of music with particular social and performance contexts was demeaned and, eventually, dismissed. This was a striking development.

Another was a reconsideration of the relation of music and texts. Even into the eighteenth century, music was paradigmatically associated with texts, and the legitimacy of purely instrumental music was still being debated. Indeed, as Carl Dahlhaus notes, even Jean Jacques Rousseau doubted that instrumental music, without the assistance of program notes, had anything intelligible to say.[35] Hanslick's formalism inverted this picture. Far from being a variant form of music, untexted music came to be seen as the paradigm case, while texted music came to be treated as the aesthetic exception.

The shift to the paradigm of untexted music was also a shift away from the traditional ground for associating music and ethics. The ethical character of music had traditionally been conveyed by means of poetry, not just the music. As music came to be seen as an autonomous structure, the association of music with ethical character began to appear more suspect. The obvious ground for the association of music and ethics—the text—was absent in the new paradigm. The general drift in musical aesthetics was away from concern with the ethical and social significance of music and toward more effete and specialized aesthetic and ontological concerns.

Musical Platonism: Formalism in Extreme

Recent musical Platonism is the most extreme development of the formalist vision of what music essentially is. As we have observed, this dominant account understands "music" as the class of (actual or possible) musical works and holds that musical works are abstract entities. Musical Platonism interprets these entities as akin to Platonic forms, in that they transcend the physical world in which performance occurs. Defenders of the Platonist position contend that performance can only imperfectly embody the musical work, which exists completely and abstractly prior to any embodiment.

I want to focus on three rather bizarre debates that have arisen in connection with the Platonist position. The questions involved are these: (1) Is actual sound essential to the existence of a work of music? (2) Does a work of music exist in any sense prior to its composition? (3) Is a musical score essential to the existence of a musical work? Not all Platonists answer these questions in the same way. Although Platonists generally consider sound inessential to music, it is possible to be a Platonist in this respect but not in others (or to be a Platonist in certain respects without acknowledging the affiliation). Thus phenomenologist Roman Ingarden, although sometimes criticized as a Platonist who considers sound inessential to the actual musical work, rejects the common Platonist position that a musical work preexists its composition. One may also, like Peter Kivy, consider "discoverism" (the view that musical works are "discovered" by their composers) to be a corollary to Platonism but reject the idea that a musical work requires a score.[36] My purpose here is not to refute any particular Platonist's views, but to show that Platonism tends toward a conception of music that is impoverished, detached from human experience, and, ultimately, demeaning to music.

Motivations for Musical Platonism

Musical Platonists all hold that the essence of a musical work is a kind of ideal entity, akin to a Platonic form. But various Platonists have offered various accounts of this ideal entity. Richard Wollheim contends, for instance, that the musical work has the status of a type (in C. S. Peirce's sense), while its performances have the status of tokens. Nicholas Wolterstorff describes the work as a norm-kind, which establishes the correctness or incorrectness of all performances of the work. Kingsley Price suggests that a work is a kind of composite Platonic entity; on his view, it is an ordered collection of essences of tones, each characterized by essences of loudness and of duration.[37]

One could marvel at the sheer abstractness of these accounts. Why would someone, hearing music, be led to such wild speculations? Unless one is similarly fascinated by the problem of the musical work's identity, a version of some longstanding problems in philosophy of language and ontology, one may find the Platonists' concern with universals a philosophical oddity, far removed from everyday musical experience. But certain everyday intuitions lend credence to the Platonists' view, or at least help us to see what the Platonists are trying to explain.

When we hear a familiar but scratchy record, for example, most of us try to listen past the scratches. We know what "the piece of music" sounds like, and we mentally tune out the scratches as irrelevant to the music. We assume that our knowledge of what the piece *should* sound like takes precedence over the details of our actual auditory experience. The Platonist might diagnose this as a recognition that a piece of music has an essence that underlies what we hear on a given occasion. Similarly, when we hear an amateur musician perform a well-known work with a few bad notes, we mentally correct for them in most cases and try to attend to "the work" despite them. A Platonist might tell us that it is our knowledge of the work's essential nature that allows us to recognize the bad notes in the first place.

Consider too the case of Glenn Gould's approach to recording. Most recordings of classical music record specific performances. A piece of music is performed start to finish, and recording equipment is used to preserve that performance. Gould, however, believed that recording techniques could be used to make a more perfect articulation of a work than could be attained by any specific performance. Recordings of Gould's performances, therefore, were often composites, which spliced together the finest articulations of a work's various parts that Gould achieved on many different "takes." Gould obviously did not consider any particular performance inviolable. Instead, he had a conception of the work, which he attempted to approximate with his best achievements in numerous performances or partial performances.

Gould's intuitions about the musical work—and the very notion that there can be a "best possible performance" of any given musical passage—could be interpreted as Platonic intuitions. And to the extent that we share his attitude, we share these intuitions. The Platonist reminds us that we often do compare actual performances of a work with a mental conception of how it ought to be performed. When we think this way, the Platonist argues, we are considering our mental *idea* to be what the work *really* is and considering performances to be better or worse depending on how well they correspond to it.

The Platonist is concerned with the essential nature of the *musical work*. Observing that we think it sensible to consider Beethoven's Fifth Symphony "real" even when it is not being performed, the Platonist worries about what kind of thing Beethoven's Fifth might be. Although performances take place in time and have both beginning and ending points in time, Beethoven's Fifth does not seem to operate on the same principles. The latter does not pop into existence when a performance begins and cease to be when it ends. Its existence does not seem to be contingent on its being performed. In fact, if Beethoven's Fifth Symphony had been composed but never actually performed, we still might want to say that it existed.

This interest in the musical composition's continued existence through time is a distinguishing characteristic of the Platonist. While an aesthetic formalist may be primarily interested in the tonal forms that he experiences on a particular occasion of listening to music, the Platonist is concerned with what endures. Both are focused on the work of music (as opposed to "music" understood more generally). But the Platonist is especially interested in the work's identity through time. The Platonist's concerns, therefore, are more strictly ontological than aesthetic.

Why, if aesthetic formalism stems from different basic concerns, do I consider Platonism an outgrowth of formalism? I do so because Platonism looks to formal structure alone as the essence of the musical work. In fact, it demands a structure of an even purer and more static sort than is demanded by formalism. A formalist like Hanslick can be satisfied, in his concern for form, with form *as heard* through the music. The typical Platonist, by contrast, considers form as heard to be a faulty embodiment of a more perfect and consistent abstract form. Insofar as musical formalism is defined by an exclusive interest in form, Platonism is more fully formalistic than most aesthetic views that are labeled "formalism," and it most completely embodies the tendencies I find objectionable in current accounts of what music is.

Assumptions of Musical Platonism

Before examining these tendencies as manifest in Platonism, however, I should point out that I do not aim to deny either the importance of the insights motivating Platonism or the need for some ontological explanation of the common denominator among different performances of the same work of music. What I take issue with is not the claim that the evidence demands some account, but the Platonist's understanding of what a good account would be. The Platonist assumes that a static, constant structure is the best explanation of what a work's various performances have in common, even if we can never find a performance that fully corresponds to it and even if we are not able to indicate it with precision.[38]

But why is this the best explanation? Ludwig Wittgenstein's notion of family resemblance, for instance, could ground an account that has important advantages over that offered by Platonism.[39] We could consider the common character of a work's various performances to be a family resemblance that is marked but not susceptible to precise specification, and thereby avoid the postulation of an abstract entity that we never fully encounter. This account would also avoid Platonist absolutism regarding which characteristics of a work's performance are essential and which are inessential. In experience, pitch, rhythm, harmony, timbre, attack, inflection, articulation, "swing," and the like are all found together. But the Platonist account christens some (usually the first three) essential, relegating the others to the status of accidents. As I argue below, this bias distorts the character of music. Certainly if we consider the standpoint of experience, this distinction is arbitrary (even if historically explicable).

And why must the "idea" with which we critically compare a performance be a rarified, timeless truth? Why should we not see it as a concretion made up of the musical elements the composer indicates, expectations that our experiences and stylistic convention have given us, and whatever ideas our own musical imaginations (as listeners) might produce? And why must the fact that an actual performance is an approximation to our idea be considered a liability? Perhaps the idea against which a performance is judged not only *is* but *should be* evolving or susceptible to redefinition.

Performance ideals do, in fact, vary among those most informed, performers themselves. In the case of present-day performances of Renaissance works, for instance, considerable debate reigns among performers and ensemble directors about whether modern or traditional instruments should be used and whether tuning should approximate that of the period or conform to modern convention. The Platonist, appealing to structure, might try to escape this debate by remaining neutral. But if this is the Platonist's solution, it fails to address some basic (and practically relevant) questions about the essence of the musical work. Or, following definitions like that offered by Levinson, the Platonist might build an abstract stipulation of performance-means into the definition of a musical work.[40] But this would still beg the practical question of whether a modern violin is enough like an eighteenth-century violin to satisfy the performance-means requirement.

For that matter, the Platonist contention that every instantiation of a work is imperfect suggests that arbitrating among degrees of quality is not a task for which Platonism is well suited. Could two Platonists, disagreeing about the relative merits of two performances of a work, use their ontology to adjudicate? It is not obvious how they could. Even if each had an ideal definitive performance sounding in his or her head, these "performances," too, would presumably be imperfect "embodiments" of a work, not the work itself. Platonism seems to dismiss most interesting practical questions as irrelevant to ontology.[41]

At the very least, the Platonist position rests on the debatable assumption that a static structure, however elusive, gives us a handle on the musical work. The Platonist insistence that a static model provides the best ontological account of the music we experience dynamically is itself a ground for controversy. The consequences of Platonism to which I turn in the next several sections, however, reveal more jarring problems with the Platonist account.

Do We Hear the Music?

Although we may share some of the intuitions that inspire it, the Platonist perspective entails a number of counterintuitive consequences, at least if its intention is to be faithful to our musical experience. One of these consequences is indicated by Price, who characterizes the essence of the musical work as "inaudible."[42] But if anything seems incontrovertible about music, it is the fact that we *hear* it. The Platonic "essence" of the musical work does not reflect this. The Platonist holds that we hear performances, not musical works themselves. The work is an abstract ideal, apparent to the intellect but not directly perceptible to our hearing.

Common sense rejects this account. It tells us that what we hear *is* music, not an inadequate and inessential replica of abstract structures. Moreover, the Platonist dichotomy between the "physical" sense of hearing and the "intellectual" recognition of form jars with our musical experience. In listening to music, we do not experience "hearing" prior to intellection. The *form* that analysis derivatively describes (and identifies as "the work") is *perceptible* through hearing. Hearing music *as music* already involves "intellectual" recognitions—recognitions of such things as themes, rhythms, and particular melodic elements.[43] As Roger Sessions observes, form "is something to be felt and perceived, and recognized, first of all, as sensation."[44] Even if it made sense in some cases to consider the human sense of hearing divorced from intellect, it would not make sense in the case of music. Sense and intellect operate as a unit as soon as one begins to hear music as music.[45]

The inadequacy of the Platonist perspective on the sensory and perceptual is indicated by Victor Zuckerkandl's analysis of our musical experience.[46] We experience musical tones, according to Zuckerkandl, as "dynamic forces" that point beyond themselves. I hear "My Favorite Things" (whether performed by John Coltrane or Julie Andrews) *as music* only when I feel a sense of direction connecting each tone with its successor. The tones are not isolated events. Instead, one tone seems a logical outgrowth of its predecessor, and successive tones convey to us a sense of forward movement. We hear not just a series of tones, but directed phrases.

Understanding music requires a recognition of this dynamic character of tones. But this recognition is perceptual, and does not depend on mediation by analysis. Our intelligent comprehension of music thus presupposes our perceptive engagement with it. If we have not perceived the dynamic tendencies in tones—if we have not preanalytically *felt* their tendencies toward movement and resolution—we have not understood the music.

One can gain an intuitive sense of the force of this point by considering the sound of a computer playing through a score or simply playing a melody (such as "Twinkle, Twinkle, Little Star"). A performer's musical understanding of a work ordinarily involves his or her impression of musical phrases, which he or she "brings out" in performance. The computer, lacking "musical" intelligence in this sense, plays the notes as written without accentuating the phrases. We have to impose a sense of the phrasing on the notes for ourselves. We find ourselves making an active effort to maintain a sense of phrasing because the computer does not give us the assistance that the performer's articulation usually does. The important point here is that we feel the *need* to think in terms of phrasing, even to impose it, in order to hear "music" in what the computer plays.

Because we perceive it as dynamic, music also makes a unique contribution to our understanding of the external world, as Zuckerkandl points out. We do not typically locate the music we listen to as occupying a specific distance from us. In this respect, our sense of hearing is unlike the senses of sight and touch, which are our primary means of establishing our relative distance from things. By contrast, hearing brings the environment to us. And musical hearing, in particular, by presenting our perception with dynamic forces, makes us aware of the world as a place of encounter and interaction between what is within and what is outside us.[47] Zucker-kandl sees this function of music as crucial to the significance music has in our lives.

The Platonic "essence of the musical work" does not encounter us in the fashion that Zuckerkandl describes. By definition, it does not depend on anyone's conscious attention to it, and thus encounter is irrelevant to its nature. But if our musical experience involves our awareness of dynamic forces and sense of being encountered, it would seem that the Platonic essence leaves something important out of the picture. Our comprehension of music *as music* involves appreciation of its dynamic character. The Platonic description, therefore, misdirects our intelligent attention.[48]

If Zuckerkandl is right that musical perception involves a sense of encounter with the external world, then Platonism's disconcern with musical context amounts to another deficiency as well, again one it shares with aesthetic formalism. And many ethnomusicologists, citing cross-cultural evidence, conclude that a sense of encounter with and connection to the larger world is one of the most important and universal contributions that music makes to the lives of its listeners.

These claims are important for my defense of a contextual account of music. For music's cultural context is crucial to the listener's sense that the world encountered through it is his or her *own* world. In the typical case of musical listening, the case in which one hears music of one's own cultural tradition, the environment one feels connected with is the intimately known environment of one's own cultural context. Catherine Ellis observes that the patterns evident in a society's music resonate with patterns that have been observable in the environment since childhood, and that these resonances make music a powerful force for societal cohesion.[49] Other ethnomusicologists have also argued that the organizational principles inherent in a society's music correlate with the principles it uses to organize other things, and that these correlations make music suited to mediate between individuals and their world. Blacking, for example, argues:

Music is . . . a metaphorical expression of feelings associated with the way society really is. It is a reflection of and response to social forces, and particularly to the consequences of the division of labor in society.[50]

And Nettl sees music's expression of basic cultural values as fundamental to its basic function in human life, a function which he takes to be "religious" in a broad sense:

The function of music in human society, what music ultimately does, is to control humanity's relationship to the supernatural, mediating between people and other beings, and to support the integrity of individual social groups. It does this by expressing the relevant central values of culture in abstracted form.[51]

Alan Lomax, who has devoted his entire career to elaborating the connections between music and societal organization, writes:

A culture's favorite song style reflects and reinforces the kind of behavior essential to its main subsistence effort and to its central and controlling social institutions.[52]

The Platonic quest for an "essence of the musical work," by radically decontextualizing works of music, overlooks an aspect of musical experience that is fundamental in the most typical case of listening (that of listening to music of one's own society). The experience of music in such cases involves not simply an encounter with "the environment," but a socially and personally intimate encounter with the specific cultural environment in which one lives and has developed.

By ignoring context and its contribution to the experience of musical listeners, Platonism excludes from its purview important grounds for believing that music can tell us something about ourselves and others. The claim that it *can* requires defense, of course. But Platonism forecloses the question before it is raised. And this points, I believe, to the most basic problem of musical Platonism. By rigidly limiting its concern in ontology of music to abstract structure, it ignores what the listener's active imagination might contribute to the music's being.

The Discoverist/Creationist Debate

The Platonist account has so little room for human involvement with music that it even has trouble explaining what the composer has to do with his work. Perhaps the debate associated with Platonism that sounds strangest to the nonphilosopher's ear is the discoverist/creationist controversy. This debate concerns the ontological status of the composer's activity. The creationist position holds that the composer brings something new into being in the act of composition. The musical work, on this view, does not exist before the act of composition.

The discoverist position, taken by some to be a corollary to Platonism, holds that the musical work does exist in some sense prior to the composer's creative activity. What the composer does is to "discover" preexistent tonal relations, selecting some, most often for possible performance. Wolterstorff, for example, describes the composer's work as a process of "selecting a certain set of properties which sound-sequence-occurrences can exemplify . . . for the purpose of their serving as criteria for judging correctness of occurrence."[53] The composer's selection of properties determines a norm-kind, which establishes the features that a correct performance of a work must have.

To our ordinary way of thinking in our musical culture, the discoverist position is counterintuitive, at least. Prereflectively it seems that the composer does something more like inventing or making than like finding. We are surprised when we hear that certain societies, such as that of the Navajo Indians, describe music as a discovery. And even in the case of the Navajo, the kind of discovery made is not an abstract discovery of the sort described by the philosophical discoverist. Navajo "discovery" is viewed as a matter of receiving a gift from the gods, which is very practical in its effect. By contrast, in American and European culture, we would probably interpret an artist's calling his or her works "discoveries" as an exercise of metaphoric license, as when Michelangelo described his sculpting as "freeing" the statues from the stones.

What arguments support the discoverist position? For many Platonists, discoverism is an innocuous corollary to their ontological position. If the musical work is an abstract entity, independent of anyone's consciousness, the composer's conscious attention can hardly be said to bring the work into being. A musical work, in the sense that it is an abstract structure, has a being much like that of mathematical entities. A mathematician who makes a breakthrough *discovers* a proof, and, similarly, a composer discovers the relational structure of his work.

When pushed, musical Platonists resort to rather contorted descriptions of *what* preexists composition. Donald Walhout, for instance, describes the work's status prior to composition as "existence as a possible state of affairs." James Anderson describes it in terms of abstract properties that together become a norm-kind in the act of composition, but which are independently describable beforehand.[54] And musical Platonists often admit that composition is an important creative activity. Nonetheless, for many it amounts to a "discovery" of musical relations that were always potentially "discoverable."

Most people's intuitions, I suspect, resist this analysis. Levinson, an adamant musical creationist, insists that creatability represents one of our most fundamental intuitions concerning art and that some of the value we place on musical compositions stems from this intuition. He goes so far as to contend that "creatability" must be included in any adequate account of a musical work. But Levinson does not offer much of a defense. Before deciding whether he is right in suggesting that creatability represents one of our most adamant intuitions about a musical work, we would need some independent idea of what he means by "a musical work." But Levinson begins his account of the musical work with the assertion, "Musical works must be such that they do not exist prior to the composer's compositional activity, but are *brought into* existence *by* that activity."[55] By foreclosing any account of the musical work that does not involve "creatability," he begs the very question we are concerned with.

Kivy, defending (although not clearly holding) the discoverist position, is quick to point this out. He observes that even if the "creatability" of a musical work represents an entrenched cultural intuition, this does not establish the validity of the idea. Moreover, he denies that it really is so entrenched. The idea that a composer is a godlike creator *ex nihilo,* he tells us, is a Romantic notion that became entrenched only in the nineteenth century. Wagner, who so admired mythology, created a myth of his own when he promoted this idea. But the more dominant historical conception in the West is that composers reveal truths about the world. And if composers are in the business of making revelations, it seems more appropriate to call their work "discovery" than to call it "creation."[56]

This final point is problematic. When people claim that a composer "reveals" something, they are not usually referring to the revelation of preexisting musical relations. Typically, they are referring to the expression of inner life that music is believed to accomplish. Or occasionally they mean revelation of the sort Zuckerkandl describes, revelation of the dynamic nature of the world and its interactive relationship with us. Or, if the claim is made by an anthropologist, it may refer to revelations of culturally specific patterns that typify a society's manner of relating to the world. Such revelations, although conveyed by means of tonal relations, are not, strictly speaking, revelations *of* tonal relations. Furthermore, this kind of revelation is not specifically the composer's aim. For the cultural patterns of thought detectable in music, if present, are so basic to the composer that one would hardly claim that he or she "expressed" them, or "presented" them with the intention of revealing them. Only rarely would someone mean by the claim that the composer reveals truth what Kivy takes it to mean, namely, that the composer achieves his goal when he "reveals" tonal relationships.

Kivy also conflates "creation" with the modern notion of "creativity," with its emphasis on originality. He is quite right that the Romantic notion of the creative genius who composes original works is historically recent. But the issue is not whether the composer is radically original (departing from the tendencies of his or her predecessors and contemporaries), but whether the act of composition brings something new into existence.

A further difficulty with the discoverist account of the composer's creative work stems from the fact that consciousness is left out of its purview. To say that a composer "discovers" musical relations would seem to imply that he or she consciously attends to them. But even if a composer might be said to "discover" musical ideas, it is not clear that this amounts to conscious focus on all relational characteristics of tones that might be consciously interesting—or "revealed"—upon analysis.

Indeed, many of the relational characteristics of the ultimate work may not be the product of the composer's "selection of tonal relations" at all. Typically, composers go through an experimental process in working out the final composition. A composer, for instance, may try various different musical phrases at a given point in a composition before deciding "that's it!" about one of them. And when he or she does decide on one of them, the criterion employed may well be that it *sounds* best, not that these are the abstract tonal relationships that he or she prefers.

Many composers describe their activity as an experimental process of elaborating a single fundamental *idea*. But this scarcely seems the same thing as a conscious exploration of the specific relations among the details "selected." Even a composer like Schönberg, whose emphasis on structure would seem akin to the emphases of musical Platonists, describes the ideational activity of composition in terms of developing a fundamental idea through a process of experimentation:

> I myself consider the totality of a piece as the *idea*: the idea which its creator wanted to present. . . . Every tone which is added to a beginning tone makes the meaning of that tone doubtful . . . and the addition of other tones may or may not clarify this problem. In this manner there is produced a state of unrest, of imbalance which grows throughout most of the piece, and is enforced further by similar functions of the rhythm. The method by which balance is restored seems to me the real *idea* of the composition.[57]

Beethoven also describes composition as the elaboration of an idea, again suggesting that the idea's "growth" is not entirely guided by a process of conscious selection:

> I carry my ideas about with me for a long time—often a very long time—before I write them down . . . then begins in my head the working-out in the broad, in the narrow, in the height, in the depth; . . . the fundamental idea never leaves me; it mounts, it grows, I see before my mind the picture in its whole extent, as it were in a single projection.[58]

The discoverist description of the composer's activity links it excessively to analytic awareness. But as many analytically trained listeners can testify, conscious analytic awareness can interfere with getting the gist of a musical passage, particularly the more one attends to musical details. It is plausible to suppose that the composer's excessive analysis of relational details could similarly interfere with his or her sustained awareness of the germinal idea. Perhaps many composers can create a musical "forest" only by being somewhat analytically oblivious of the trees. To the extent that a composer makes certain musical decisions intuitively, analytic focus on detail seems unnecessary or even undesirable.

Kivy, however, has another argument in defense of the discoverist position. "Creation" and "discovery," he points out, are not mutually exclusive concepts. Taking scientific discovery as a paradigm, he argues that discovery involves a certain amount of invention (often the invention of new instruments of observation), while human creation depends on and departs from what has been discovered. The analogy between scientific discovery and musical composition is, however, questionable. Science is driven by the quest for experimentally verifiable truth; and any candidate for the appellation "true" is expected to cohere with the entire body of other scientific truths. A "discovery" in science is so designated when it successfully passes these tests of experiment and coherence with other truths. No similar tests entitle us to call specific selections of tonal relations "discoveries" in this sense. In fact, it seems that *any* selection of tonal relations would qualify as a discovery in Kivy's usage. But if that is so, "discovery" is hardly an honorific. And it is very hard to believe that composers set as their goal simple "discovery" in this sense.

Even if Kivy's science analogy were reasonable in this context, his use of it represents a concession. For to the extent that his defense requires it, he, too, appeals to our intuition. Our custom of thinking of composition as "creation" does not logically preclude our acknowledging an element of discovery. Thus, our entrenched belief does not categorically deny the character of composition that discoverists view as most important. But at this point, the debate becomes largely verbal. The same aspects of the composition process can be described with either term, depending on what the speaker wants to emphasize.[59]

Renée Cox uses this point in defense of the creationist view. "Creation," she argues, is simply a better word for describing the composition process than "discovery" or "selection." "There is a seemingly infinite array of possible choices involved in the compositional process," she points out, and it hardly seems that composition is a straightforward selection from among them.[60] The composer does not have the range of choices laid out like candy jars from which to make selections. The part of the composer's work that seems "selection" in any usual sense is the process by which several possible passages, experimentally toyed with, are compared and one is ultimately selected.

Is musical composition more a matter of an integral idea that comes to the composer or a matter of selecting from myriad musical relations that are always abstractly available? Cox's creationist answer, I think, is closer to experience than that offered by the discoverist view. Only abstractly considered could the composer's work be described as "selection" from among the range of possible musical elements. As most composers describe their work, composition emerges from germinal ideas.

Cox makes another important criticism of the discoverist view as well. By analyzing composition as the selection of eternally available musical relations, the discoverists ignore "the dynamic nature of musical elements, relationships, and systems, all of which take on new meaning in different historical and cultural contexts."[61] The discoverist position has no room for meanings that are not inherent in the musical structure itself. Once again, context is utterly ignored. But even formal significance, as Cox observes, depends on a work's situation within a historical context. Thus, the discoverist view cannot sustain even an intellectualist account of musical meaning.

Again we find an absence of concern with what musical structure might mean *to us*. This is not in itself a refutation of the discoverist view, but it nevertheless indicates the narrowness of that view's conception of music, and even of "the musical work" that so concerns it. Abstracting the musical work from our experience, the discoverist view strips it of all but self-contained significance. The discoverist "work" is perhaps an admirable structure from an analytical point of view, but it is divorced from any meaning that depends on context or human response. The discoverist view ignores the fact that even the significance of formal elements is affected by historical context. Thus, it is not surprising that it completely ignores another kind of musical meaning, the experienced meaning that might answer the question "Why do people love music?"

The Score and the Musical Work

The third problem involved in many articulations of Platonism stems from an explicit or implicit requirement that a musical work be notated in a score. Platonists often take the score for granted. Levinson, for instance, remarks, "Scores are generally taken to be definitive of musical works, at least in conjunction with the conventions of notational interpretation assumed to be operative at the time of composition." Stephen Davies goes further, suggesting that scores are not only capable of defining a work, but also necessary (at least in Western music): "particular compositions . . . are independently identified with event-specifications which, in the case of the Western cultural tradition on which I shall concentrate, take the form of musical scores." Certain ontologists explicitly link Platonism with the requirement that musical works have scores. Wolterstorff, for instance, stipulates that a work can properly be described as "composed" only if it is notated in a score, and he argues that a corollary to his account of composition is "that to improvise is not to compose."[62] Not only is a score authoritative, but it is the only means by which composition can occur.

It is not difficult to see why a Platonist might adopt this position. The beauty of the Platonic model is that a musical work endures through time. But we are hard put to say what endures without some kind of enduring designation. And even if a musical work consists of abstract properties and relations on the Platonist account, we would like to be able to say something about them. A Platonist who is also a discoverist has an additional reason for concern with the score. If a composer is a kind of discoverer, who selects from the range of possible musical elements and relations, there must be some means by which he or she indicates which ones are selected. The score provides an obvious vehicle for designating selected musical properties.

One problem with this position, however, is that it ignores the fact that the score is not the only means through which structures of musical properties can be indicated. Broeckx criticizes the common failure to see this:

> I strongly reject the assumption that scores must constitute a theoretical necessity, or that they are the only practicable means of composing. The composition forms the mental aspect of the musical work, as distinguished from its material or sonorous aspect. But both aspects may be harmoniously blended in one and the same set of activities, whereby the purely imaginative process of composing is immediately materialized in sonorous results—either fixed on tape or improvised on musical instruments.[63]

To the extent that improvised pieces or unnotated recordings are musical works, a score does not appear to be a necessary condition of a musical work.

Another problem involved in the association of musical works with a score stems from the score's character as an idealization. In relation to performance, a musical score is an idealization in a double sense. It is both an abstraction and a normative guide for performance. The problem with the Platonist position is that it conflates these two senses and views the score's idealization as normative in a restrictive sense. The common-sense notion of a score's normative role takes the score to establish minimal conditions that must be approximated in order for a performance to be a performance of the work. The Platonist interprets the score as normative in a different sense, however: the score indicates the correct set of musical relations, which a performance can only approximate. This departure from the common-sense view involves a misguided understanding of our culture's actual musical ideal.

The discrepancy between the score and any performance is indisputable. The typical score indicates which pitches and rhythms the performer ought to realize, and it does so with a precision that no performer could actually realize in practice. Even when the level of precision and regularity desired is simply that detectable by the ear (as opposed to more scientifically determinable precision), no one's timing is absolutely regular. And on many instruments and in voice, pitch is not an absolute constant, either, even for the most competent performers. "The human touch" that perceptibly distinguishes human performance on instruments from performance by machines is largely a product of the less than perfect regularity of human timing and the less than perfect stability of pitch.

Many (I suspect most) listeners find human performance more aesthetically satisfying than music performed by machines. And this fact points to the problem in conflating the idealizing and normative functions of a score: the idealization of the typical score does not reflect our actual normative ideal for music. Certain irregularities in both pitch and rhythm are viewed, in many styles of music, as desirable vehicles for expressiveness. In certain styles, such departures from the precision of the score are not only positively valued, but indispensable. Many basic techniques of jazz improvisation, for instance, involve deliberate deviation from the types of regularities that conventional scores notate. Tonal instability, rhythmic "swing," spontaneous ornamentation of notes, deliberate moments of being out of tune, glissandos, and the like are part of the basic jazz vocabulary. As an improvised tradition, jazz works are not typically notated in standard score form. But the range of jazz techniques that defy the regularity indicated by standard notation reveals that uniform correspondence between performance and the score is not essential to good music and may even be undesirable.

So far I have suggested that the typical score notates primarily pitch and rhythm. This assumption is somewhat inaccurate. There are, in fact, many scores of a conventional format that indicate phrasing and fingering, and many that suggest less measurable aspects of a performance as well—mood, for instance. However, since the purpose of a score is the clear conveyance of certain information, it is not surprising that virtually every score leaves out certain other kinds of information. And this poses a further problem for the Platonist, one I briefly suggested earlier. What we take to be a performance *of* a musical work involves many factors that are not fully indicated by a score.

The traditional score, for instance, does not indicate much about articulation or about manipulation of timbre. These omissions do not indicate that there is no agreement on these matters. To a large extent, these matters are subject to orally transmitted conventions. Even Kivy, who considers Platonism sympathetically, argues against Wolterstorff's claim that a score is necessary to the existence of a musical work, observing that scores are meaningless without conventions for using them. He also points out that such conventions change over time.[64] If this is true, the score does not absolutely establish the unchanging essence of a musical work even in styles of music that rely heavily on musical scores.

Moreover, the role of convention in interpreting scores varies from one musical style to another, with some styles depending more heavily on oral/aural tradition than on scores. Even different musical styles within our own musical culture view the authority of the score very differently. The amount of information conveyed by the score is usually a rough index of how much authority the score is given. The typical jazz "score," not surprisingly, is exceedingly sparse. The notation of jazz "pieces" in fakebooks (anthologies of popular jazz works) consists of simple indications of pitch and rhythm for the basic opening melody. Jazz charts can be as minimal as a sequential list of chord changes that are to serve as the basis for improvisation.

The relationship of the work as notated to the work as performed is never one of identity. The gap between the two, however, may be informative. Observing the gap between what is recognized in performance of a jazz work and what can be indicated in a transcription can give one a strong intuitive sense of what is meant, say, by "swing." And this suggests the biggest problem with the view of Platonists who take the score to define the essence of a musical work. The musical work that we hear and value involves what Charles Keil calls "vital drive." Vital drive gives us an impression of lively musical intelligence and feeling guiding what we hear performed. Although such features are clearly more prominent in some styles than in others, the impression of a guiding musical intelligence behind performance is, I believe, essential to our enjoyment of music in any style.[65] The Platonic account considers "vital drive," articulation, style of attack, and even an active musical intelligence irrelevant to the existence of a work of music;

but our experience suggests that a work understood without such "life" is absolutely dead.

A Word on Formalism

The Platonist positions in each of the debates we have considered exhibit the same basic problem. Abstract definition of a musical work is valued for its own sake at the expense of the sensual, social, and "human" aspects of the music that we hear.

But is it fair to focus an attack on the musical Platonists? After all, Platonism is an extreme position. And although musical aesthetics is currently dominated by formalism, Platonism as such is not the consensus view. Should I not focus attack on formalism instead?

I have focused on Platonism because it is the culmination of a long history of answers to the question "What is music?" It is an ontological view that is taken very seriously by some of the leading theorists in the field of musical aesthetics, and its understanding of the musical work diametrically opposes that which I am defending here. My criticisms of Platonism also have a bearing on the more pervasive formalism that dominates the current aesthetic scene. For formalism is a presupposition of musical Platonism, and some of Platonism's confusions about the nature of the musical work are problems for its presupposition as well. Only in consequence of the formalist understanding of the musical work as formal structure can Platonism locate it in a nonsensory world apart. Although Platonism makes the most extreme division between the musical work and its performance, formalist insistence since Hanslick that aesthetic appreciation concerns form alone already implants a wedge between the two. Context is already dislodged from the concept of the musical work when formal structure is treated as the work's essential character. And although non-Platonist formalists are typically not discoverists, they share with the Platonist the idea that the musical work is a set of musical relations that retains constant identity throughout all its instantiations.

The peculiarity of this idea is suggested by the scene in the movie *Back to the Future* in which Chuck Berry's cousin introduces him to one of Berry's own works, being played before its composition by a time-traveling teenager of the 1980s.[66] This instantiation of the discoverist view strikes the movie's audience as humorous for its implausibility, and it might strike the average formalist that way, too. But the formalist view treats the work as independent of historical and social context, so that if a formalist could accept time travel, he or she would have to accept the identity of time-traveling musical works as well.[67] As it is, to the extent that one is a strict formalist, one must consider it contingent that the same formal structure has not been produced at various periods of history. And if this had happened, the strict formalist would be obliged to consider it the same piece of music, even if one society used it for sacred ritual and another used it as Muzak.

The formalist view that formal structure constitutes the musical work also tends to overemphasize the importance of the score. This is not a necessary correlate of formalism (or of Platonism, either). But to the extent that the work is understood as a set of structural relations, the score can easily come to seem the schematic of what is most important in a piece of music.

Although formalist understandings of music are often beset with some of the problems I have tied to Platonism, I will not further itemize them here. My arguments against formalism, and against certain conceptions of "form," emerge in the next chapter. Before presenting them I should reiterate that I do not mean to deny that analysis of musical form is important for some purposes, including the proper performance of classical works in our musical tradition. What disturbs me in many formalist accounts is not their focus on form but the exclusivity of this focus. In general, I reject the tendency, most emphatic in Platonism but also evident in aesthetic formalism, to regard "music" as something independent from its historical, cultural, and sensory context. I take issue with specific formalist accounts to the extent that they, like Platonism, leave context in the broadest sense out of consideration.

Thus, I do not mean to underplay the importance of formal recognitions to understanding and appreciating music. To the extent that emphasis on form is of an instrumental nature, assisting the comprehension and appreciation of music, I have no quarrel with it. The discourse of formal analysis is one of several kinds of discourse about music that can aid our understanding. Formalism, in my view, becomes misleading only when it adopts the ontological pretension that Platonism most emphatically promotes: the pretension that analytical abstraction from the full texture of experience is the royal road to legitimate understanding of music, and that the move toward abstraction necessarily increases or improves one's grasp of the music.

Conclusion

Whatever our intuitions and experiences may tell us about the importance of "form" for an understanding of music, it is clear that musical Platonism goes too far. Like the forms of the historical Plato, "form" for musical Platonists is divorced from everyday musical experience—and from the everyday world of our other activities as well. Not only is musical Platonism antithetical to the view that music has a practical role in our ethical lives—it is antithetical to the view that music is properly seen as an immanent part of everyday experience at all.

The ambivalent view of music taken by Platonism's historical namesake reveals the inadequacy of this ontological account. For while Plato did see music as a branch of mathematics, and hence as a study of formal relations apprehensible by the intellect, he also saw music as a volatile social phenomenon with impact both on emotional states and on ethical behavior and character. Like his self-proclaimed descendants in philosophy of music, Plato admired music as transcendent mathematics, and his appreciation of practical music's ethical role was hesitant. But he recognized the ethical, experiential character of music even when he subordinated it to his abstract characterization of music as ideal.

In the next chapter, we consider in further detail the rationale of those responsible for philosophy's rejection of the ethical in favor of the formal view of music. By examining the formalist theories advanced by Kant and Hanslick, we see that recent structural accounts of form are extreme even within the spectrum of formalism, and that the philosophical pioneers of musical formalism found it necessary to give considerable latitude to nonstructural features of music.

2 ‖ : The Many Faces of Form

*Energy is eternal delight; and from the earliest times human
beings have tried to imprison it in some durable hiero-
glyphic. It is perhaps the first of all the subjects of art.*
— Kenneth Clark, *The Nude*

*A terminology is a kind of photographic "screen" which
will "let through" some perceptions and "filter out" others.
I began to suspect that this fact about the nature of "ter-
ministic screens" is the sheerly technical or "logo-logical"
counterpart of the theological formula, "believe that you may
understand" (crede ut intelligas). Technically, the choice of
a terminology in terms of which to state one's proposition is
equivalent to the "act of faith" (credere) through which one
can arrive at understanding (intelligere).*
— Kenneth Burke, "On Form"

The terminology of "form," applied to music, is am-
biguous. "Form" can refer to structure, either static or unfolding. It can
mean the genre of a work, or the details of a work's configuration. "Form"
might oppose some musical "content." Or "form" can refer to the medium
employed to communicate: "music" itself might be considered a "form" for
artistic communication.[1] "Form" can have the minimal meaning of "any recognizable organization." Or "form" can represent the application of selective
principles: the "form" is whatever is "essential" as opposed to "ornamental."

I have been criticizing the excesses of formalism in musical aesthetics,
but the identity of my target has been only casually defined. My short description of the "formalism" I attacked was "the insistence that music is
essentially structure"; and by "structure" I meant a complex of tonal relations of notatable detail. But the only formalist view I have considered is
musical Platonism; and few philosophers are thoroughgoing Platonists. And
only the most adamant promoters of musical structure would deny the importance of performance entirely. So the reader may well wonder why I find
aesthetic emphasis on "structure" so pernicious.

I am disturbed by the structuralist approach to musical form because it screens out and ignores (even if it does not deny) much that is essential to musical experience. Most important, "form" in such accounts is insufficiently wed to activity, whether that of the composer, performer, improviser, or listener. The effect of these formalist commitments is, I believe, a constraining of musical attention and understanding. Attention solely to the literal significance of the speaker's words would constrain one's understanding of an emotionally heated diatribe. But we are encouraged by formalist injunction to do something similar—namely, to censor our own responses to music and to ignore emotive and imaginative reactions in favor of intellectual interpretation.

This approach to music loses sight of one of the greatest values that our own and other cultures find in musical experience: the fact that we experience music as temporally, dynamically *alive*. The "ethical" functions that music has performed in the majority of cultures around the world have typically played upon this character of music. Music is interpreted in these cultures as an experiential metaphor for and an inducement to a particular approach to living.

It would indeed be foolish to suggest that "content" should replace "form" as the major concern of musical aesthetics. In discussions of music, this very distinction is debatable and at best situationally defined.[2] We are often compelled to speak of "formal" features, not because of ideological commitment, but in order to make particular distinctions at particular times, for example, between a melody and the instrument playing it, or between the form of the classical sonata and a particular sonata by a particular composer.

My purpose in this chapter is not to dispense with form, but to consider some of the alternatives available in understanding it. I argue that exclusive or predominant preoccupation with structure is insidious and unnecessary, and that the field of Western aesthetics since Kant has taken some wrong turns. The focal figures in this discussion are Kant and Hanslick, the two theorists most responsible for the formalist bent in musical aesthetics.

A comparative consideration of Kant's and Hanslick's versions of formalism reveals a number of interesting differences. Among them are the specific motivations that prompt these two thinkers to embrace formalism; the extent to which their formalist aesthetics are designed to account for music; the degree to which dynamism is built into their models; and the extent to which anything beyond formalist appreciation is considered a legitimate aspect of musical experience. My aim here is to open up the notion of "form" to encompass a broad range of perceivable patterns, some of which recent formalists have ignored. Equipped with a broader notion of musical pattern than is afforded by structuralist accounts, we will be in a position to recognize that "form" itself can underlie an association between music and ethics.

Kant's account of music, as I suggested in the previous chapter, is constructed in accordance with his general aesthetic theory. I therefore begin my discussion of the Kantian version of musical formalism with an overview of the premises of his basic aesthetic account.[3]

Kant's Account of Aesthetic Experience

In the *Critique of Judgment*, Kant's explicit task is to establish aesthetic judgment on an intersubjective basis. Here as elsewhere, Kant sets out to refute David Hume, who tied experience of the beautiful to an inner sentiment and thus held that disagreements about taste were in a strong sense unresolvable. In the "Four Moments" which open the body of the book, Kant isolates four crucial aspects of the beautiful. Taken together, these four aspects indicate how it is that the beautiful, which is experienced subjectively, is nevertheless intersubjectively recognized by human beings.

According to the Four Moments, the beautiful (1) is the object of "a liking or disliking *devoid of all interest*"; (2) "is what, without a concept, is liked universally"; (3) exhibits in its form what Kant describes as "purposiveness . . . without the presentation of a purpose"; and (4) "is what without a concept is cognized as the object of a *necessary* liking."[4] Consideration of these requirements reveals that "form" provides the Kantian basis for an intersubjective *experience* of an aesthetic object. The central role of form for Kant, then, is social and experiential, even though form is contrasted with the contextual in his theory.

In the first moment, Kant establishes that an aesthetic experience of an object involves a stance of disinterestedness. Unlike sense pleasure, which provokes an interest in sensuous appropriation of the object, and unlike satisfaction in the moral law, which inspires interest in bringing the moral ideal into actuality, appreciation of the beautiful inspires no desire with respect to the object. Instead, the judgment of the beautiful is content with mere contemplation. Kant thus distinguishes a sensuous from an aesthetic comportment toward an object. A sensuous experience of an object is, in Kant's view, a purely private experience. Thus, in the first moment he rules out one possible reason for regarding aesthetic experience as a completely personal matter; but this requirement precludes any further attention to the sensuous character of aesthetic experience or concern for the active nature of response to music.

The second moment focuses directly on the intersubjectivity of aesthetic experience. Kant observes that the judgment of the beautiful carries with it an expectation that others besides the subject will agree with the judgment. This perplexes Kant because the universality assumed in such a judgment does not, as he puts it, depend on concepts. In aesthetic judgment we refer the object immediately to our feelings of pleasure and pain. Thus our judgment is grounded in our subjective state; its correctness cannot be demonstrated by universally valid conceptual arguments. A judgment that a thing is beautiful *means* that it provokes aesthetic pleasure within us—and argument is beside the point.

But where does this universality of aesthetic experience come from if not from compelling argument? It comes, Kant argues, from our universal capacity to contemplate suitable objects with our mental faculties in an extraordinary mode of operation. Kant describes this mode of operation as "free play." The faculties that are involved in free play are the very faculties that Kant takes to be essential to the possibility of human cognition: imagination and understanding. In order to make sense of Kant's idea of free play, therefore, we must consider the most familiar mode of interaction between imagination and understanding, that of ordinary cognition.

In the *Critique of Pure Reason*, Kant describes the roles of imagination and understanding in the act of knowing an object. Imagination integrates the manifold of intuition (the multiple impressions that the senses provide the mind) into definite representations. Kant describes this process as "blind but indispensable," and he asserts that while "we should have no knowledge whatsoever" without it, we are "scarcely ever conscious" of it.[5] The understanding forms definite concepts that give analytic unity to these representations, and when it has yielded these concepts, we have objective knowledge regarding the object to which they refer. The end product of an act of cognition, therefore, is a determinate concept of the object: one knows what the object is.

Let us consider a concrete example. When a flower is approached from the standpoint of cognition, the representation of the flower that the imagination presents to the understanding is "understood" by means of a definite concept: let us say that of a petunia. Once the understanding has determined the appropriate concept with which to designate the represented object, the process of cognition is over. We now see "a petunia" before us, and we can go about our business.

In aesthetic experience, the same two faculties again operate together. However, the end result is not a determinate concept. Instead, the two faculties interact in free play. In this case, again, the imagination forms a representation of the object by synthesizing the manifold of intuition. But unlike in the case of cognition, the representation generated by imagination is not cognitively enshrined in a definite concept. Indeed, in aesthetic experience, we feel that no definite concept could adequately define what we observe. Thus, the two faculties do not neatly finish their work in aesthetic experience. Instead, they play by mutually enlivening one another.

Kant does not elaborate much on his evocative image of "play." But presumably, he sees the imagination's activity as the formation of an open-ended series of representations, which brings now this and now that aspect of the object into relief. The understanding, meanwhile, apprehends these various representations, gaining a foothold here and there, but not consummating the entire process with the formation of a concept. This, at least, seems phenomenologically to reflect the way in which the mind shifts about in aesthetic contemplation. And we have every reason to believe that Kant, while not concerned to elaborate on the phenomenological, intends not to contradict our phenomenological experience.[6]

When we view our petunia aesthetically, our minds are not statically contemplative, but actively so. We leap from focusing on one aspect of the flower's form to focusing on another; and in the midst of all this we find our understanding sufficiently engaged that we often do seek words to communicate about features of what we notice: "Isn't the way that petal flips up interesting? It almost seems perky." We probably make such comments more often in the case of art than in that of nature. Such comments do not explain our enjoyment—in this case, of the flower's form. Yet they do reveal that our understanding in its own way is at work while our imagination reworks its presentation.

The understanding's shifting emphasis, too, seems to encourage imagination to further reformulate the image that it produces for the mind. Imagination may present us with a differently focused representation of the petunia in light of the understanding's stumbling description "perky." Because no conceptual classification confines the imagination, it can attend to more and more features of the object. It thus enhances our experience of the object's particularity as opposed to its generically classifiable features.

While Kant is not forthcoming with phenomenological accounts of specific aesthetic experience, it is clear that some assessment of the phenomenological character of the experience is integral to his determination of what we experience intersubjectively. According to Kant, the intersubjective aspect of our experience is neither representational nor conceptual. The beautiful object is but an occasion for what is basic to aesthetic experience—the condition of free play between the faculties. What we share, when we experience aesthetic delight intersubjectively, is this condition of free play:

But the way of presenting [which occurs] in a judgment of taste is to have subjective universal communicability without presupposing a determinate concept; hence this subjective universal communicability can be nothing but [that of] the mental state in which we are when imagination and understanding are in free play (insofar as they harmonize with each other as required for *cognition in general*).[7]

Free play of imagination and understanding depends on the observer's situational freedom from any need to analyze the object in terms of definite concepts. Superficially, this requirement seems minimal and apt as regards aesthetic experience. Anyone who has analyzed a piece of music knows that attempting to give a comprehensive analysis is not identical with being aesthetically moved. Indeed, the two often seem to be unrelated activities. Kant, however, means something far more extreme. Strictly speaking, he insists, even a determinate concept of the type of thing an object is precludes a pure judgment of taste. Thus, if we have a well-defined notion of "petunia" in our conceptual arsenal, we cannot appreciate the beauty of the petunia with a *pure* judgment of taste. Our experience includes, instead, an admixture of something alien—namely, our judgment regarding whether or not the object accords with our preconceived concept of what this type of thing (a petunia) ought to be.

Preconceived concepts certainly affect our ability to appreciate a thing aesthetically; for it would be difficult to assume an aesthetic stance toward an object that appeared deformed with respect to our concept. But the more Kant says about the inadmissibility of definite concepts in pure judgments of taste, the more obvious it becomes that few objects that we encounter are suitable objects for such judgments. Kant admits this and distinguishes between free beauty, which "does not presuppose a concept of what the object is [meant] to be," and dependent beauty, which "does presuppose such a concept." His list of free beauties is scanty: flowers, many birds, many seashells, "designs *à la grecque,* the foliage on borders or on wallpaper," what Kant calls "fantasias in music (namely, music without a topic [*Thema*])," and "indeed all music not set to words."[8]

The latter two inclusions suggest Kant's own limited conception of musical form. But the list as a whole indicates that pure judgments of beauty, which consider form alone, without reference to concepts, are rare and, in fact, impossible with respect to representational art. And the inclusion of musical examples in the list of free beauties, coupled with the fact that Western music is not typically "representational" on the model of the visual arts, might suggest that music is paradigmatically "aesthetic" on Kant's criteria. Kant himself does not see music in this way, however, for reasons I consider later.

Kant's third moment, which limits pure judgments of the beautiful to those that contemplate mere form, also characterizes the nature of the form that is contemplated without the mediation of concepts. The beautiful object reveals to the contemplating observer what Kant calls "purposiveness without a purpose." The object, in other words, forms an organic unity that coheres as if toward a definite *telos,* or purpose (sometimes translated "end"). But our contemplation reveals no such determinate end. If we did discover such a determinate end, or purpose, it would provide the key to a conceptual account of the arrangement of elements in a beautiful object. A botanical account of the parts of a flower would be a conceptual explanation of the function of each element with respect to a definite end (the continued life of the plant and its species). But no such definite end accounts for the aesthetic form of an object.

> Therefore the liking that, without a concept, we judge to be universally communicable and hence to be the basis that determines a judgment of taste, can be nothing but the subjective purposiveness in the presentation of an object, without any purpose (whether objective or subjective), and hence the mere form of purposiveness, insofar as we are conscious of it, in the presentation by which an object is *given* us.[9]

Form, for Kant, is the primary object of aesthetic experience. But Kant characterizes "form" in terms of *overall effect.* Form, in whatever medium, is that organized configuration of parts that conveys the impression of organic coherence in the service of a teleological end. This understanding of form leads Kant, in the case of some media, to disregard certain features of an aesthetic object in ways that are counterintuitive. Most strikingly, Kant insists that "design" is the essential aesthetic focus in painting, while color is of aesthetic value only in clarifying design and can even have an aesthetically harmful effect if its charm distracts from proper formal concern. Kant takes a similar view of musical tone (by which he seems to mean instrumental timbre). Significantly, Kant analyzes both color and tone as merely charming, not beautiful, because they engage sense without engaging the cognitive faculties. He concedes, however, that

> if, following *Euler,* we assume that colors are vibrations (*pulsus*) of the aether in uniform temporal sequence, as, in the case of sound, tones are such vibrations of the air, and if we assume . . . that the mind perceives not only, by sense, the effect that these vibrations have on the excitement

of the organ, but also, by reflection, the regular play of the impressions (and hence the form in the connection of different presentations), then color and tone would not be mere sensations but would already be the formal determination of the manifold in these, in which case they could even by themselves be considered beauties.[10]

Aesthetic form, then, is for Kant essentially bound up with active reflection. Scientifically analyzable form—such as that Euler assigns to color—is not aesthetic form unless it becomes itself the occasion for free play of the mental faculties.

In the fourth moment Kant accounts for the fact that our aesthetic judgments implicitly demand assent from others. His analysis here depends again on the identity of the faculties that are employed in aesthetic experience with the faculties that are employed in cognition. Insofar as we can communicate with others—something that we assume in the case of all mentally competent human beings and something that depends on our common ability to form concepts—we assume their reliance on the same processes of cognition as those we employ. In making this assumption, we presuppose that their cognitive faculties do function harmoniously.

But to the extent that we have presupposed this, Kant argues, we have presupposed in every human being the active capacity for aesthetic experience. For aesthetic experience depends only on the active harmonious free play of the cognitive faculties. As Kant says later in the *Critique of Judgment*, the pleasure accompanying aesthetic experience is a satisfaction taken simply in the adequacy of the presentation "for [giving rise to a] harmonious (subjectively purposive) activity of the two cognitive powers in their freedom, i.e., in order [for us] to feel the presentational state with pleasure." Kant goes on to argue that this state is universally communicable:

> This pleasure must of necessity rest on the same conditions in everyone, because they are subjective conditions for the possibility of cognition as such, and because the proportion between these cognitive powers that is required for taste is also required for the sound and common understanding that we may presuppose in everyone. That is precisely why someone who judges with taste (provided he is not mistaken in this consciousness and does not mistake the matter for the form, i.e., charm for beauty) is entitled to require the subjective purposiveness, i.e., his liking for the object, from everyone else as well, and is entitled to assume that his feeling is universally communicable, and this without any mediation by concepts.[11]

Kant feels justified therefore in calling taste a kind of "common sense," for this "sense" is a responsive, harmonious condition of the cognitive faculties that can be activated in any aware human being.

Surveying the Four Moments, we can see that they work together as a package. In Kant's aesthetic picture, a disinterested intellect contemplates the form of an organically coherent and purposive representation, and does so through a play of the cognitive faculties of imagination and understanding. Form is central to this picture, but its role is bound essentially to the experience of free contemplation, unconfined by the project of conceptual understanding.

Kant's Analysis and Music

Having outlined Kant's model of what is involved in aesthetic experience in some detail, we are now in a position to ask what it does and does not illuminate about musical experience. Most strikingly, Kant positively suggests an *active* intellectual basis for aesthetic appreciation of music and for the intersubjectivity of musical experience. But his species of formalism trivializes the sensual and socially conditioned aspects that (beyond any satisfaction they yield in themselves) contribute to our intellectual assessment of what is happening in music.

The relevance of the first moment—the beautiful is the object of a disinterested satisfaction—to musical experience is problematic. On the one hand, the pleasure taken in music is, in keeping with Kant's analysis, contemplative. The musical work is not "consumed" by the listener. Nor does the musical work motivate the listener to action by appealing to his or her conceptual understanding. (If the listener is a composer, the musical work might inspire him or her to attempt something similar. But Kant argues that aesthetic inspiration, even when it stems from exposure to exemplary works, is itself a matter of free interplay between the cognitive faculties, not a matter of conceptual understanding.) [12]

Kant himself, however, recognizes a difficulty in applying the criterion of disinterestedness to music. The crux of the problem is that music is sensuous. Perhaps more than any other art, music typically provides direct sensual pleasure along with what Kant understands as purely aesthetic satisfaction. Thus our pleasure in listening to music is, from Kant's aesthetic standpoint, virtually always impure.

An empirical consequence of music's sensuous character is that we can expect less actual agreement about the beauty of music than about beauty in other arts, which are less inherently bound to sense pleasure:

One person loves the sound of wind instruments, another that of string instruments. It would be foolish if we disputed about such differences with the intention of censuring another's judgment as incorrect if it differs from ours, as if the two were opposed logically. Hence about the agreeable the following principle holds: *Everyone has his own taste* (of sense).[13]

Because Kant aims to secure a universal basis for aesthetic judgment, he finds the sensuous character of music worrisome. He resorts to classifying most musical judgments as aesthetically impure, and to placing music low in his hierarchy of the arts.

Kant links the sensuous aspect of music with instrumental timbre. This indicates the narrowness of his conception of music's sensual character. Other sensuous features of music—rhythm, vital drive, and so on—are prominent in certain musics, and one might argue that in the music of Kant's own era, harmonic rhythm and teleological formal organization have an inherent sensual appeal. Some of these other kinds of sensuous appeal might be used to ground a biologically based argument for intersubjective appreciation of music. But this type of argument would be far afield from Kant's intellectualist defense of intersubjective aesthetic experience. And it would not undercut his basic point, which is that music's sensuous appeal conflicts with his demand for disinterestedness.

Kant emphasizes the sensuous character of music more than its emotional influence, but he also treats all emotional satisfaction derived from art as an impediment to pure aesthetic judgment. Both exclusions make music a problematic case for Kant's aesthetics. From my point of view, these exclusions indicate his willingness to sacrifice a realistic account of experience for the sake of sharp theoretical distinctions. Kant may be right to withhold the name "aesthetic judgment" from cases in which a listener has become so enthralled in a musically stimulated emotion that new musical events make virtually no impact. But to insist that aesthetic experience of music is bought at the expense of both sensuous and emotional satisfaction is to make it an abstraction that few listeners would want to instantiate.

And even if one wanted music to provide pure, Kantian aesthetic experience, one would not have much luck. The verdict of modern psychiatry is that any intellectual experience has an emotional aspect.[14] Hence, Kant's notion of disinterested contemplation, divorced from emotional "interest," no longer appears tenable as a description of any, let alone aesthetic, experience. Kant may have a rather crude conception of emotion in mind, so that he ignores all but the overwhelming cases of emotional distraction.

But in excluding emotion from aesthetic experience, he undercuts a realistic description of the intellectual contemplation he insists on.

Kant himself, moreover, is incapable of divorcing sense from intellectual appreciation of music. While intellectual contemplation is the focus in his discussion, he concedes a role to sense even in his discussion of imagination. The representations that imagination formulates from the manifold of intuition are synthesized from the data provided by the senses. The active senses are already in play before aesthetic "free play" can commence. While Kant argues for clean analytic distinctions between the sensuous and the aesthetic, he himself cannot fully maintain them. On his own account, the "sensuous" is a danger to aesthetic experience only when it floods consciousness with so much immediate pleasure that one fails to engage in "aesthetic" contemplation.[15]

In summary, Kant's first moment draws attention to the contemplative satisfaction to be taken in music. But insisting on exclusively contemplative satisfaction, it distorts aesthetic experience generally and renders music, in particular, a dubious mode of aesthetic experience.

Skipping to the third moment—the beautiful exhibits "purposiveness without the presentation of a purpose"—we find Kant more apt with respect to music, at least in regard to "purposelessness." To the extent that music engages us, it makes us feel a kind of indeterminacy as we listen. The listener approaches the next musical event that he or she will hear with uncertainty. Even though resolution tendencies have (in most cases of Western music) been developed over the course of the work that precedes the musical present, these tendencies can be variously resolved.[16]

This is true even in the case of a work or recording that one knows well. Although the listener in such a case does not have any rational doubt about what the next note or chord will be, appreciative listening involves a kind of suspension of this knowledge. One assumes a stance of expectancy, even virtual uncertainty (as one does when one watches one's favorite old movie or a rerun from a previously seen detective series).[17]

Musical works are thus independent of "purpose" in Kant's sense. At the same time, traditional works of music are *purposive*. Musical compositions of the Western classical tradition aspire to a kind of organic unity—and this is precisely the "purposiveness" that Kant describes. Some sense of the traditional work's coherence is essential to one's ability to experience it as a musical work. Moreover, a criterion of musical success in composition is often taken to be the listener's sense that every musical event is exactly as it should be.

The main limitation of Kant's third moment as applied to musical experience is that it reflects traditional values that need not be accepted by musicians. Many recent instances of both improvised and composed music in the West consciously reject precisely the values that Kant assumes are invariant. One of these values is a demand for closure. The demand for closure in music involves an insistence on definite boundaries and on fulfillment of all the tensions developed during the course of the work. A clear example of conformity to this demand can be heard in the final cadence of Beethoven's Fifth Symphony or virtually any symphony of the classical or early Romantic period.

Defiance of musical closure has become almost a canon of faith for many twentieth-century musicians. (Indeed, Beethoven's late string quartets, especially opp. 130–32, are often described as already defying the conventions of closure.) Broeckx's previously cited list of aberrant musical instances that do not easily fit our preconception of "a musical work" includes many cases that do not aspire toward closure—or even toward the development of tensions to *be* closed. (Steve Reich's "Come Out" serves as an example.) For that matter, every time we hear a "fade-out," we hear a departure from the traditional demand for a clearly defined "beginning, middle, and end."[18]

Had he lived during the era of such antitraditional forms and techniques, Kant might have claimed that his moments establish requirements for *beauty,* and that these modern innovations, while interesting, aspire toward something else, to which the term *beauty* does not apply. Always a pioneer in the resources of technical vocabularies, Kant is well equipped to maintain that he is concerned only with precisely delimited cases that he takes to be "standard." And in the aesthetic case, Kant has tradition behind his "standard"; Aristotle demanded closure and organic unity in his aesthetics of tragedy. Kant might have employed this defense. But the more he claims to have circumscribed his field of inquiry to what suits his precise categories, the less he can claim to offer a complete aesthetic account.[19]

The demand for *organic unity* is another traditional value embedded in Kant's demand for "purposiveness without a purpose." The image of every part contributing to the life of the whole is aptly metaphoric for our sense that every detail of a great work is just as it should be. But as Kenneth Burke's comment cited at the head of this chapter suggests, this metaphor serves as a screening device as well as a tool for analysis. Kant instructs us to see the particular arrangement of elements of an aesthetic object (or, more strictly, "representation") as necessary to aesthetic success. This arrangement, he suggests, is as necessary as is the arrangement of our physical organs to our biological life. But in making such comparisons, Kant subtly directs us to treat structure as aesthetic essence. Kant's third moment thus encourages a bias toward structure in our aesthetic exploration of the musical work, despite the vitality of the "organic" image.

More aptly, from my point of view, the metaphor of the biological organism also calls attention to the mutual adjustment of musical elements. It thus invites comparison with other kinds of harmony, after the fashion of ancient "ethical" considerations of music. While Kant himself does not pursue this comparison in connection with music, he does consider the symbolic potential of beauty in connection with moral life.[20] His emphasis on structure diverts attention from certain connections between musical experience and the ethical sphere, but he defends a connection between nonrepresentational art and morality that most of his recent successors deny.

Turning now to the model of aesthetic experience suggested by the second and fourth moments, we find more suggestions that illuminate musical experience than Kant himself fully develops. These moments characterize aesthetic experience as a harmonious interplay of imagination and understanding. Aesthetic experience for Kant *is* this interplay, and what pleases us is this active harmony of our own faculties. Moreover, what we experience commonly, and what we thereby experience as communicable, is this subjective condition.

How does this condition illuminate musical experience? What Kant describes in terms of "imagination" and "understanding" *are* fundamental features of the conscious enjoyment of music. If our earlier example of the operations of imagination and understanding while contemplating a petunia is at all on the track, I think musical experience on Kant's analysis would involve something like this: imagination apprehends fleeting musical forms (or, in more Kantian terms, organizes the manifold of intuition) and presents organized representations of these forms to the understanding. Imagination (in Kant's sense) must be at work in the experience in order for us to apprehend any musical form at all. Understanding, meanwhile, gains footholds at various points in listening. This "gaining a foothold" is what is involved when aspects of the musical work become more or less articulate, in the sense that one has sufficient grasp of them to be able to verbally allude to them. Recognition of the return of the principal theme in a sonata, for instance, is an indication that the understanding is at work.

Significantly, the intellectual recognitions involved in such enjoyment need not employ a sophisticated vocabulary for identifying what is recognized. Recognition of a musical theme does not presuppose formal musical training (although it may presuppose a certain degree of listening experience). One would hope that musical training would extend the listener's range of musical recognitions, and at the same time enlarge the understanding's facility for actively engaging in free play with the imagination. But the experience of free play in listening to music does not presuppose prior analytic knowledge.

The imagination, meanwhile, is kept active in the experience of music, because the form being apprehended is itself evolving as the work unfolds. What imagination presents to the understanding as the musical work proceeds is a changing sequence of particular representations that collectively function to shed light on the particularities and nuances of the work.

The free play model is valuable to musical aesthetics for a number of reasons. In the first place, it reflects something important about the intellectual processes that are involved in understanding music. Listening to music (where "listening" connotes some degree of conscious comprehension) does seem to involve a complicated interplay of imaginative apprehension of form and quasi-conceptual recognitions.[21]

Moreover, the two fundamental activities that seem essential to any appreciative experience of musical listening correspond to the two that Kant emphasizes. On the one hand, we must synthesize clear musical "images" from the flux of sound. In other words, we must have the kind of clear apprehensions that imagination affords on Kant's analysis. We might describe this mental process, which is scarcely conscious enough to seem a mental activity at all, as involving a mental stance of receptivity to the music. On the other hand, we must engage in the more active process of making the elements and figures observed sufficiently distinct from one another to attend to their musical roles both with respect to one another and within the context of the musical texture as a whole. This is the process that Kant associates with the understanding, and we might well describe this activity as the basic process involved in "understanding" the music. These two processes also interact with one another. A vague new awareness of some musical element can pave the way for a new understanding of what is happening in the musical work, while one's overall understanding of what is happening at any given point strongly influences what one is likely to notice.

Some such interplay characterizes the listening experience at all levels of sophistication, insofar as the listener can be said to "understand" what is going on. Any degree of musical "understanding" requires as a precondition that one reach a certain "imaginative" threshold of apprehending musical "shape." I can recall the sense that I was beginning to understand Indian music when I began to think of quarter-tone movements as perfectly normal in the context, not as alien dissonances. Similarly, at a higher level of understanding, I reached a new threshold of understanding the Mbira music of Zimbabwe when I began to apprehend in specific recorded pieces the typical pattern that had been described to me: basic chords, followed by increasingly more complicated variations on the chords, then a climax, followed by variations of gradually reduced complexity, and finally a return to simple chords. In this latter case, more conceptual training was presupposed for my apprehension of something about the music than in the former. But in all such cases, something mentally apprehended becomes "understood" because it has been consciously recognized (whether or not theoretically articulated).[22] The basic intellectual moves described by Kant's "free play" model seem to be basic to the *thinking* involved at every level of understanding.

Kant's insistence that we *enjoy* the simultaneous and interactive play of the activities of imagination and understanding also accurately describes our enjoyment of music. But Kant's claim goes too far, for he contends that our experience of this interactive play is the only genuine aesthetic enjoyment. Clearly, we do enjoy precisely the kinds of things that Kant takes pain to eliminate from the "pure" judgment of taste: the sensuous "feel" of musical materials, the emotions experienced in connection with the musical stimulus, and the feeling of social participation that listening with others involves. Kant himself acknowledges the presence of each of these elements in our experience. Concerning the pleasure of social participation in aesthetic experience, Kant goes so far as to say that

> someone abandoned on some desolate island would not, just for himself, adorn either his hut or himself; nor would he look for flowers, let alone grow them, to adorn himself with them. Only in society does it occur to him to be, not merely a human being, but one who is also refined in his own way (this is the beginning of civilization). For we judge someone refined if he has the inclination and the skill to communicate his pleasure to others, and if he is not satisfied with an object unless he can feel his liking for it in community with others. . . . in the end, when civilization has reached its peak, it makes this communication almost the principal activity of refined inclination, and sensations are valued only to the extent that they are universally communicable. At that point, even if the pleasure that each person has in such an object is inconsiderable and of no significant interest of its own, still its value is increased almost endlessly by the idea of its universal communicability.[23]

But although aware of the importance of such "empirical" elements in our actual evaluation of the beautiful, Kant circumscribes his term *aesthetic* in such a way as to exclude aspects of musical pleasure that are familiar to virtually everyone.

Nonetheless, Kant is surely right in claiming that a major source of musical enjoyment is the very active intellectual state in which we apprehend, recognize, and rework our sense of the form. Indeed, the intensity of this enjoyment, particularly for those of an intellectual bent, might largely account for the extent to which philosophers of music have embraced musical "cognitivism" (a matter that I discuss further in Chapter 4).

Another virtue of Kant's model for an understanding of the intellectual character of our musical experience is its inherent temporality. The dynamic activity suggested by the free play model seems particularly well suited to music. Music necessarily unfolds itself over a span of time, and listening requires mental attentiveness across this span. Our experience shows us that in listening our minds are not engaged in a single, continuous activity throughout the work's duration. Instead, our mental activities vary and interact with each other. Dahlhaus characterizes aesthetic contemplation in a manner that accords with this description:

> Absorption in a work of art, no matter how self-forgetful, is seldom a mystical state in a literal sense, seldom a motionless and hallucinatory fixation. More likely it is a to-and-fro between contemplating and reflecting, and, if so, then the level it reaches depends on the esthetic and intellectual experiences contributed by the listener, experiences into whose context he can fit the work that he is now appreciating.[24]

Ironically, the temporal character of Kant's model does not strike him as particularly useful for understanding music. In fact, Kant's emphasis on the mind's own free activity in contemplating the aesthetic object may lead him to undervalue the temporal demands that music qua phenomenon places on the person who experiences it. At any rate, the form that Kant envisions as the object of aesthetic contemplation is described in static terms. This fact, coupled with the structural metaphor suggested by Kant's adoption of the organic model, makes Kant's aesthetics partly responsible for the emergence of a tendency toward structural reduction in musical aesthetics.

But Kant himself found music deficient when considered from an exclusively formal perspective. In light of the later tendency of aestheticians to view music as particularly suited to formal appreciation, an explanation of Kant's notorious undervaluation of music is in order.

Kant's Problem with Music

Kant sometimes treats music with little short of disdain:

Music has a certain lack of urbanity about it. For depending mainly on the character of its instruments, it extends its influence (on the neighborhood) farther than people wish, and so, as it were, imposes itself on others and hence impairs the freedom of those outside of the musical party. The arts that address themselves to the eye do not do this; for if we wish to keep out their impressions, we need merely turn our eyes away. The situation here is almost the same as with the enjoyment produced by an odor that spreads far. Someone who pulls his perfumed handkerchief from his pocket gives all those next to and around him a treat whether they want it or not, and compels them, if they want to breathe, to enjoy at the same time, which is also why this habit has gone out of fashion.[25]

Kant has difficulty treating music on a par with other art forms. In the *Critique of Judgment*, he vacillates between describing music as an agreeable art (which pleases through mere sensation) and describing it as a fine art (which affords pleasure through its form alone and which alone can be the object of aesthetic appreciation). Even when he treats it as a fine art, moreover, he finds that the timbres involved in music, although often means by which musical form is clarified, threaten to distract attention from musical form to themselves. He even emphasizes, with apparent admiration, the social function that music can perform independent of anyone's aesthetic experience, describing the agreeable "table-music" at large banquets as "a strange thing which is meant to be only an agreeable noise serving to keep the minds in a cheerful mood, and which fosters the free flow of conversation between each person and his neighbor, without anyone's paying the slightest attention to the music's composition."[26] While perhaps ahead of his time in admiring background music, Kant refrains from granting such skill the status of fine art.

Various factors contribute to Kant's low assessment of music. Kant seems not to have been overly sophisticated in his musical appreciation; and this might be one reason music did not seem to him as evocative of free play of the mental faculties as did other aesthetic phenomena. He himself found that timbre distracted from attention to musical form; but perhaps, additionally, apprehension of unfolding musical form was an activity for which Kant was not particularly gifted.[27]

The fact that Kant is so quick to add "indeed all music not set to words" to "music without a topic (*thema*)" in his list of free beauties suggests that he considered the words of vocal music to play a significant role in the definition of form. And the fact that Kant, in discussing the possibility of a mathematical basis of music, focuses on the frequencies of individual tones, instead of the proportions of larger formal elements, does not suggest a sophisticated acquaintance with the temporally unfolding structure more typically designated "form" by musicians and theorists.[28] Ironically, while he demands purely formal appreciation in aesthetic judgment, what Kant seems unable to appreciate in music is precisely musical form.

The same inability is more comically suggested by the report that Kant's favorite song, which he once described as "the highest of musical compositions of its kind," was a drinking song called "Crown with a Garland the Dear, Full Cup." Rudolf Weingartner, who notes this song for readers of the *Journal of Aesthetics and Art Criticism*, draws special attention to the final verse, which he translates:

> So drink it then, and let us all the time
> Enjoy ourselves and merry be!
> But if we knew where sadly someone pined,
> We should give the wine to him! [29]

Even in his musical tastes, we might conclude, Kant treasured the beauty of the moral law.

We have already mentioned another of the grounds for Kant's low assessment of music. He accepts the common prejudice that the visual and literary arts are less intrinsically sensual than music. Beyond any prudish disdain for the sensual, Kant had systematic reasons for being disturbed by this. His entire aesthetic project aimed to establish the intersubjective validity of aesthetic judgments. Music's inherent sensuousness threatened to make appreciation too privately subjective to qualify as a matter of universal, intellectual judgment.[30]

Another explanation for Kant's undervaluation of music, however, gives him more credit. Kant occupied a peculiar moment in the history of Western thought on music. The *Critique of Judgment* appeared in the wake of instrumental music's rise to ascendancy and at the very historical moment when it was first being legitimated theoretically. Indeed, this is reflected in the third *Critique*, for as Herbert Schueller observes, it is instrumental music that Kant primarily discusses. Kant's acceptance of instrumental music as legitimate music is thus a progressive view for the time.[31]

Yet the pivotal moment in musical history that Kant occupies is reflected by his simultaneous skepticism toward instrumental music. In some of his remarks, Kant seems strongly influenced by the adamant critics of instrumental music who see it as "empty sound devoid of substance." Thus, while admitting that "agreeable" music of minimal content exists, Kant judges it harshly.[32]

That Kant is taking pains to treat his subject fairly is suggested by his discussion of the possibility that music might have a mathematical basis. In section 51 of the *Critique of Judgment*, Kant reconsiders the argument (earlier suggested in connection with his comment on Euler) that the frequencies corresponding to perceived musical tones provide the basis for appreciation of form. If we did directly perceive the vibrations of the air that correlate with tones, he acknowledges, we might be capable of intelligibly distinguishing between them and judging form on the basis of them. But Kant is skeptical: "the rapidity of the vibrations of . . . the air" involved in tones "probably far exceeds all our ability to judge directly in perception the ratio in the temporal division [produced] by these vibrations." However, Kant concedes that the evidence might convince someone that our perception of musical tones does indeed involve the judging of form.[33]

Again, in this discussion, we see Kant searching in vain for a musical form that he understands. Given Kant's premises, it is no wonder that he found music to be of dubious aesthetic worth. The only admissible ground for aesthetically valuing it—its formal characteristics—reveals little of interest to Kant. It took someone with more understanding of music's formal possibilities—namely, Hanslick—to see Kantian formalism as a doctrine that could vindicate the status of music.

Before considering Hanslick's alternative formalism, however, we should consider a further explanation for Kant's attitude toward music, one that is central to my purpose. Kant was more concerned with morality than with aesthetics. And he had more difficulty relating music to morality than he did the other arts.

After delineating what a pure aesthetic judgment would be, Kant makes it evident throughout the rest of the third *Critique* that he prefers dependent to free beauty, and that the ultimate value that he finds in the beautiful is that it serves as a symbol of morality. No sensible intuition is adequate to morality, according to Kant, but we can nonetheless represent the moral ideal to ourselves indirectly by means of analogy. Beauty naturally serves this role for us, so much so that Kant claims that "only because we refer the beautiful to the morally good . . . does our liking for it include a claim to everyone else's assent."[34]

Beauty can serve this role because we appreciate it freely, without being determined by sensual pleasure; and our recognition of this freedom directs our attention toward the "intelligible," noumenal realm in which we are free moral agents, similarly capable of resisting sensuous inclinations. Moreover, in the case of beauty, nature itself harmonizes with human freedom; and this unity suggests the harmony of freedom and nature to which the moral ideal compels us despite the apparent conflict between the two on the phenomenal plane.[35]

Kant deems the other arts more valuable for this symbolic function than music. Poetry, for instance, dependent as it is on concepts, is well adapted to reminding us of our freedom from determination by sense (and thus of our vocation as moral agents):

> It expands the mind: for it sets the imagination free, and offers us, from among the unlimited variety of possible forms that harmonize with a given concept, though within that concept's limits, that form which links the exhibition of the concept with a wealth of thought to which no linguistic expression is completely adequate, and so poetry rises aesthetically to ideas. Poetry fortifies the mind: for it lets the mind feel its ability—free, spontaneous, and independent of natural determination— to contemplate and judge phenomenal nature as having [*nach*] aspects that nature does not on its own offer in experience either to sense or to the understanding, and hence poetry lets the mind feel its ability to use nature on behalf of and, as it were, as a schema of the supersensible.[36]

Kant concludes that poetry is the art of the first rank.

Music, by contrast, although it enlivens the mind nearly as much as poetry, does so "through nothing but sensations without concepts, so that unlike poetry it leaves us with nothing to meditate about." Thus, "if . . . we assess the value of the fine arts by the culture [or cultivation] they provide for the mind, . . . then music, since it merely plays with sensations, has the lowest place among the fine arts."[37] It certainly does not remind us of our freedom from sensuous determination. Its ability to charm depends precisely on our susceptibility to being sensuously moved. And because Kant's moral theory, like his aesthetic theory, insists on the human mind's freedom from sensible determination, the sensuous character Kant sees in music renders it a poor candidate for moral symbolism.

We should note, however, that although Kant's specific symbolic requirements marginalize music as an aesthetic symbol of the ethical, he considers it "natural" for human beings to find analogies for moral life in aesthetic experience. To seek such analogies in our musical experience, then, is in keeping with Kant's general aesthetic findings, even if his own understanding of music and his picture of morality do not allow him to discover useful analogies.

Again, Kant's position in musical history must have helped to shape his moral assessment of music. For the traditional association of music with morality, which had been dominant in the West since Plato, had long been supported by the assumption that typically music was joined with poetry, which provided the kind of ethical material that Kant praised so highly.

Although ambivalent regarding music, Kant made laudable efforts to do it justice within his own historical context. Any attempt to do justice to music in any context is noteworthy in modern Western philosophy. Schueller observes that Kant was the first modern Western philosopher to include "a theory of music as an integral part of his system."[38]

One must conclude, nevertheless, that Kant's understanding of music was severely limited. Despite many common assumptions, therefore, Kant's account differs markedly from that of the music critic Hanslick, to which I now turn.

Hanslick's View of Musical Form

Hanslick is most responsible for musical aesthetics' preoccupation with structure to the exclusion of interest in music's ethical character. In opposition to Kant's concern to wed the aesthetic to the ethical, Hanslick divorces the two: those interested in music's moral effects, he tells us, are not concerned with aesthetics. Yet Hanslick and Kant are often linked as formalists. The reason is that Hanslick builds his musical aesthetics on a Kantian analysis of aesthetic experience.[39]

Like Kant, Hanslick treats aesthetic contemplation as a purely intellectual activity enjoyed for its own sake. While sense is the medium through which the intellect comes into contact with music—its very role in Kant's aesthetics—it is "imagination" that aesthetically appreciates: "The auditory imagination, however, which is something entirely different from the sense of hearing regarded as a mere funnel open to the surface of appearances, enjoys in conscious sensuousness the sounding shapes, the self-constructing tones, and dwells in free and immediate contemplation of them." While Hanslick does not employ the "free play" model, he grants "understanding" a Kantian role: "Certainly with regard to beauty, imagining is not mere contemplating, but contemplating with active understanding, i.e. conceiving and judging." And again like Kant, Hanslick denies that musical contemplation depends on concepts: "Every art has as its goal to externalize an idea actively emerging in the artist's imagination. In the case of music, this idea is a tonal idea, not a conceptual idea which has first been translated into tones."[40]

Despite these similarities, however, Hanslick's orientation toward music differs from Kant's. While Kant aimed to establish the ground for universal subjective experience in aesthetics, Hanslick wanted to get away from subjectivity altogether. Aesthetics, he contended, should aspire to the condition of a science: it should aim to give us objective laws. This quest for an objective basis for aesthetic principles led Hanslick to concern himself with the structure of unfolding tonal relations in music. Structure, for Hanslick, is first of all an objective basis for the construction of a musical aesthetics.

Structure is also a means of legitimating music's status. Sensitive to the charge that music is excessively sensuous, Hanslick argues that it is properly appreciated through the intellect. Music can be so appreciated because it has its own "sense and logic":

> As the creation of a thinking and feeling mind, a musical composition has in high degree the capability to be itself full of ideality and feeling. This ideal content we demand of every artwork. It is to be found only in the tone-structure itself, however, and not in any other aspect of the work.[41]

Significantly, structure is the basis even of the "feeling" content that we demand from music.[42]

Hanslick sees structure as the supreme tool through which the intellect imposes itself on the materials of sense. Although he makes the striking concession that musical materials have a symbolic character, he contends that the aesthetic value of music depends on the subordination of these elements to structure:

> Tones, like colours, possess symbolic meanings intrinsically and individually, which are effective apart from and prior to all artistic intentions. . . . It is the same with the basic ingredients of music: different tonalities, chords, and timbres have their own characters. . . . Yet these ingredients . . . follow laws entirely different in their artistic application from the laws of their effects as isolated phenomena. No more than every bit of red in an historical painting means joy or every bit of white means innocence will every bit of A-flat major in a symphony arouse an ecstatic mood or every bit of B minor a misanthropic one or every triad satisfaction or every seventh despair. At the aesthetic level, all such rudimentary differentiations are neutralized through subordination to higher principles.[43]

Implicit in Hanslick's talk about structure is an atomistic interpretation of musical elements. He asserts that "music is a kind of kaleidoscope, although it manifests itself on an incomparably higher level of ideality." That he means to limit structure to the components of music that are atomistically notated in standard scores is indicated when he describes timbre as providing the "charm" to "enhance" the more essential materials of music—melody, harmony, and rhythm.[44]

Hanslick's atomistic bias is linked to his "scientific" pursuit of precision and determinacy. He considers its precision to be one of the great merits of structural language: "What makes Halévy's music bizarre and Auber's charming, what brings about the peculiarities by which we at once recognize Mendelssohn and Spohr, can be traced to purely musical factors without reference to the obscurities of the feelings." In light of its capacity for precision, structural language should be fundamental in philosophical discussions of music:

> The "philosophical foundation of music" would have to try first of all to find out which necessary ideal determinants are connected with each musical element, and in what manner they are connected. The double requirement of a strictly scientific framework and the most elaborate casuistics makes the task a very formidable but not quite insurmountable one: to strive for the ideal of an "exact" science of music after the model of chemistry or of physiology.[45]

Hanslick recognizes that there is a price in the quest for "exactitude." After sketching a structural analysis of the opening of Beethoven's *Prometheus* Overture, he acknowledges that this procedure "makes a skeleton out of a flourishing organism." Beauty is destroyed along with the organism's life—yet such analysis is justified, Hanslick contends, for it also destroys "all misguided interpreting."[46] He describes his goals for structural analysis as modest: such analysis corrects for the tendency to project irrelevant subjective states on music.

But Hanslick's rhetoric belies this pose of modesty. Filled with polemical fervor, Hanslick employs a jargon of snobbery, which he uses with flair. Discussing those who do not experience music with intellectual contemplation, Hanslick insists:

> The number of people who hear music (or, strictly speaking, *feel* it) in this fashion is very considerable. While they in passive receptivity allow the elemental in music to work upon them, they subside into a fuzzy state of supersensuously sensuous agitation determined only by the general character of the piece. . . . Slouched dozing in their chairs, these enthusiasts allow themselves to brood and sway in response to the vibrations of tone, instead of contemplating tones attentively. . . . These people make up the most "appreciative" audience and the one most likely to bring

music into disrepute. . . . Incidentally, for people who want the kind of effortless suppression of awareness they get from music, there is a wonderful recent discovery which far surpasses that art. We refer to ether and chloroform.[47]

By contrast with this uncouth majority, "only . . . the cultivated understanding" can perceive music's ideal content.

Who are these "cultivated" perceivers? They are those who intellectually contemplate the tonal structure of music. Hanslick denies that structural analysis can substitute for listening. But his rhetoric implies that the best listeners are the ones who *can* analyze in this fashion. The more structural recognitions the listener has, the better, according to Hanslick. But this suggests that analytical training is a privileged access to aesthetic experience. At the very least, it is hard to imagine that anything approaching a "good" level of musical appreciation, on Hanslick's criterion, could be reached by someone who lacked both training and experience in employing some type of structural terminology.

In fact, many of Hanslick's most pointed sarcasms are directed against those who use the wrong sort of terminology:

> "Music has to do with the feelings," we are told. This expression "has to do" is a characteristically vague utterance of previous musical aesthetics. In what the connection between music and the feelings . . . might consist, according to what natural laws music might work, and according to what laws of art it may be shaped—about all this the very people who "have to do" with it leave us entirely in the dark.[48]

It is revealing that Hanslick devotes so much attention to how we talk about music. Defending his own practice as a critic (which is replete with emotional terminology),[49] he acknowledges the aptness of metaphors from the life of feeling to describe musical characteristics, so long as one has enough "cultivation" not to take them too seriously. But he insists that feelings are "only one source among others which offer similarities," and he considers use of emotional terms legitimate only so long as "we never lose sight of the fact that we are using them only figuratively." Those who assert that definite feelings comprise the content of music are sloppy with their language: "Music can, in fact, whisper, rage, and rustle. But love and anger occur only within our hearts."[50]

Hanslick's Restrictions on Musical Experience

Hanslick's "scientific" approach to music has ironic results. He aims to vindicate musical experience as something that admits of intellectual articulation. But he privileges the experience of those who are both verbally and structurally articulate. In so doing, he privileges those "experts," like himself, who are in the business of verbalizing about music. Hanslick aims to give an "objective," "scientific" account of musical beauty, as opposed to Kant's account based on "universal subjectivity." But while Hanslick pretends to eliminate the merely subjective from aesthetics, he actually legitimates a certain kind of subjective experience: that of musically trained intellectuals.

Another irony is evident when one considers how such intellectuals would fare in an attempt to extend their expertise into areas of foreign musics. Would it even be possible to begin such an activity without assuming a listening condition that Hanslick vigorously denounces: that of the person who recognizes the instances of the same basic style but cannot distinguish among them?[51] And what of those cases in which Hanslick's preferred structural terminology misses fundamental values embodied in a music? Kaluli music in Papua New Guinea and many African musics view resonance as a positive value. Javanese music is built upon an "inner" melodic "structure" that is conceived differently by different musicians, any one of whose conception may not determine what is sounded.[52] Hanslick's terminology of the musical kaleidoscope cannot even recognize these values, let alone provide precise articulations.

One might attempt to maintain Hanslick's aesthetic ideals by maintaining a staunch ethnocentrism.[53] But unfortunately, even within Western society, Hanslick's ideals also exclude as aesthetically worthless the experiences of all but those trained as "experts." The effect of this is the impoverishment of everyone's musical discussion.

Even from the standpoint of his attempt to establish aethetics on an objective basis, Hanslick's intellectualist bias impoverishes his analysis. For it cannot account for one of the most "objective" facts about musical experience: the fact that musical experience is typically intersubjective. The problem is this: On Hanslick's account, intersubjective enjoyment of music as such varies directly with the listener's sophistication in recognizing "musical ideas." For beauty, the intersubjective basis for our enjoyment, is a function of musical relationships which, to be recognized, must be appreciated intellectually. This is not to say that appreciation of musical relationships presupposes that one has mastered a standard analytical vocabulary. But the appreciation that Hanslick seems to equate with musical appreciation and musical aesthetic experience varies directly with intellectual grasp of musical elements and their interactions.

The problem with this account is that Hanslick's model emphasizes analytic appreciation of formal and structural elements of music at the expense of any preanalytic or Gestalt understanding. In radically isolating emotion and intellect, and in maintaining intellectualist and atomistic biases in his account of proper musical appreciation, Hanslick makes music too much the exclusive province of "the cultivated ear" and "the trained judgment."[54] His account does not leave much room for the claim that listeners with very different levels of musical sophistication can in some sense share an aesthetic experience of music. This claim, however, strikes me at least as correct and important. In fact, I do not see how the musical educator could *develop* musical sophistication in students unless a common basis of shared aesthetic experience were presupposed.

Furthermore, Hanslick's account, by linking aesthetic experience of music directly with analytic (although not necessarily linguistic) recognition of structural elements, creates a rift even between listeners of the same level of musical sophistication and training. For can we really suppose that different listeners are actively recognizing the same musical structure? Certainly our experience as listeners, even when we are utilizing our musical training to the highest degree, involves not a static appreciation of structure but a very dynamic stance of shifting observations. The shifting observations we make are so idiosyncratic and continuous that, in the age of recordings, we entertain very different sequences of observations on different hearings of the same performance of the same work. What, then, can be the common denominator of aesthetic experience of music on Hanslick's account? If we tie aesthetic experience directly to intellectual recognition of structure, we have neither commonality with the appreciative experience of others nor even commonality with our own experiences from one listening occasion to the next.

A Comparison of Formalisms: Kant versus Hanslick

The Superiority of Kant's Model

If we now compare the two formalist accounts just considered, we find that Kant's model is less wed to atomistic structuralism and more accommodating to the character of our actual experience in listening to music than Hanslick's. In particular, Kant's analysis is more faithful to the social dimension of musical experience, for it is concerned with the intersubjective basis of aesthetic value.

Some of the differences between Kant's and Hanslick's accounts can be traced to the thinkers' respective positions in intellectual history. Kant, as an Enlightenment philosopher, consistently sought the universal conditions of human experience. In his aesthetic theory, he argued that a universal basis for aesthetic experience could be found in one of the human mind's essential modes of functioning. Insofar as music affords aesthetic experience, musical experience has a universal "shape." Fundamentally, the state of mind involved is the same for all human beings.[55]

Hanslick, writing during the Romantic era, is not so much concerned with finding a universal common denominator for human experience as with attacking the excesses of his time. When he defends a demystifying, nonsubjectivist approach to aesthetics, he reacts against tendencies of Romanticism. His orientation is in certain ways shaped, however, by his era's adulation of the privileged experiences of the artistically elite. While explicitly rejecting the musical values that Wagner employed in his own quest for the status of artistic godhead, Hanslick accepted the Romantic elitism that Wagner nurtured. Wagner taught that he had transcendent experiences that his music could communicate. Hanslick taught that the musically educated intellectual alone had *aesthetic* experiences of music, and that these transcended the experience of most listeners.

Hanslick sees no conflict between his attempt at an "objective" aesthetics and his conclusion that most people's musical experiences do not conform to it. Kant's theory, in principle, is similarly unconcerned with the empirical facts about actual experiences. But Kant insinuates that it is appropriate to seek to minimize the discrepancy between an aesthetic theory and contradictory empirical evidence. He claims that we are justified in demanding the assent of others in our aesthetic judgments *and* in presupposing the possibility of such experience in every human being whose mind is functioning well enough to use language. Thus Kant's account takes the experience of the nonexpert as the paradigm case that aesthetic analysis seeks to understand. As a result, his aesthetic theory is much more adaptable than Hanslick's to the project of understanding aesthetic experience of music in everyday and non-Western contexts.

In the first place, Kant's aesthetic model is able to account for musical intersubjectivity much more adequately than Hanslick's. Kant goes some way in making sense of our confident attitude that despite our very different musical biographies and levels of talent, the most fundamental aspect of music is something that we share. What we share, on Kant's analysis, is a state of mind. I think that Kant is correct in claiming a shared intellectual basis for the shared character of musical experience. The mentally active state of mind that Kant describes *is* more fundamental to musical experience than the particular details of what flashes through our minds on any occasion of listening. Because he is committed to an intellectualist aesthetic position and allegedly demonstrates the universal character of aesthetic experience, he does not avail himself of physiological or culturally conditioned bases for intersubjectivity in musical experience. But he offers a persuasive defense of an intellectual grounding for musical intersubjectivity.

Kant's account is also superior to Hanslick's in that the latter makes the possibility of aesthetic experience of music hinge on the quasi-conceptual or analytic appreciation of specifically musical relations. Hanslick's account, as I have suggested, limits the intersubjectivity of musical aesthetic experience to those who have reached a threshold of musical "competence" (as defined by his society's musically elite) which is far from universal. Perhaps even more important, it creates problems for the claim that any two listeners are sharing an aesthetic experience. For it links such experience to sequential intellectual recognitions that are not plausibly simultaneous for two listeners. Even if it is conceded that perhaps on this account only the most basic structural features need be observed by two listeners in order for us to call their experience concurrent, the account still seems to rule out the possibility that the experience of two listeners attending to different basic features at a given moment can be shared. And although Hanslick allows room for less than fully articulate apprehension of musical coherence,[56] his insistence that aesthetic experience involves an intellectual appreciation of musical ideas seems to demand that aesthetic appreciation engage consciousness in a way that would not seem simultaneously possible for any two listeners.

Of course, Hanslick does not explicitly make such outrageous demands. By making aesthetic appreciation of music a matter of intellectually apprehending form, he seems to feel he has dissociated appreciation from subjective mental conditions and tied it to something objective. He therefore does not devote much attention to the conscious condition of a genuinely musical listener (although he does recount the failures of those who enjoy music "pathologically"). But by assuming that intellectual appreciation of form is objective (and not, as Kant has it, the medium by which experience of the musically beautiful is possible), Hanslick exposes his account to the absurdity that either two listeners must appreciate form to the same degree (or at least to the same threshold degree) or they are not sharing aesthetic experience. And as soon as one considers the temporal dimension of musical experience, one is hard put to imagine what shared aesthetic experience could amount to on Hanslick's account. The inherent temporality of Kant's model again shows its superiority to this alternative view. For it faithfully describes musical comprehension and explains how shared experience is possible.

Kant's analysis does not deny that those who have reached higher thresholds of musical competence might have more interesting things to say to one another than listeners who approach music with radically different levels of sophistication. But it does insist that every human being is capable of aesthetic enjoyment of music, and that this enjoyment proceeds by means of a common "sense," which is the intersubjectively enjoyed state of mind that Kant describes as "free play." Because free play does not depend on determinate concepts, Kant also avoids Hanslick's difficulty in accounting for the shared aesthetic experience of two attentive listeners who are entertaining different observations about the music's structure. Kant's account suggests that, regardless of our level of musical sophistication, in an important sense we share our aesthetic experience of a musical performance with every other aesthetically open listener.

But perhaps I am still unfair to Hanslick. After all, he explicitly states that the content of music cannot be subsumed under concepts. And it was not Hanslick, but Kant himself, who bequeathed to aesthetic history the idea that form alone was the legitimate concern of a pure judgment of taste. Perhaps, in light of the resonances between Hanslick's claims and Kant's own, we should consider whether Hanslick embraced the Kantian overview of aesthetic experience.

The primary reason for rejecting this assumption is that Hanslick does not build "free play" into his model. The only possible justification I can see for believing that Hanslick simply assumes the Kantian model would be a demonstration that his theory is deeply and consistently indebted to Kant. And no such demonstration is available. Hanslick's translator Geoffrey Payzant asserts that "we have neither internal nor collateral evidence upon which to make a positive claim for an influence from the one to the other, except perhaps indirectly by way of C. F. Michaelis."[57] We are thus not justified in assuming that Hanslick simply adopts Kant's general account of aesthetic experience without comment. On the contrary, it is entirely possible that he never read Kant.

Another question that might be raised regarding my fairness to Hanslick concerns the degree to which his position is intellectualist. Perhaps his intellectualism is not as severe as I have suggested. After all, Payzant, Dahlhaus, Gordon Epperson, and others have observed that Hanslick does not claim that the experience of music is or ought to be unemotional. Hanslick's claim is that there is no regular, necessary effect of music on emotion and that therefore emotion cannot be the ground of any aesthetic principle. And his own belief that the experience of music is inherently emotional is evident both in his practice as a music critic and in the text of *On the Musically Beautiful*. Had he believed that musical experience absorbed only the intellect, he would certainly not have written a whole chapter entitled "Musical Perception: Aesthetic versus Pathological."[58]

To the objection that I caricature Hanslick, I concede that I have here emphasized only the most striking features of his approach to form in music. Our picture of Hanslick is further developed in the next chapter, where his mixed remarks on feeling in music concern us. If I simplify here, however, I believe that my simplification does justice to Hanslick's view. Hanslick's turn from emotion to musical form as the basis of aesthetic experience was motivated by a desire to make aesthetic judgment "scientific."[59]

The only intersubjective basis of musical aesthetic experience, according to Hanslick, is therefore to be sought in the formal structures that may be described "scientifically," not in the emotions that listeners may experience. Thus, the ground of intersubjective aesthetic experience of music in his account *is* intellectualist, even if he acknowledges that intellectual enjoyment of form is not all that the listener experiences.

"Form" in Kant and Hanslick

I have suggested that Kant's aesthetic theory does greater justice than Hanslick's to actual musical experience. The root of the latter theory's relative deficiency, I now wish to suggest, is its structural interpretation of "form."

"Form," in Kant's theory, is understood in terms of the organic metaphor implicit in the third moment. According to this model, formal components serve the "life" of the entire aesthetic object. But Kant does not presuppose that such "elements" need share more of a "family resemblance" than do organs of the human body. Even his vagueness in describing the aesthetic focus in painting as "design" reveals an open attitude toward what composes the design. One can imagine Kant, if better acquainted with the musical possibilities his tradition afforded, applauding an appreciation of the diversity of formal levels in music. Such appreciation would not only be compatible with Kant's "free play" model, it necessarily involves the shifting movements of conscious attention in musical contemplation that Kant's model casts as central.

Hanslick, with his penchant for precision and his concern for "relations between tones," locates musical "form" on one formal level only, that of the basic unit of Western musical notation. He describes musical events atomistically in terms of formal "recognitions" and of "following" an unfolding musical structure. The resulting image of musical appreciation depicts the listener's mind as passively and evenly processing units of musical data as they go by. Hanslick's account misses the lively movements of attention that occur during the course of even the most focused experience of listening. It also fails to reflect the complicated nature of "formal" recognitions when they occur in actual musical experience.

"Form" itself can be understood as a matter of pattern recognition. Insofar as Hanslick stresses form, his emphasis on "recognition" is unremarkable. In fact, "recognition" is the one feature of his model that allows for an active mental stance on the part of the listener. But "recognition" is ambiguous here. My brother as a child, seeing a necktie hung over a doorknob, called it a cuckoo clock, for he noticed a resemblance between the lengths of the necktie and the chains suspending the weights from our clock. Surely this was a "recognition." But did my brother recognize something that was latently "there"?

The "recognitions" involved in attentive musical listening may be more like my brother's than Hanslick's account suggests. Hanslick implies that what is recognized is already "put" into the score by the composer and correctly identified by "the trained judgment." Music comes off as a kind of secret code. Much like a telegraph operator's translation of Morse code, musical understanding is depicted as a step-by-step decoding by a musical elite that knows the language.

To use Kantian terms in a non-Kantian sense, Hanslick sells out "imagination" in listening for the sake of objective "understanding."[60] His description of musical aesthetic experience flattens the experience while it narrows the audience. It ignores some of the positive and very active roles played by imagination in musical experience.

Feld points out that imaginative takes, which he describes as "interpretive moves," are fundamental to a listener's making sense of any music:

As one listens, one works through the dialectics by developing choices and juxtaposing background knowledge. I call this process "interpretive moves." Interpretive moves involve the action of pattern discovery as experience is organized by the juxtapositions, interactions, or choices in time when we encounter and engage obviously symbolic objects or performances.[61]

Feld itemizes a number of such interpretive moves. In discussing "Spangled Banner Minor," by Carla Bley Band, which involves a performance of the "Star-Spangled Banner" in a minor key, he lists the following:

> For instance, one kind of move is *locational,* relating the object that one is hearing to an appropriate range within a subjective field of like items and events or unlike items and events. Such a move would, in this case, vary significantly if the listener were an American.
>
> One might also have certain more specific *categorical* interpretive moves, relating this to a class of things—anthems, patriotic songs. . . . Moreover, one might additionally make various *associational* moves, relating or analogizing this item to particular visual, musical, or verbal imagery. . . . Additionally one might make a variety of *reflective* moves, relating this item to some personal and social conditions, (like political attitudes, patriotism, nationalism) and related experiences where things like and unlike this can be heard, mediated or live. . . . Perhaps one also makes some *evaluative* interpretive moves, instantly finding this funny, distasteful, inappropriate, or immoral.[62]

Pattern discovery in listening occurs on a number of levels simultaneously. While the recognition of "pattern" might be called "formal recognition" in some sense, Feld emphasizes the social and symbolic interpretations in response to musical pattern and the role these play in our getting our bearings in music. Does this anthem represent my nation or a foreign one? Does this orchestral form symbolize the reconciliation of all nature (as in Beethoven's Ninth Symphony) or disintegration? Is this music straightforwardly religious (as in Josquin's *Missa Pange Lingua*)? Such questions are fundamental to any interpretation of music, and they require active judgment and awareness of relationships not fully contained "in the notes."

Feld acknowledges that such mental activities, which accompany any effort to interpret encountered music, can stifle fresh listening (a concern reminiscent of Hanslick when he complains about the listening habits of "pathological listeners"). But they need not. Interpretive "frames," he argues, can either "lock in or compact a summary of all interacting interpretive constructs, or . . . let them scatter and draw more attention to [the frame's] own position among these elements."[63] A recognition of the various conscious moves that are enlisted in active listening can in fact alert one to the limitations of too rigid an adherence to any one of them.

Hanslick describes musical experience as a kind of step-by-step processing of musical events in sequence. He acknowledges a role for unconscious recognitions, admittedly; but his model depicts the listener's mind as serially "catching" the relations that the composer puts before it. He makes no room in his account for the mental play that we all experience while listening, a play that Feld points out is fundamental to our getting our mental bearings in a musical work. Nor does Hanslick acknowledge extramusical awareness or the comparison of music with extramusical patterns as basic to our appropriation of patterns while we listen.

Because he builds mental play into his model, Kant has room for some of the active mental operations that Feld describes. In making "free play" his fundamental model of aesthetic experience, Kant gives us a different picture of the listener's appropriation of musical form. Form, to paraphrase Sparshott's remark cited earlier, is "an opportunity" in Kant's system. Believing that it is an opportunity that can engage any human being, so long as that person is capable of speech, Kant stresses the active play of the mind on the occasion of encountering form. Form is not, as in Hanslick's account, a musical "tracking" of the listener's mind. Instead, form is an occasion for the listener's imagination to engage itself with the music. In this respect, Kant's account is more accommodating to our actual listening experience.

Of course, Kant himself does not go out of his way to encourage the range of "interpretive moves" that Feld describes. Kant restricts the role of empirical conditions in aesthetic judgment (seeing them as impediments to aesthetic purity) and seeks a universal foundation of aesthetic appreciation. A sense of one's belonging to one nation or another or an awareness of the social context that grants a pattern a local symbolic meaning would, from Kant's point of view, be extraaesthetic distraction. Nor can we credit the empirical Kant with imaginative openness to musical possibilities. But my point is that Kant's aesthetic theory appropriates "form" much more broadly and realistically than Hanslick's. Unfortunately, it is the Hanslickean spirit of "science" that has guided the development of musical aesthetics over the past century.

But even Hanslick should be credited for quietly acknowledging that "form" has an ethical aspect. "Form," as Hanslick uses the term, has a relationship to spiritual life. Hence "the forms which construct themselves out of tones are not empty but filled; they are not mere contours of a vacuum but mind giving shape to itself from within."[64] It is worth asking Hanslick, or the contemporary formalist who stresses "attending to structure," why it is that the great musical structures of our classical canon continue to live for us. Might it not be that the very formal complexity of these works prevents us from ever entirely attending to the form? Even in relatively form-centered attention to Mozart's Fortieth Symphony, I think, any listener's attention makes leaps from one concern to another, if only because one cannot attend to everything. But if this is so, and if, as I suspect, this active immersion in listening is itself enjoyable, then even formal focus transcends itself.

Perhaps a similar intuition prompted Hanslick, while defending musical experience as mentally active, to the remarkable claim that

> music['s] . . . achievements are not static: they do not come into being all at once but spin themselves out sequentially before the hearer, hence they demand from him not an arbitrarily granted, lingering, and intermittent inspection, but an unflagging attendance in keenest vigilance. This attendance can, in the case of intricate compositions, become intensified to the level of spiritual achievement.[65]

This admission that following an unfolding form can be a "spiritual achievement" is, I think, the key to the repressed in musical formalism. The ultimate value that even Hanslick discovers in attending to form extends beyond mental exercise to a broader integration of the listener's powers.

Both Kant and Hanslick overemphasize the intellectual aspects of listening at the expense of the more holistic enjoyment that listening, for most of us, involves. In this respect, both of their accounts are disturbingly incomplete. In the next chapter, we consider the affective aspects of musical experience and its connection with ethical experience. Later I return to the "intellectual" features of music that Hanslick emphasizes and suggest that he was right in claiming that these, too, have a role in spiritual life.

3 ‖: Music and Emotions: The History

The joy of the heart begets song.—The Talmud

Through the mid-nineteenth century, emotion provided a theoretical link between music and ethics in Western philosophical thought.[1] From the time of Plato and Aristotle, music's influence on the listener's emotions was thought by most philosophers who discussed it to have a powerful effect on ethical outlook and behavior. The history of theories connecting music and emotion, accordingly, corresponds to the development of Western attitudes toward the relationship of music and ethics.

There are three predominant historical Western explanations of the relationship between music and emotion. These are (in the order of their emergence and respective dominance): (1) music *imitates* or *represents* emotion; (2) music *arouses* emotion; and (3) music *expresses* emotion. The shift from imitation to arousal to expression parallels a move away from implicit assumptions grounding the shared character of musical experience in aspects of the experience that can be termed "contextual."

This tendency reaches a new threshold in the nineteenth-century theory of Hanslick. Hanslick's theory represents not so much a denial of any relationship between music and emotion as a shift toward an exclusively structural account of music, which in turn renders the emotion–music connection problematic. His account allows for some connection between emotion and music, but only *if* this connection is subordinated to a structural account of music, and thus divorced from an analysis of context.

Hanslick's orientation has influenced the accounts of the music–emotion connection developed in this century. The most influential accounts have typically aimed to forge links between emotion and structural features of music, subordinating any explanatory contribution that might be made by contextual features of music. But these efforts ignore the emotional impact of many other factors, including the emotional attitudes assumed by the listener on the basis of style, performance situation, and audience affiliation, as well as the listener's empathetic stance toward emotions suggested by music.

History

Imitation Theory

The theory that music imitates emotion is familiar to almost every student of philosophy through the writings of Plato and Aristotle. Both believed that music accomplished its imitative purpose by means of modes and rhythms, and that such imitation had an ethical impact on listeners. In the *Republic*, Plato suggests that specific patterns of intervals (which distinguish modes) evoke particular emotions, and that specific rhythms recall the dynamic character of particular feelings. In light of these associations, the state should regulate music, restricting it to modes and rhythms that have a benign ethical influence:

> Leave us that mode that would fittingly imitate the utterances and the accents of a brave man who is engaged in warfare or in any enforced business, and who, when he has failed, either meeting wounds or death or having fallen into some other mishap, in all these conditions confronts fortune with steadfast endurance and repels her strokes. And another for such a man engaged in works of peace, not enforced but voluntary, either trying to persuade somebody of something and imploring him— whether it be a god, through prayer, or a man, by teaching and admonition—or contrariwise yielding himself to another who is petitioning or teaching him or trying to change his opinions, and in consequence faring according to his wish, and not bearing himself arrogantly, but in all this acting modestly and moderately and acquiescing in the outcome. . . . upon harmonies would follow the consideration of rhythms; we must not pursue complexity nor great variety in the basic movements, but must observe what are the rhythms of a life that is orderly and brave, and after observing them require the foot and the air to conform to that kind of man's speech and not the speech to the foot and the tune. . . . seemliness and unseemliness are attendant upon the good rhythm and the bad.[2]

Aristotle similarly ascribes emotional characters to modes and rhythms in the *Politics*, and concludes that music has a profound impact on character and spiritual state. After discussing music's recreational character, he remarks:

> In addition to this common pleasure, felt and shared in by all (for the pleasure given by music is natural, and therefore adapted to all ages and characters), may it not have also some influence over the character and the soul? It must have such an influence if characters are affected by it.

And that they are so affected is proved in many ways, and not least by the power which the songs of Olympus exercise; for beyond question they inspire enthusiasm, and enthusiasm is an emotion of the ethical part of the soul. Besides, when men hear imitations, even apart from the rhythms and tunes themselves, their feelings move in sympathy. . . . Rhythm and melody supply imitations of anger and gentleness, and also of courage and temperance, and of all the qualities contrary to these, and of the other qualities of character, which hardly fall short of the actual affections, as we know from our own experience, for in listening to such strains our souls undergo a change.[3]

Is this association of musical elements with emotions a prototypical theory of music as structure? There are decisive differences between the ancient Greek perspective and the modern structural notion. In the first place, the ancient Greeks did not share our expectation that a musical work will be structurally complicated. Greek music consisted primarily of songs with a single basic scale-pattern and a single dominant rhythm. Thus one did not need to examine structural nuance in order to determine the emotional content of a piece of music. Emotions were associated with the broadest features of a song (or other musical form) and were thus constant for the whole "piece" of music.[4]

Plato and Aristotle also assumed that the specification of emotion proceeded in large part from contextual elements. Although some of the associations between modes and emotions were probably conventional (for example, the Dorian mode sounded "warlike" and "manly" because military music was always composed in it), both assumed that such associations would be reinforced by the emotional tone of poetic texts.[5] Ancient Greek music was almost always associated with words and dance. Plato so completely assumed that music was paradigmatically texted that he categorized music as a part of poetry.[6]

The imitation theory of Plato and Aristotle is thus not bound to a structural conception of music. On the contrary, it assumes the role of an active, responsive audience. In fact, this theory might be termed an "arousal" theory were it not for its emphasis. Both Plato and Aristotle believed that music, by imitating states of mind, aroused similar states in the listener. Music's capacity to convey passions through imitation was, in fact, precisely what Plato found so suspect about it, while Aristotle considered it the means by which music could serve as a vehicle of ethical education.[7]

Nevertheless, although mindful of music's impact on inner life, Plato and Aristotle stressed its external effects. The Socrates of the *Republic*, in his discussion of music, is exclusively concerned with responsive behavior of listeners. And although Aristotle considered a wide range of music's effects and functions, he, too, devoted considerable attention to music's effect on character and behavior. Both thinkers also believed that imitation was objective. There is no room in the account of either for doubt as to what state of mind any given passage of music conveys. If one recognizes the mode and rhythm, one recognizes the emotional content of the music.[8]

Arousal Theory

Imitation theory was superseded during the medieval period. Arousal theory came to dominate philosophical thought about music in the West, until imitation theory was revived by certain theorists of the eighteenth century. The shift at first amounted only to a change of emphasis. Medieval arousal theory presupposed an imitation theory. Music was thought to have the power to arouse emotion because of its imitative character.[9]

Saint Augustine was an early proponent of the arousal theory. He saw value in music's power to inspire a devotional state of mind. But Augustine admired the orderly, "numerical" proportion inherent in music more than its arousal potential. Music's highest purpose, on his view, was to serve as a vehicle for intellectual appreciation of divine order, as reflected in numerical relationships.[10]

Influenced by Plato in his respect for music's orderly proportions, Augustine also followed Plato in acknowledging music's power to arouse emotion. The shift in emphasis from imitation to arousal might well reflect Augustine's particular concern, as a Christian bishop, with the promotion of virtue as opposed to sin. The music that Augustine associated with emotion was specifically texted music connected with worship. He apparently had no doubt that such music would have similar effects on all hearers, owing to the character of the melody. Augustine saw music's capacity to inspire emotion as a mixed blessing. Even in religious music, melody could become too sensuously interesting in itself. To the extent that it did so, melody constituted temptation: "the sense . . . having for reason's sake gained admission, . . . strives even to run before and be her leader. Thus in these things I sometimes sin unawares, but afterwards am aware of it." Augustine insisted that melody employed in worship should be reduced to simplicity so that the intellect could stay attuned to the prayerful words that it accompanied.[11]

Augustine obviously considered some melodies to be more sensuously appealing than others, since he viewed simplicity as an ideal. But he contrasts the music that exhibits it not with music of more complicated or more ornamental structure, but with music that features "warbling of the voice," something more technically described as a matter of articulation than of structure. Apparently, when Augustine refers to the "temptation of the flesh" afforded by the sensuous quality of some music, he refers literally to physical attraction provoked by the sensual and appealing qualities of the human voice:

> Whenas I am moved not with the singing, but with the thing sung (when namely they are set off with a clear voice and suitable modulation), I then acknowledge the great good use of this institution. . . . And yet again, so oft as it befalls me to be more moved with the voice than with the ditty, I confess myself to have grievously offended.[12]

Augustine's emphasis on the mathematical aspects of music as opposed to its practical emotional aspect reflects his Neoplatonic interests. The development of Western thought on the music–emotion connection can be seen as the ultimate domination of this Platonic–Augustinian preference for the mathematical over the emotional. But the recent version of this hierarchy is more estranged from the ethical sphere than were Plato's and Augustine's version.

Plato still valued the practical use of music to effect emotional responses and ethical dispositions, and his mathematical realm was akin (although inferior) to the realm of forms, which was the true ground of ethical insight. Augustine drew an even closer connection between ethics and mathematical insight into music, for he believed that music reflected the order of divine law, itself the basis of ethical conduct. Moreover, he believed that melodies, when properly subordinated to religious texts, could positively dispose a worshiper to prayerful emotion. Thus, despite the preference for the "mathematical" that links recent philosophers of music with Plato and Augustine, these ancient thinkers appreciated music—in both its mathematical and its emotional character—as an ethical medium in a way that recent philosophers typically do not.

The theory that music arouses intersubjective emotion held sway throughout the medieval period. Historically, René Descartes was one of the most adamant proponents of arousal theory, for he considered music's very purpose to be "to please and to move the various affections in us."[13] But Descartes added some new twists to arousal theory. He denied that musically aroused emotions were intersubjective. He also denied that arousal stemmed from musical imitations. Instead, he argued that the emotions aroused by music were the products of purely personal associations. Writing to Marin Mersenne, Descartes asserted:

That which moves some to dance, causes others to wish to cry. The reason for this is that certain images in our memories are aroused: those who once found pleasure in dancing to a particular melody will want to do so again, when they hear it anew. And conversely, if someone has suffered while listening to the sounds of a *galliarde,* he will certainly be sad when he hears it again. If one were to thrash a dog five or six times to the sound of a violin, when he heard that sound again, he would surely whine and run away.[14]

Descartes, who first developed the modern theory of the isolated cognitive subject, considered emotive experience in conjunction with music to be a similarly private, individual matter. Thus, skepticism regarding the intersubjective character of music's emotional content appeared along with the basic subjective turn that ushered in modern philosophy.

Part of what Descartes challenged was the traditional assumption that contextual cues secured the commonality of audience emotional experience. Certain contextual features of listening remained important to Descartes, for these were the bases of the personal emotional associations that his theory described. But he treats these features and associations as biographical accidents, not as customary concomitants of musical performance. Perhaps, like Kant, Descartes was particularly interested in the range of reactions to specific instrumental timbres and developed his association theory as an explanation. At any rate, he underplays the emotional responses to immediate features of context (such things as vital drive, social occasion, and details of articulation), emphasizing instead the importance and fixity of memory in the formation of emotional reactions.

Indeed, Descartes treats the music as almost an unstructured stimulus. On his account, instrumentation (which is usually constant through a whole performance, or at least through a given piece) can establish a listener's emotional response to a piece of music. Internal changes in musical structure, on the other hand, seem incapable of shaking a generic emotional reaction to a particular instrument or compositional form. As Rowell observes, Descartes' theory of music "implied that the response to beauty is a kind of conditioned reflex."[15]

Descartes' rationalism had considerable influence on music theory, as did his basic account of emotion, which he viewed as a perturbation of the "vital or animal spirits," a particular physical medium within us.[16] But his skepticism regarding the intersubjectivity of music-based emotions did not attain dominance. Perhaps his influential model of the individual conscious mind, coupled with this skeptical outlook, provoked his intellectual descendants to seek an objective basis for musically elicited emotion. At any rate, the resurgence of arousal theory in the Renaissance took inspiration from Plato and Aristotle. Despite Descartes, arousal theory was again linked to the idea that music imitates emotion.

Imitation and Arousal Go Structural

The difference between this later arousal theory and that of the Middle Ages was that the later theory was wed to detailed analysis of music. A tendency to analyze music on the model of rhetoric and poetics developed in the Renaissance along with the expansion of interest in Aristotle's writings on music in the *Poetics* and *Politics*. In the years spanning the medieval period and the Renaissance, as we observed in Chapter 1, developments in notation had made possible increasingly structured musical compositions. As a consequence, the sixteenth and seventeenth centuries had a relatively "objective" conception of music, which was analyzed in terms of specific melodic, rhythmic, and harmonic patterns.

This "objectified" and structural conception of music had an impact on the correlations seen between music and emotion. A number of seventeenth-century treatises modeled on Aristotle's theories of music and rhetoric developed theoretical systems of "feelings" correlated with musical intervals and rhythmic–melodic patterns, which in turn were correlated with rhetorical devices and figures. According to Edward Lippman, the stereotyped "feelings" were supposed to be "aroused in the listener when the tonal pattern to which they were correlated produced analogous motions in the corporeal fluids, or 'vital spirits.'" Because they allegedly occasioned biological responses, these patterns were believed to have essential connections with emotional states; they were not understood as merely conventional. Moreover, these "affections" were not linked to the expression of an individual artist's feelings; they were taken to be emotions in the abstract and not at all arbitrary.[17]

Thus, while Descartes' theory of the vital spirits found its place in the post-Renaissance version of arousal theory, his view that musically aroused emotions were radically private was firmly rejected. Instead, the emotions aroused by music were understood to be universal and intersubjectively accessible to everyone. Significantly, these universal emotions were comprehended in terms of musical structures. One did not have to analyze the context of musical listening to apprehend emotional content. Descartes' association between certain contextual factors and private subjective states

was, in a sense, inverted by the later theory. It was precisely because context was *not* viewed as a relevant factor that the emotions aroused could be
securely pinpointed and claimed to be intersubjective.

The Renaissance interest in antiquity revived imitation theory while
giving impetus to arousal theory as well. But in the eighteenth century,
imitation theory began to flourish on its own, without any corollary theory
regarding arousal. One basis for this shift was a theoretical desire to establish a common goal for all the arts. Charles Batteaux defended the view that
all arts had the same basic aim by enlisting the Aristotelian theory that art
aims at imitation. In the case of music, the object of imitation is emotion:
"The passions are the principal object of music and of dance." [18]

Despite Aristotle's role in the revival of imitation theory, the theory's
eighteenth-century formulation contrasted with its ancient counterpart.
Eighteenth-century theorists believed that instrumental music, by then a
significant musical phenomenon, could provide objective imitations of emotion. The poetic text was no longer assumed to be decisive in musical communication of emotion. The growing prominence of untexted music meant
the decline of one traditional link between music and ethics, the ethically
significant texts that music supported.

Eighteenth-century imitation theory also diverged from its ancient predecessor—and from a conception of music as an ethical influence—in its
association with a "natural language" view of musical meaning. Batteaux
was a spokesman for this position. Music, he claimed, is a natural language,
which uses signs modeled on nature. Because its meaning is grounded in
nature, moreover, music can unproblematically communicate passion:

> Music speaks to me through tones: that language is natural to me: if I do
> not understand it at all, art has corrupted nature rather than perfected
> it. . . . All feeling, says Cicero, has a tone, a proper gesture that announces
> it; this is like the word attached to the idea.[19]

In defense of this natural language theory, Batteaux appealed to intuition
more than argument. Admitting that we cannot name the passions imitated
by most music, Batteaux claims that this is unimportant. "It suffices that
one sense it, it is not necessary to name it. The heart has its intelligence independent of words, and when it is touched it has understood everything."
And unlike the arousal theorists of the seventeenth century and the expression theorists of his own era, Batteaux did not attempt to link emotion to
any specific structural features of music. Indeed, he sides with feeling over
structure:

Let us conclude then that the music the best calculated in all its tones, the most geometric in its harmonies, if it happened that with these qualities it had not a single signification, it could be compared only to a prism, which presents the most beautiful colors and forms no picture at all. It would be a species of chromatic clavecin, which would present colors and transitions, perhaps to amuse the eye, and certainly to bore the mind.[20]

Another divergence between ancient and eighteenth-century imitation theory was the latter's divorce from arousal. Like other artistic depictions, music was thought by most of the eighteenth-century theorists to represent objective reality for the detached listener.[21] This view of music was even more pronounced in another eighteenth-century contingent: the proponents of expression theory.

Expression Theory

The theory that music expresses emotions is a product of the Enlightenment. It reflects both Enlightenment glorification of the universal and the Kantian emphasis on the subjective character of experience. The expressionist theory of music and emotion located the emotional significance of music in the subjective state of the musician, but it understood this state to be universally accessible.

Enlightenment expression theory developed in opposition to the renewed interest in imitation theory. Batteaux had contended that the common goal of the arts was to "imitate" reality. But as instrumental music became a more important musical phenomenon and imitative cues provided by texts more infrequent, the idea that music imitates reality on a par with representational arts became less convincing. A growing movement rejected Batteaux's theory that all the arts had the same aim.

Music's aim was different—it sought to express the inner world, not to represent external reality. Such expressionists as J. G. Herder, C. P. E. Bach, Daniel Schubart, and Heinrich Heine argued that the composer's task was to express his innermost being in music. Not mimicry but communication of inner life was the composer's chief concern. Music was to be an "actual outpouring of the heart."[22]

The private individual self was not, however, the being whose emotions concerned these composers. Instead, they sought to express the "intelligible self." "The intelligible self" was a universal self, free from the empirical constraints and practical motives that distinguish one person from another.

The subjective state expressed in music was thus conceived as a universally available stance, not as the reflection of a private subjectivity.

Because it was understood as universal, this emotional expression was considered an effective means of communication between composer, performer, and listener. In fact, it was *the* means by which communication was achieved. C. P. E. Bach's maxim of performance was that a musician "could not move others unless he himself was moved."[23]

This maxim itself reflects an irony involved in the development of expressionist theory. Premised on the notion of a universal selfhood, expressionist theory nonetheless paved the way for skepticism regarding the communication of inner states. If music aimed to express the inner state of the musician, how could one be certain that the audience recognized that inner state? For that matter, how could a composer be sure that his intelligible self, not his private self, was the source of his expression? Eventually such questions were employed by Hanslick in an effort to undercut expressionist theory.

Eighteenth-century expressionists also contributed to the move toward structural accounts in accepting the legitimacy of instrumental music. When Hanslick later raised skeptical questions regarding the basis for claims about universal emotional content, textual evidence could not be used in rebuttal. Defenses resorting to structure were, by contrast, tenable and arguably invited as a valid response by Hanslick.[24]

The eighteenth-century emphasis on universality also resulted in a less contextual understanding of music. The earlier notion that the "ethos" of different human types and contexts could be reflected in music was not consonant with the Enlightenment ideal of transcending differences between human beings. By contrast, the general tendency to associate rationality, so glorified in the eighteenth century, with basic, universal structures of the human mind made structuralist analyses the preferred intellectual approach.[25]

The expressionist theories of the nineteenth century intensified these tendencies to take untexted music as paradigmatic and to regard as universal the expressive content of music. Instrumental music was considered the ideal artistic medium by the Romantic age. More divorced from everyday experience than either texted music or more representational arts, instrumental music could suggest the yearning inner life of the human Spirit (or Will) and the boundlessness of the transcendent.[26] Although the Romantics underplayed the connection between music and practical behavior, they considered music a medium for transcendent spiritual experience.

Wagner, high priest of nineteenth-century expressionism, was typically Romantic in considering music the finest vehicle for emotional communication. Of all the arts, music most ideally achieves art's basic aim, which is to serve as a medium for the artist's vision to speak to the emotions.[27]

Although essentially an expressionist, Wagner embraced a kind of imitation theory; for he believed that music revealed inner life through a kind of emotional depiction.[28] Wagner was also concerned, in his operatic art, with arousing emotion in his listeners. But, being prototypically Romantic, Wagner had no interest in either imitation or evocation of everyday emotion. Music, on his view, had a transcendent vocation. It portrayed the elemental life force beneath everyday human reality, and by stirring what is fundamental in the listener, it could effect the union of man and God, soul and body.[29]

Modesty was not Wagner's strong suit. Although unconcerned in his art with the personal emotions of the private self, he nonetheless glorified the personal power of the composer. Overturning the Kantian notion of genius, which considered the possessor of genius a vehicle for a force of nature, Wagner promoted a theory of genius as a power with personality, a power that entitled its possessor to unrestricted license. This did not strike the Romantics as inconsistent, however, for the composer's personality itself was seen as a manifestation of an inner life in touch with the transcendent.[30]

A more musically significant irony lay in the fact that Wagner, the most ardent defender of the evocative power of music, considered music a mere *ancilla* to drama. "My primary aim," he insisted, "is to compel the public to focus its attention upon the dramatic action so closely that it is never for a moment lost sight of: all the musical elaboration must be experienced simply as the presentation of this action." Although Wagner had no doubt that music without words communicates emotion, he was unwilling to rely on music's own power. Without words, Wagner argued, music's emotional potential remained sterile: "*But every musical organism is by its nature—a woman. . .* ; it is merely a *bearing,* and not a *begetting* factor; the begetting force [drama] lies clean *outside it,* and without fecundation by this force it positively cannot bear."[31]

It was only in the twentieth century that an expression theory of music and emotion concerned itself with the personal emotions of the private individual. This theory was not descriptive; instead it was a prescriptive theory about legitimate compositional aims. Expression of the composer's personal feelings and states of consciousness, according to this theory, was an appropriate aim for music.[32] Following expressionists in the visual arts, who reflected the rift between external and inner reality by distorting and exaggerating depictions of the external world, expressionist composers departed from musical *terra firma* by abandoning traditional tonality.

Before the expression of private emotion became a compositional aim, however, its possibility became a philosophical problem. How, asked Hanslick, can we be sure that any music expresses intersubjective emotion? What grounds are there for the earlier expressionists' claim that music is a universal language of emotions? When instrumental music is taken as paradigmatic, Hanslick argued, no vocabulary of emotions can be found. Hanslick dislodged intellectual faith in the idea that music has an emotional content.

Hanslick on the Emotions

Despite his reputation, Hanslick is remarkably tolerant of claims linking music to emotion. As Payzant observes: "He by no means claims that music cannot arouse, express, or portray feelings; obviously it can do all these things. He merely says that to do so is not the defining purpose of music." Payzant acknowledges the influence of *On the Musically Beautiful* on twentieth-century readers, presumably including those who have questioned these powers of music. But he observes that "there is a remarkable disproportion between its influence and the author's modest intentions in writing it."[33]

Hanslick's views on music's relation to emotion are, as we have noted, the result of his effort to make musical aesthetics objective and "scientific." A scientific musical aesthetics must be based on necessary laws that link form (understood as structure) to beauty. But no necessary connection between music and definite emotions can be established, since the "thought" that specifies each definite emotion cannot be communicated by music. Thus, associations between music and emotions have no place in musical aesthetics, and they are irrelevant to proper aesthetic appreciation.

This is the basic form of Hanslick's attack on each of the three basic theories we have considered. He attacks them only insofar as they are asserted as *aesthetic* theories of music. In each case, he allows great latitude for the theory's basic premise, so long as it is recognized as extraneous to aesthetic considerations.

In his consideration of music's capacity for imitation or representation, for instance, Hanslick makes remarkable allowances. He acknowledges that "music can, with its very own resources, represent most amply a certain range of ideas":

These . . . are simply all those ideas which relate to audible changes in strength, motion, and proportion and consequently they include our ideas of increasing and diminishing, acceleration and deceleration, clever interweavings, simple progressions, and the like. Moreover, it would be possible for the aesthetic expression of a piece of music to be called charming, soft, impetuous, powerful, delicate, sprightly. These are pure ideas which have their corresponding sensuous manifestation in musical tonal relationships. So we can apply these adjectives to music without regard to their ethical significance, which has a way of becoming insidiously confused with purely musical qualities.

Even a description of what Hanslick terms "purely musical qualities" can thus involve considerable use of emotive terminology. And Hanslick grants that our imagination naturally leaps from musical qualities to affective associations:

> Just as every actual phenomenon points to the generic concept or idea which includes it, and this in turn to the idea which includes it, and so on higher and higher to the concept of the absolute Idea, so it is with musical ideas. Thus, for example, this calm adagio, harmoniously dying away, will bring the general idea of calm harmoniousness to the beautiful phenomenon. Imagination, which gladly refers artistic ideas to the peculiarly human inner awareness, will interpret this dying away on a higher level, e.g., as the expression of mellow resignation by a person of equable disposition, and can perhaps ascend instantly to an intimation of everlasting bliss in the world beyond.[34]

Why, then, does Hanslick criticize the theory that music imitates or represents emotion? Because music, in his view, cannot specify *definite* emotions. In order for emotions to be specified, mental representations of emotional *objects* would have to be established by music. But music, instead, gives us only "unspecified stirrings," and these cannot serve as a basis for aesthetic law:

> Instrumental music cannot represent the ideas of love, anger, fear, because between those ideas and beautiful combinations of musical tones there exists no necessary connection. Then which moment of these ideas is it that music knows how to seize so effectively? The answer: motion. . . . Motion is the ingredient which music has in common with emotional states and which it is able to shape creatively in a thousand shades and contrasts. . . . Whatever else in music seems to portray specific states of mind is symbolic.[35]

Hanslick's case against imitation theory, therefore, is grounded in his insistence on necessary connections. The associations between musical "behavior" and emotion that imitation theory asserts are conceded by Hanslick but, in the same breath, demeaned. Associations and symbolisms, while perhaps common to virtually all listeners, are not sufficiently grounded to be an "objective" basis for musical aesthetics.

Regarding *arousal theory,* Hanslick distinguishes the claim that music arouses feelings (a matter that he considers indisputable) from the claim that this is "the task of music." "Once we grasp that the active imagination is the real organ of the beautiful, feeling will be admitted to be a secondary effect in each of the arts." But in Hanslick's opinion, emotional arousal cannot be the primary *purpose* of music, for failure to arouse emotion does not constitute musical failure. "Beauty is and remains beauty even if no feelings are aroused." Hanslick also argues that music cannot be explained as being designed to arouse emotions, for emotions are much more emphatically aroused by other experiences. (This is obviously more a polemical point than a persuasive one. We might enjoy artistic control over emotional arousal and thus devise ways to accomplish it even if other experiences do result in more intense arousal.)

> Joy and sorrow can in the highest degree be called into life by music; to this we entirely agree. But could not even more intense feeling be caused by winning a big prize in a lottery or by the mortal illness of a friend? So long as we are reluctant to include lottery tickets among the symphonies or medical reports among the overtures, we must not treat the feeling it in fact produces as an aesthetic specialty of music or of a particular composition. How such feelings will be aroused by music depends entirely upon the circumstances of each particular instance.[36]

This last sentence reveals Hanslick's determination to remove the concerns of aesthetics from the contingencies of circumstances—and thus from all matters of context. Context figures prominently in emotional arousal, but because Hanslick treats music as structure independent of context, this is all the more reason to dismiss arousal from musical aesthetic concern.

Again the search for necessary aesthetic laws leads Hanslick to deny arousal a place in musical aesthetics. Observing that the emotions associated with given works have varied over time, he insists that musical value and beauty have remained unaltered. "Thus," he concludes, "the effect of music upon feeling possesses neither the necessity nor the exclusiveness nor the constancy which a phenomenon would have to exhibit in order to be the basis of an aesthetic principle."[37]

Hanslick treats *expression* theory much as he does the other theories. He both acknowledges music's expressive potential and insists that expression is irrelevant to aesthetics because it is insufficiently lawlike:

> I share completely the view that the ultimate worth of the beautiful is always based on the immediate manifestness of feeling. However, I hold just as firmly the conviction that, from all the customary appeals to feeling, we can derive not a single musical law.[38]

Expression, like arousal, cannot be the purpose of music, according to Hanslick. To claim that music expresses emotion would make it a mere means, comparable to speech:

> The essential difference is that in speech the sound is only a sign, that is, a means to an end which is entirely distinct from that means, while in music the sound is an object, i.e., it appears to us as an end in itself. The autonomous beauty of tone-forms in music and the absolute supremacy of thought over sound as merely a means of expression in spoken language are so exclusively opposed that a combination of the two is a logical impossibility.[39]

Music is thus not a mere communicative means, as expression theory suggests.

Nor is "emotion" the concern of composers, as expressionists claim when they assert that the composer conveys inner experiences. Composers are primarily concerned with tonal relations. A composer *may,* while composing, focus on the idea of an emotion, Hanslick concedes, but only as an organizing technique:

> It is often said that Beethoven, while sketching many of his compositions, must have thought of specific events or states of mind. Where Beethoven or any other composer followed this procedure, he used it merely as a device whereby the coherence of an external event makes it easier to keep hold of the musical entity. If Berlioz, Liszt, etc., believed they got more than this out of the poem, the title, or the experience, this was a self-delusion.[40]

So much for appeals to the testimony of composers!

Hanslick concedes the role of contextual features in emotional expression but denies the relevance of either to musical aesthetics. He acknowledges that the *performer* expresses feeling through particular musical performances:

The act in which the direct emanation in tones of a feeling can take place is not so much the fabrication as the reproduction of a musical work. . . . To the performer it is granted to release directly the feeling which possesses him, through his instrument, and breathe into his performance the wild storms, the passionate fervour, the serene power and joy of his inwardness. The bodily ardour that through my fingertips suddenly presses the soulful vibrato upon the string, or pulls the bow, or indeed makes itself audible in song, in actual fact makes possible the most personal outpouring of feeling in music-making. Here a personal attitude becomes directly audibly effective in tones, not just silently formative in them. . . . Thus the emotionally cathartic and stimulating aspect of music is situated in the reproductive act, which coaxes the electric spark out of its obscure secret place and flashes it across to the listener.

Hanslick goes on to acknowledge "the highest degree of immediacy" in expression, which is achieved by the improviser who is motivated "not with formally artistic but with predominantly subjective intent," so that "love, jealousy, rapture, and grief come roaring, undisguised yet unbidden, out of their night."[41] Hanslick describes this as one of the most magical phenomena in music. And his abrupt shift, after these remarks, to a discussion of the subjective condition of the listener might be seen as a rhetorical admission of the importance of what his aesthetics omits. At any rate, Hanslick does not, as usual, denigrate this "nonaesthetic" phenomenon after citing it.

But Hanslick concludes the chapter in which this discussion occurs by reiterating a dichotomy that underlies his restriction of the scope of musical aesthetics: the opposition of the *physical* and the *intellectual*. He contrasts the "physical" features of music (including physiological effects as well as the bodily based expression of emotion in performance) with the contemplative aspect of listening. This intellectual side of music is the exclusive basis for aesthetic appreciation of music. Emotional expression, Hanslick admits, is a component of musical phenomena; but because it is tied to the physical rather than the intellectual side of music, he does not consider it a matter with which aesthetics need concern itself.

Hanslick's relegation of emotion to the category of the "nonaesthetic" leads directly to his dissociation of musical aesthetics from ethics. Analyzing the alleged "moral effects" of music as consequences of its neurophysiological influence, he denies that these effects are worthy of being called "moral." Morality is a matter of free, intellectually guided choice, not of physiological manipulation. Again, the dichotomy between the intellectual and the physical comes down against the ethical and emotional:

The creditor who, when pressing for repayment, was so moved by the sound of his debtor's music that he forgave the whole debt is activated in no other way than the sluggard who is all of a sudden prompted by a waltz tune to dance. . . . Neither proceeds out of free self-determination . . . ; neither is yielding to the promptings of spirit or of love for beauty, but both are stirred as a result of neural stimulation. Music loosens the feet or the heart as wine the tongue. Such conquests tell us only about the vulnerability of the vanquished. To undergo unmotivated, aimless, and casual emotional disturbances through a power that is not *en rapport* with our willing and thinking is unworthy of the human spirit.

Far from being morally desirable, music in such cases is potentially harmful, for it can impede the moral independence of the intellectually enlightened will:

When people surrender themselves so completely to the elemental in an art that they are not in control of themselves, then it seems to us that this is not to the credit of that art and still less to the credit of those people. . . . Beethoven insisted that music should "strike fire in the soul." Note carefully that word *should*. It is open to question, however, whether or not a fire produced and nourished by music might inhibit the development of a person's willpower and intelligence. . . . Just as the physical effects of music stand in direct relation to morbid irritation of the nervous system accommodating itself to them, so the moral influence of tones increases with coarseness of mind and character. . . . As is well known, music exercises the strongest effect upon savages.[42]

Hanslick's disinterest in emotional and ethical responses to music stems from his view that aesthetics should study and develop laws regarding precisely defined relationships between tones. His defense of this disinterest, however, is not particularly compelling, as Malcolm Budd's recent critique of Hanslick indicates. Budd concurs with Hanslick that listening in which reverie obstructs any notice of musical events is not "aesthetic" experience. But Hanslick fails to establish "that an emotion in a person's response is never aesthetically relevant, or never required, or of no importance."[43] Budd analyzes the possibilities ignored by Hanslick's account in great detail. In my view, Budd treats Hanslick's book as a more thoroughgoing argument than it sets out to be, with the result that Budd's discussion at times reads like a catalogue of Hanslick's sins of omission. But Budd valuably establishes that Hanslick's achievements, whatever his goals might have been, are quite modest.

Budd also points out that Hanslick himself lays the foundations for defending certain "objective" connections between music and emotion. For example, Budd cites Hanslick's mention of the "general feeling of satisfaction or discomfort" that music affords:

> If music could represent the experience of satisfaction and dissatisfaction, in the sense that it could in some way reproduce or copy them, there would after all be a connection, of the kind Hanslick denies, between music and at least something integral and peculiar to emotions and other allied phenomena. Or if, at least, there are musical analogues of pleasure and pain and the different ways in which they arise and develop, then a musical work might stand in a significant symbolic relation to an important element of the emotions. . . . And if this essential element of emotional experience can in some way be made manifest by music, its appearance in a musical work might be sufficient to endow the work with musical value or to make the music intrinsically rewarding from the listener's point of view.[44]

Moreover, dissonance and consonance and the movement from tension to resolution are integral features of Western tonal music; and these dualities "naturally" correspond to the duality of dissatisfaction and satisfaction. Why not expect an affect registering satisfaction or dissatisfaction to be a constant concomitant of purely tonal displays of dissonance or consonance, tension or resolution?

I have already mentioned other reasons for thinking that musical aesthetics should not be restricted as Hanslick suggests. I would therefore quarrel with Hanslick's premises, which underlie his case against aesthetic concern with emotion in music. Below I consider some additional reasons for rejecting Hanslick's premises, reasons which bear more directly on the "ethical" functions of music. I proceed to these arguments, however, by way of a critical consideration of some recent theories that set out to defend music's emotional character within the framework that Hanslick develops.

4 ‖: Music and Emotions: Theories, Problems, and Suggestions

Imitation, arousal, and expression theory have all been reincarnated in twentieth-century musical aesthetics. But proponents of these revivals have obviously read and been influenced by Hanslick. Accustomed to Hanslick's doctrine that music is a collection of autonomous structures, recent theorists have typically sought to tie emotional content directly to musical structure. Thus, even the aestheticians who defy Hanslick's dismissal of emotion from musical aesthetics strive to make their theories "respectable" in essentially Hanslickean terms. They build on the restricted parallels between music and emotion that Hanslick accepts—those based on music's dynamic characteristics.

The three theory types we have considered have been revived in the twentieth-century theories of music and emotion proposed by Susanne Langer, Leonard Meyer, and Peter Kivy. Each of these theories more or less conforms to the pattern I have just described. And although each offers hints that might be fruitfully developed in the direction of recognizing an ethical dimension of music, these hints are not pursued by their originators. The explanation, I am convinced, is that Hanslick's ideals still determine what counts as professionally acceptable musical aesthetic discussion. Kivy virtually says as much when he describes Meyer's *Emotion and Meaning in Music* (which develops an arousal theory based on structure) as "the book which taught many of us for the first time that you can talk about music without talking nonsense."[1]

As a result of the reigning emphasis on structure in accounts that link music to emotion, any connection between musically associated emotion and the practical sphere of ethical life is radically deemphasized or ignored. Significantly, the recent theorists who most eagerly seek a structural basis for an emotion–music connection (Langer and Meyer) tend not to be much interested in characterizing the emotion they discuss in extramusical terms. Not surprisingly, the possible link between musical emotion and ethical life is a topic that rarely comes up.

Recent Imitation Theory: Susanne Langer

Susanne Langer's theory, although akin to imitation theory, is more accurately described as a "representation theory." Her claim is that music "represents" emotion.[2] I believe that it is fair to group Langer's theory with imitation theories, however, because she argues that music is isomorphic with emotional life. Although Langer is less than clear as to what she means by "isomorphism," her basic point is that the structures of music and those of our emotions are similar in basic "shape." As a consequence of this similarity, we take music to be symbolic of our emotional life.

What does Langer mean by a "symbol"? On her view, a symbol has a similar structure to what it symbolizes and is used to think of the latter. Langer thus places emphasis on form, understood as structure:

> Let us look at music from the purely logical standpoint as a possible symbolic form of some sort. As such it would have to have, first of all, formal characteristics which were analogous to whatever it purported to symbolize; that is to say, if it represented anything, e.g. an event, a passion, a dramatic action, it would have to exhibit a *logical form* which that object could also take.[3]

Symbols can be, in Langer's terminology, either "discursive" or "presentational." The musical symbol is, for Langer, a "presentational" symbol. That is, music presents an image whose basic structure directly parallels that of the emotional world it symbolizes. The "discursive" symbolization of language, by contrast, is subservient in its structure to grammatical rules that dictate how the sequence of words must be arranged within a sentence of a given language. Music is, therefore, a freer mode of symbolism than language, for it is able to mimic fluidly the sequential and dynamic structure of feelings:

> *Music articulates forms which language cannot set forth.* . . . Because the forms of human feeling are much more congruent with musical forms than with the forms of language, music can *reveal* the nature of feelings with a detail and truth that language cannot approach.[4]

Langer's emphasis on symbolism and structure are in keeping with her formalism. She characterizes "the real problem" of art as "the *perfection of form,* which makes this form 'significant' in the artistic sense." Langer accordingly describes the aesthetic experience of music in essentially cognitive terms:

> If music has any significance, it is semantic, not symptomatic. . . . Music is not the cause or the cure of feelings, but their *logical* expression. . . .

If music is really a language of emotion, it expresses primarily the composer's *knowledge of human feeling.* . . . This is the most persistent, plausible, and interesting doctrine of meaning in music. . . . music is not self-expression, but *formulation and representation* of emotions, moods, mental tensions and resolutions—a 'logical picture' of sentient, responsive life, a source of insight, not a plea for sympathy.[5]

This "logical picture" description would probably surprise many musicians, composers and performers alike. Did Bach or Beethoven or Dvořák attempt to present a "logical picture"? What about Scott Joplin—or Janis Joplin? Pete Townshend, at least, voiced the opposite point of view when he announced that he and the rest of The Who "never let the music get in the way of the performance." It is not the orientation of musicians, but that of Hanslick that Langer's formalism and cognitivism reflect. Hanslick, after all, receives considerable (and mostly favorable) mention in her discussion. And Langer's musical symbol attains its symbolism by means of the very "dynamic qualities" that Hanslick acknowledged.[6]

According to Langer, these dynamic features of a given passage of music may represent emotions of radically different content, so long as these emotions have dynamic features in common with the passage. "*What music can actually reflect is only the morphology of feeling; and it is quite plausible that some sad and some happy conditions may have a very similar morphology.*"[7] Musical passages do not symbolize specific (that is, verbally specifiable) emotional content. Again, Langer agrees with Hanslick.

Langer totalizes the concept of "music" in her account, speaking of music as a general phenomenon rather than of discrete pieces or instances of music. Thus the "logical picture" to which she refers is hard to pinpoint. The vagueness of her musical "image" is exacerbated by her contention that the musical symbol does not represent definite feelings, nameable by common emotional terms: "A composer not only indicates, but *articulates* subtle complexes of feeling that language cannot even name, let alone set forth." Instead, "*Music at its highest, though clearly a symbolic form, is an unconsummated symbol* . . . , a significant form without conventional significance."[8] In other words, the musical symbol is open-ended, and the same passage of music is in principle capable of symbolizing various emotions, some of which may not be delineated by our everyday emotional vocabulary.

The representation offered by Langer's theory is thus representation of a nebulous sort. Langer offers no correspondence theory of musical elements and emotional content. Nor does she really explain what (if anything) the listener gets from the musical symbol apart from a reminder of general dynamic features of emotional life.

Langer, however, attempts to turn her theory's vagueness into a virtue. "The real power of music lies in the fact that it can be 'true' to the life of feeling in a way that language cannot; for its significant forms have that *ambivalence* of content which words cannot have."[9] Because the emotional content of any given passage of music is not definitively established, she argues, music can symbolize the ambivalent, transient character of feeling. One suspects that the transience of musical form is of more concern to Langer than anything in particular about emotion; for in her later work on music, she characterizes music as an "image of time" and emphasizes its value for our understanding of temporality more than its specifically "emotional" character.[10]

In *Philosophy in a New Key*, Langer defends the value of music's open-ended symbolism for our understanding of feeling. Because the same morphology can represent feelings of various affective tones, it is possible to understand form in music ambivalently, or to change one's emotional "take" on it in response to successive musical events. Thus, we can often interpret a passage of music as symbolic of the ambivalent character of many of our emotions.[11] One wonders, nonetheless, how frequently this possibility is important in our experience of a given passage of music.

Budd questions, too, whether listeners typically, or even often, do experience music as a symbol in Langer's sense. The opposite, he argues, is more likely. In attributing a symbolic function to music, Langer treats music as primarily a vehicle for thinking about emotional life. But more often, Budd suggests, "the music fills our consciousness and no thought of anything else is present to our mind. . . . The music is intrinsically appealing, and there is nothing we find more interesting and are listening to the music to acquire knowledge of." Budd seems to endorse the traditional ideal of disinterested contemplation, which is not applicable to all kinds of music. But his more general point that music is typically valued as intrinsically enjoyable, independent of its usefulness as a symbol, seems a fair description of most Westerners' approach to their musical experience.[12]

Significantly, the "symbolic" function of music, in Langer's theory, is aimed at assisting our *understanding* of the basic character of our emotional life. Music presents certain dynamic features of affective life for our contemplation. It is not primarily described as a basis for emotional satisfaction. Instead, its appeal is primarily cognitive.[13] One wonders, again, how often this cognitive function is actually fulfilled in listeners' experience. Do most of us take such a detached intellectual approach to the emotions we find suggested by music?

Cognitive in emphasis, Langer's theory, for all its talk of emotion in music, ignores the possibility that music appeals primarily, or even importantly, to the emotions. At most, it makes room for an experience of emotional resonance with what music is intellectually taken to symbolize. But it is not obvious that music is designed as an intellectual tool for the understanding in the way that Langer's theory suggests.

Langer's theory emphasizes the structural patterns that can be used to characterize either music or emotion, not the experience of either. Her avoidance of particular examples of both cases reflects this remove from the experiential. Her failure to provide examples also raises questions about the alleged similarity between musical and emotional "shape." What are these shapes, and how do they resemble each other?

Langer's Isomorphism

Let us consider the pattern or "shape" of an emotion. It is not clear precisely what Langer has in mind. What is the structure of an inner, "emotional" state?

One historical account of the "inner" condition that music resembles is straightforwardly physiological. Music perturbs us physically, according to this view, and our physical response to music resembles emotional response. Dahlhaus observes that such accounts have been offered since antiquity. In the sixteenth-century version, our "animal spirits" (or "vital spirits," discussed in the previous chapter) were "supposed to account for the transfer of physical stimuli into psychic reactions." They were thought to "either stretch or contract, either reach out toward some object or withdraw from it." On this view, particular rhythms or intervals caused emotional responses that had the same basic "shape" as the music. Major intervals, for instance, were considered "stretched" or "expanded" by comparison with minor intervals. In this respect, they could be said to resemble the vital spirits in an "expansive" state, that is, in a condition of joy or happiness.[14]

Deryck Cooke has recently extended this type of analysis to all of the intervals available within major/minor tonality. While he does not postulate a specific physical substratum, comparable to "animal spirits," he does contend that such physical sensations as expansion, exertion, dragging, and lifting are suggested by the intervals built on the overtone series, and that musical structures composed of these intervals can suggest the physiological correlatives of specific emotional tones.[15]

Like Hanslick, Langer dismisses physiological stimulus–response mechanisms as irrelevant to aesthetic effect. But it is unobvious what she means by the "morphology of feeling," which is suggested by music's "dynamic qualities," beyond the physical processes that we experience in conjunction with emotion. Are we given, on Langer's account of music, more than stimulus–response patterns as a basis on which to contemplate emotional life? If not, her attitude toward such physiological reactions seems self-contradictory. These physiological patterns cannot be both irrelevant to aesthetic experience and the ground of aesthetic contemplation.

Furthermore, if Langer wants a full-fledged isomorphism between the structures of emotion and music, then she must show how music provides more than an image of physiological processes. For if physiological conditions are all that music imitates or represents, music does not provide an imitation of a full emotional structure. Although merely physiological changes can, in some cases, result in a feeling that we associate with emotion (the feeling of rage, for example, induced by localized brain stimulation), this is not what is properly called an "emotion." The term *emotion* refers, not to all kinds of feeling, but to feelings of a particular sort. Emotions are identified in terms of particular orientations that the mind assumes (either consciously or unconsciously) and the object toward which it comports itself. Simple physical provocation may remind us of the physical "feel" of an emotion—and, indeed, the brain, when so provoked, may seek an object to explain this subjective reaction. But this is not fully developed emotion, which is based on an assessment of an object. Instead, the brain stimulation provokes the construction of an imaginary assessment as a rationalization after the fact. Does music provide patterns that are isomorphic with the full texture of our emotions? Langer does not demonstrate that it does.

The musical patterns of concern to Langer are similarly problematic. Even if conventions for identifying musical patterns are more clearly established than those that identify the structures of emotions, Langer's sense of "musical pattern" remains unclear. In the first place, it is not obvious which features of music we should look at. Should we focus on the broad aspects that Plato considers? Or should we consider the finer details of a musical structure? And if the latter, how fine-tuned do we want to get?

"Musical pattern," moreover, may refer either to "pattern that is consciously observed by the listener" or to "pattern that is analytically discerned" (perhaps structurally notatable). The importance of this distinction is evident when one considers serialist music of this century, which employs intricate patterns observable in the score by a trained musician but not necessarily perceptible even to the trained ear.

In light of her emphasis on perception, Langer's theory would seem concerned with "pattern as consciously observed." But this kind of pattern is much more difficult to pinpoint than analytically observable pattern. Particularly when a musical work is notated, one can examine analytically observable patterns at leisure and repeatedly. But "pattern as consciously observed" is not so easily examined or specified. It is difficult even to describe one's own consciousness attending to an ongoing pattern, let alone to establish intersubjective features of consciously observed pattern.

Budd raises another problem regarding musical pattern. We might, Budd observes, see the structures of music as reflecting the structures of processes in general, in that all processes have dynamic qualities of the sort that Langer makes so much of. We have no reason to believe that the dynamic patterns we associate with feelings are unique to feelings. But if this is true, we have no more reason to believe that music represents emotional life than to believe that it represents any other process whose form it resembles.[16]

Langer's correlation between basic musical pattern and emotional pattern seems tenuous. As Langer herself observes, nothing precludes the possibility that very different emotions might share general structural features. But with this we are back to the question of what music can show us about the structures of emotional life.

A Defense of Langer's Vagueness

In my view, however, Langer's vagueness is not the primary problem with her theory. The basic problem is that she relies on the language of structural isomorphism in her account of music and emotion, and thereby raises expectations of precise correlations of music and emotional pattern that her theory is unable to fulfill. She thus succumbs to one of the worst temptations for imitation theory. The more the imitationist seeks to connect detailed musical structures with specific emotions, the less defensible imitationist theory becomes.

The specification of such detailed connections, however, seems more important to theoretical tidiness than to the project of making sense of our experience. Langer is right in refusing to specify any such connections. The problem is that Langer, with her "unconsummated symbol," suggests that the consummation to which we are invited is nevertheless an isomorphism of structure and structure.

Such "structural" precision is not necessary for an imitation theory to make some sense of our musical experience. We do not typically move from emotion to emotion with every new musical figure, although some striking musical figures may provoke a change in our feeling response. More often, a general feeling color characterizes a whole "expanse" of music, and the longer the same feeling color continues, the more it is reinforced. The persistence of dynamic effects (of the sort that Hanslick accepts as suggestive of feeling) can be one of the most powerful means by which affect is suggested. An autonomous work of music that constantly shifted emotional gears at every new figure would probably not strike many of us as emotionally very gripping. Perhaps this insight motivated the ultimate predominance, in the seventeenth- and eighteenth-century music influenced by the *Affektenlehre*, of compositions dominated by one reigning affect.

In this connection, Plato's failure to elaborate on fine structural details in Greek music may reflect a studied conclusion about which musical patterns suggest emotion. In identifying such broad, or "primitive," elements as basic rhythm and mode as the determinants of affective content, Plato contends that these elements can imitate features of the external display of emotion. Indeed, one wonders whether Plato might not have had in mind essentially the same "dynamic" features that Hanslick accepted as reminiscent of emotion. If so, perhaps Plato's "imitation theory" and Hanslick's concession are remarkably similar, despite the very different interpretation the two thinkers put on the same phenomenon.

Langer's vagueness remains a problem, not because she fails to achieve structural precision in describing the similarities between music and emotion, but because she obviously expects us to discover plenty of cognitive content to contemplate. But she does not explicate what sorts of contents (presumably patterns) she expects us to attend to in listening. She encourages us as listeners to seek rich symbolizations of our emotive life in music. But although she claims to offer a theory of isomorphism, it is unclear how we are to measure, or even what we are to measure against what.

Langer's Theory and Ethical Life

Langer's discussion of music in *Philosophy in a New Key* refers frequently to "insight," "revelation," "vitality," and "inner life." One might suspect that such references signal a connection between her theory of musical significance and our ethical lives. If Langer intended such a connection, however, her theoretical statements do not support it. Instead, her formulations indicate a divorce between musical meaning and ethical life.

In discussing the positive cultural role the arts were once expected to play, for instance, Langer describes as "natural" the tendency to view music as an inferior artform:

> The problem of the nature and function of music has shifted its center several times; in Kant's day it hinged on the conception of the arts as

cultural agencies, and concerned the place of music among these contributions to intellectual progress. On this basis the great worshiper of reason naturally ranked it lowest of all art-forms.[17]

Langer similarly dismisses the alleged "moral effects" of listening to music in a manner reminiscent of Hanslick. What influence music does have on behavior, she claims, is mostly by way of physiological reactions which are little related to ethical behavior; and at any rate it is sound, not music, that produces these effects:

> Music is known, indeed, to affect pulse-rate and respiration, to facilitate or disturb concentration, to excite or relax the organism, *while the stimulus lasts;* but beyond evoking impulses to sing, tap, adjust one's step to musical rhythm, perhaps to stare, hold one's breath or take a tense attitude, music does not ordinarily influence behavior. Its somatic influences seem to affect unmusical as well as musical persons . . . , and to be, therefore, functions of *sound* rather than of *music.*[18]

Langer is presumably influenced by Dewey in her emphasis on the parallels between musical tensions and resolutions and the dynamics of our emotional life.[19] But while Dewey also considers such tensions and resolutions to parallel the tensions experienced in our ethical life and the resolutions our actions attempt to accomplish, Langer does not extend the analogy to the practical sphere. This seems rather arbitrary on her part, as the argument by Budd cited earlier suggests. The entire basis of Langer's isomorphism theory is recognizable similarity of pattern, and the patterns of tension and resolution in music can be seen as analogous to the patterns of practical life. Why, then, does Langer fail to pursue this analogy?

The explanation seems to be that Langer takes psychic distance or disinterestedness to be a corollary to aesthetic formalism. Hence, she stresses that music makes emotions "*conceivable,* so that we can envisage and understand them without verbal helps, and without the scaffolding of an occasion wherein they figure."[20] Our comprehension of musical significance is thus linked to the music's representation of emotions *detached from everyday experience.* Music achieves its artistic purpose precisely when it diverts our attention away from the practical sphere. Langer cites Edward Bullough's discussion of the importance of psychical distance in art:

> "Just as an artist, if he is to move his audience, must never be moved himself—lest he lose, at that moment, his mastery over the material—so the auditor who wants to get the full operative effect must never regard

it as real, if his artistic appreciation is not to be degraded to mere human sympathy.

". . . distance . . . describes a *personal* relation, often highly emotionally colored, but *of a peculiar character*. Its peculiarity lies in that the personal character of the relation has been, so to speak, filtered. It has been cleared of the practical, concrete nature of its appeal."[21]

Art is degraded, on this view, when it becomes associated with "mere human sympathy." Emotion experienced in connection with music is taken to be legitimate, but only insofar as it is disconnected from concrete experience.

Langer accepts these platitudes from Bullough without criticism, and she uses them in defense of her theory of musical symbolism. Her admission of emotion into a discussion of music's aesthetic value is thus premised on a denial of the connection of both with practical life. She closes her discussion of music with an insistence on the importance of consciously "abstracting" the symbolic forms of music, lest they be confused with the emotions they represent. As we see in a later chapter, symbolic representations of emotion for thought might themselves be of value to ethical life; but Langer emphasizes the distance between the two. Whatever revelations her account of music might promise, it does not encourage our expectation that they might assist us in our ethical experience.

Recent Arousal Theory: Leonard Meyer

One of the most noteworthy and recent proponents of arousal theory is Leonard Meyer. Meyer's theory of music's relation to emotion provides a detailed account of the arousal mechanism. Perhaps the most philosophically striking achievement of Meyer's theory is that it avoids a problem that challenges most other arousal theories: that of empirically establishing that the allegedly aroused emotions do occur in listeners' subjective experience.[22]

Meyer's theory begins with a theory of emotion. An emotion, he claims, presupposes a stimulus that produces a tendency to think or act in a particular way. "Emotion or affect is aroused when a tendency to respond is arrested or inhibited."[23] In other words, when an internal tendency to think or act is not followed immediately by thinking or acting in accordance with it, we experience emotion. Meyer's model, therefore, considers the frustration or inhibition of a tendency to be crucial to the occurrence of an emotion. Emotion occurs only when gratification is somehow delayed.

One might question the appropriateness of Meyer's model as a characterization of all emotions. Love for someone and pride in one's achievements are emotions, but they do not obviously involve frustration of a tendency. Counterexamples like these suggest that Meyer's theory does not explain the common denominator among emotions, or at least that it is overly simplistic. Indeed, Meyer's model seems designed with the musical case in mind, for its virtue is that it makes it easy to see how music would arouse "emotion."[24]

Meyer's use of the model, however, does not focus on differentiating emotions according to common, everyday categories. Meyer does not even attempt to distinguish various kinds of emotion aroused by music. He is concerned only to indicate *how* affect is aroused by music. The restricted nature of Meyer's concern, in his account of music's relation to emotion, is both a virtue and a limitation. The strength of Meyer's theory is to pinpoint when affect occurs; its weakness is its inability to distinguish among the varieties of affect produced. Again we see a recent theorist prefer structural specificity to a connection with the everyday emotional world.

How, then, does music arouse affect, according to Meyer? In the first place, formal structures set up tendencies toward specific resolutions. "One musical event (be it a tone, a phrase, or a whole section) has meaning because it points to and makes us expect another musical event." (Obviously, this analysis best describes teleologically structured musics. It does not appear well suited to aleatoric music, or other avant-garde music that defies conventional canons of closure.) Meyer describes a range of basic tendencies suggested by Gestalt psychology (the tendency of a figure toward completion, and the tendency for the starting point to return, for instance). He also considers more localized tendencies within a phrase to move, for example, toward tones of greater tonal stability, or to reiterate patterns previously encountered. When such tendencies are not immediately satisfied, both affect and uncertainty result. The uncertainty produced may itself create additional tendencies toward clarification. Uncertainty heightens our curiosity as to how a tendency will be satisfied as well as our desire for satisfaction. Structural production of uncertainty produces in the listener both affective response and interest in the music:

> Once it is recognized that affective experience is just as dependent upon intelligent cognition as conscious intellection, that both involve perception, taking account of, envisaging, and so forth, then thinking and feeling need not be viewed as polar opposites but as different manifestations of a single psychological process.[25]

The difference between analytic and emotional response to music is most often a difference between the personalities and backgrounds of listeners, and with respect to comprehension of music, this difference is less significant than it appears:

> Whether a piece of music gives rise to affective experience or to intellectual experience depends upon the disposition and training of the listener. To some minds the disembodied feeling of affective experience is uncanny and unpleasant and a process of rationalization is undertaken in which the musical processes are objectified as conscious meaning. Belief also probably plays an important role in determining the character of the response. Those who have been taught to believe that musical experience is primarily emotional and who are therefore disposed to respond affectively will probably do so. Those listeners who have learned to understand music in technical terms will tend to make musical processes an object of conscious consideration. This probably accounts for the fact that most trained critics and aestheticians favor the formalist position.[26]

Unlike Hanslick and many other formalists, Meyer elevates emotional responses to music to the level of intellectual response. Acknowledging the difference that musical training makes in the listener's response, Meyer does not favor the response of those with greater training as the more legitimate one. Emotional and analytical responses are two modes of comprehending the same thing. But Meyer resembles other formalists in his characterization of the thing comprehended. Emotional and analytical listeners, he argues, are both responding to musical structure.

Meyer is not concerned to label the emotions that music arouses. We differentiate our affective experiences, he tells us, by reference to the stimulus situation, that is, to objects and our assessment of their relation to us. We describe a certain affective state as "fear" because it is aroused in the course of a situation in which an external object is seen as threatening to us. In music, however, no extramusical stimulus situation differentiates affect into the categories that we label with common emotional terms. In music, the stimulus that encounters us is consistently music.[27]

Significantly, the tendencies that music provokes in us are also inhibited by music, not by anything extramusical. The structure of the music produces the inhibition of tendency that results in affect; and the eventual resolutions of tendencies are also *musical* resolutions:

> In musical experience the same stimulus, the music, activates tendencies, inhibits them, and provides meaningful and relevant resolutions for them. This is of particular importance from a methodological standpoint. For it means that granted listeners who have developed reaction

patterns appropriate to the work in question, the structure of the affective response to a piece of music can be studied by examining the music itself.[28]

This conclusion is crucial to Meyer's theory. By linking the production of affect to purely formal musical movements, he makes the emotional content directly observable through musical form.

Meyer's theory acknowledges the need for some musical knowledge in affective response to music. In order to have expectations that are not immediately satisfied, a listener must be aware of the conventions characteristic of the style in which the work is written. "Because expectation is largely a product of stylistic experience, music in a style with which we are totally unfamiliar is meaningless." If a listener has assimilated the conventions of a style, he or she will have developed appropriate reaction patterns and will thus experience the tendencies and uncertainties built into the structure of a work in that style. Given the listener's awareness of the work's stylistic conventions, his or her affective patterns will correspond to the structure of the work.[29]

Meyer accomplishes a number of theoretical feats by this final move. He enables us to examine the structure of affective patterns aroused in listeners by examining the formal structure of the work. He avoids the need to ask listeners themselves what they are experiencing. All we need to do is to determine the expected progression of sounds within a stylistic convention to determine which musical moves in a work are deviations; we can then regard these deviations as affective stimuli.[30]

Meyer ingeniously deflects the objection that the same emotions are not consistently aroused in various listeners by constructing a theory that does not enlist the support of empirical data with respect to arousal. His analysis also allows him to dismiss specific empirical cases that seem to counter the theory—for example, the case of a listener who fails to experience affect at musical points predicted by the theory. Such a listener, on Meyer's account, is either (1) not paying attention to the music, (2) listening analytically (and thus responding to emotionally significant events with the intellect instead of the feelings), or (3) insufficiently familiar with the stylistic conventions that inform the work. Meyer's claim that emotional arousal corresponds to musical structure is, thus, virtually unfalsifiable. By insisting that the listener must be abreast of the ever changing conventions of a given style, Meyer implicitly assumes the role of judge of the qualifications of any given listener.

Meyer has not completely avoided the need for empirical support of his theory of emotion. It is convincing only if people actually *experience* emotion as a consequence of being incapable of acting in response to a tendency. Experimental investigation of this hypothesis would be difficult, however. What would count as evidence? And how would one construct a "demonstration" that did not itself presuppose implicit acceptance of questionable features of Meyer's theoretical framework? We might, for example, want to test whether "tendencies" were impeded in certain circumstances. But could we do this without accepting Meyer's view that "tendency" is an appropriate designation of a basic operation in mental life?

Sufficient empirical evidence might undercut Meyer's theory. The theory would be discredited if the inhibition of "tendencies" never seemed a plausible characterization of human emotional experience. The same would be true if listeners acquainted with a given style of music consistently failed to experience affect in response to the structural characteristics that Meyer emphasizes. The practical problems in attempting to establish such patterns, however, would make an empirical attack on Meyer's theory difficult. And in most cases, one would not expect empirical data to be so overwhelming that everyone would acknowledge their sufficiency to outweigh Meyer's theory.

A stronger challenge to Meyer's theory is suggested within it. Meyer's theory succeeds in obviating the need for empirical confirmation only insofar as it removes the connection between music and emotion from the empirical realm and ties emotional content to structural features. But Meyer's own concessions regarding the importance of association in emotional arousal undercut the force of the structural basis he aims to establish.

Association

Meyer acknowledges a variety of ways in which associations can affect our emotional response to music. Emotions experienced in connection with music can, he tells us, be the product of "contiguity; i.e., some aspect of the musical materials and their organization becomes linked, by dint of repetition, to a referential image." He cites harp music as an example. Although culturally associated with religious subjects in the Middle Ages, the harp later became associated with the "tender vagueness" characteristic of late nineteenth-century French music. Modern Western listeners consequently tend to respond to harp music with one of these associations. (Meyer claims that "tender vagueness" is the more common association, but I suspect that for the American audience Bugs Bunny cartoons have tipped the balance in favor of "heaven.") Although the development of a contiguous association within a culture is contingent, even a matter of chance, such associations can be extremely tenacious. "Once such an association has become firmly established," Meyer observes, "our response to it will be just as direct and forceful as if the response were natural."[31]

Associations based on isomorphism between musical phenomena and extramusical ideas can also exert a marked influence on emotional responses to music. These are, according to Meyer, the most common kind of association:

> Most of the connotations which music arouses are based upon similarities which exist between our experience of the materials of music and their organization, on the one hand, and our experience of the nonmusical world of concepts, images, objects, qualities, and states of mind, on the other.[32]

An example of such an association is the aural image of a thunderstorm in Beethoven's Sixth Symphony (by now an association reinforced contiguously by Walt Disney's *Fantasia*). Another such association is Moussorgsky's musical self-depiction as a strolling museumgoer in *Pictures at an Exhibition*. These associations may respond to such "objective" features of music as the dynamic qualities that Hanslick observes, or they may be rooted in the basic materials of music:

> In experience even single musical tones tend to become associated with qualities generally attributed to non-aural modes of sense perception. . . . In Western culture, for example, tones are characterized with respect to size (large or small), color value (light or dark), position (high or low), and tactile quality (rough or smooth, piercing or round).[33]

In any event, even when connotations are attached to structurally describable features of music, structure does not determine or specify the connotations. Meyer concludes that "no particular connotation is an inevitable product of a given musical organization," even in cases in which members of various societies make similar associations.[34]

Meyer concedes so many associative possibilities for the arousal of affect that one wonders whether these might not ultimately be more basic in emotional arousal than the structural elements that he emphasizes. By making room for societal and transsocietal association, he escapes the burden of linking all affect aroused by music with structure. But he goes so far as to deny inevitability in the relationship between *any* structure and a particular emotional connotation. In so doing, he leaves open the possibility that the nuance of affect experienced at any point may be a function of association rather than structure. We may reasonably wonder, in response to Meyer's admission, how basic structure is to the composite affect experienced in connection with music.

Structure Dominates Context

Dependent on both structural and contextual considerations, Meyer's theory of emotion rests on a tension. On the one hand, his structural theory of emotion in music relies on contextual factors for its plausibility. In order for emotional arousal to actually correspond to structure, as Meyer contends, listeners must already be aware of stylistic features of the work in question (an awareness derived from previous experience, not from the work in question) and sensitive to the work's position within the broad context of historical stylistic change. The extent to which Meyer relies on context is thus enormous; and if it has been underappreciated, I am convinced that this stems from the common tendency to associate such awareness with technical musical training, which itself typically emphasizes structure.[35]

In tension with this dependence on the contextual is Meyer's attempt to account for many basic contextual factors in terms of his structural model. An example is his effort to systematize the stages through which a given musical style passes. Meyer claims that it is the evolution of what counts as structural deviance that dictates the development of a style:

> Deviation, originating as expression, may after a time become normative, and when this occurs it is necessary either to invent new deviations for the sake of aesthetic effect or to point up those already in use. This means that once a style is established there is a constant tendency toward the addition of new deviants and toward pointing up, through emphasis or exaggeration, those deviants already present. In short, the nature of aesthetic communication tends to make for the eventual destruction of any given style.[36]

Meyer is suggesting, albeit in cautious language, that composers' deviations from norms are more or less rule-bound, and that the "rules" in question are appropriately analyzed in terms of his structural model.[37] Granted, Meyer talks here in terms of "tendencies," not of necessities. But the effect is to suggest that the factors most important in accounting for stylistic change are structural features of music.

This same tendency to treat the structural as key to the contextual is evident in Meyer's discussions of non-Western music. In chapter 7 of *Emotion and Meaning in Music*, Meyer describes several non-Western musics in terms of "simultaneous deviation" (evident in heterophony, the practice of singing multiple versions of the same melody simultaneously) and "successive deviation" (the performance of various successive versions of previously presented melodic material). Meyer's claim that "aesthetic effect" in the non-Western styles he considers depends on the listener's "awareness of the basic ground plan" and of what constitutes departures from it seems unproblematic.[38] But the idea of "norms," as Meyer uses the term in his account of structural tendencies, is not obviously applicable to all musics.

One might reasonably describe the music of Java, one of Meyer's examples, in terms of "norm" and "deviation." But applied to Javanese music, these terms refer to something different from what Meyer typically means when he uses them. The "norm" from which Javanese performance deviates is not structurally definable. It is an "inner melody," understood by all participants, but not explicitly stated by any one of them, or even necessarily by the entire group. Ethnomusicologist Susan Walton observes:

> The instruments and voices play polyphonic lines that are expressions of an underlying melody, that the Javanese call *lagu* or the inner melody. The inner melody is never stated literally, never fully sounded. It exists in complete form only in the minds of the musicians and they frequently have somewhat different conceptions of it.

Walton believes that "deviation" is an appropriate term for what occurs in a Javanese performance:

> Each instrument has its own way of expressing the inner melody. Some instruments have more responsibility than others in manifesting it. Furthermore, the melodies of some instruments deviate occasionally from the inner melody. It is possible to speak of "deviation" even though none of the instruments play the inner melody, because there is a generally accepted notion of that melody, especially at crucial points.[39]

Nonetheless, the type of structural norm that Meyer proposes in his theory of musical meaning seems oddly applied to Javanese music. For as Walton describes it, Javanese music reflects a process of group thinking, which alone can manifest the "inner truth" of the melody. The Javanese understand music as comparable to meditation, which is also conducted in groups. "It is believed," Walton reports, "that absolute truth can be perceived by individuals, but it can be 'confirmed' only by a group and expressed as consensus achieved during group meditation." This conception of group consensus is also manifested in the relationship of musical performers to the inner melody:

In both mystical and musical practice, the task of uncovering the absolute truth or making manifest the inner melody is the responsibility of a group, not an individual. Although an individual musician can write down his conception of the inner melody, other musicians would not agree with it in every detail. Furthermore, although it is theoretically possible to play the inner melody on a single instrument, no one instrument ever can play it without breaking rules of style and range. The inner melody can be realized only by all the instruments of the ensemble playing the piece together. . . . In playing a piece, the musicians both follow their own conceptions of the inner melody and listen to the suggestions from other instruments that express the inner melody.[40]

Perhaps Meyer intends "norm" to encompass such an implicit basis for music-making as the "inner melody." But certainly the inner melody is not the kind of well-defined structure that defines the listener's expectations in Meyer's account. At least explicitly, it would be hard to classify as a definite structure at all. Here the norm is neither a particular presented melody nor a structural pattern clearly established by previous statements. And the suitability of a statement is as much dependent on what other musicians are doing as it is on a preestablished expectation of what the melody ought to be.

The approach the Javanese take to their norm is also quite different from that suggested by Meyer's account. The Javanese aim to manifest an inner insight by means of a musical group mutually attuning themselves to one another. Each musician's deviation from the inner melody is a reflection of the insufficiency of the individual to attain inner truth through his or her own resources, not a stimulating inhibition of a basic tendency. To the extent that one can speak here of a "tendency," it is the tendency toward achievement of group coordination that is needed for the manifestation of the inner melody, with its various demands on the musicians. Meyer's model of the frustrated tendency, ultimately gratified after delays, does not readily fit the Javanese musical situation.

Meyer admits that his theory does little to address the music of certain non-Western societies. This music he labels "primitive music," which he characterizes dismissively:

Unfortunately little of the extensive research done in the field of primitive music is of value for this study. First, because the primitives themselves do not make musical creation a self-conscious endeavor, they have neither a theory of music nor even a crude "aesthetic" which might serve to connect their musical practices to their responses. It seems clear that on the most primitive level music is, on the one hand so intimately connected with ritual and magic that its aesthetic content is severely restricted and, on the other hand, that it is so closely associated with bodily effort that its shape and organization are to a considerable degree products of the physical activities connected with ritual, labor, or expressive behavior. And second, because music ethnologists have tended to collect and classify tunes and instruments, compile statistics, and concern themselves with the sociology of primitive music, the aesthetic meaning, if any, which music has for the primitive musician or listener, has for the most part been ignored.[41]

In his essay "On Value and Greatness in Music," it becomes obvious that Meyer *defines* primitive music in terms of its lack of structurally based expectation tendencies, the basis of his theory of music and emotion. Meyer goes out of his way to point out that many non-Western musics are not "primitive" in his sense.[42] But this shows that he deems non-Western music worth analyzing precisely to the extent that it conforms (or appears to conform) to his structural theory. The passage just cited also reveals Meyer's subordination of contextual features of music-making to structure. For it treats "primitive" music's association with "ritual and magic" and "bodily effort" as deficiencies that interfere with the development of the structural (and teleological) features that Meyer values.

Meyer's fundamental subordination of context to structure is evident, finally, in the fact that he discusses mood and associational affective factors only in the final chapter of *Emotion and Meaning in Music*. Even the title of that chapter—"Note on Image Processes, Connotations, and Moods"—suggests that these generators of affect are to be treated as an afterthought. But his admissions in that chapter, as we have seen, concede tremendous importance to these factors. It appears that Meyer's relegating them to a final, seemingly tacked-on chapter is a rhetorical acknowledgment of a tension within his own theory. It also indicates his own recognition that structure cannot do as much in an account of music and emotion as his basic theory purports to do.

On balance, Meyer's laudable efforts to do justice to contextual factors in musical comprehension are overshadowed by the structural focus of his basic theory. He tends to treat contextual features either as structurally analyzable, as afterthoughts, or, at best, as secondary factors in the musical arousal of emotion. His elevation of emotion to a response on a par with intellectual analysis is achieved by making emotion primarily dependent on structural features of music. Structure allows us to say when emotion will be aroused by music, but the emotion aroused is not akin to everyday emotion. Meyer's theory resuscitates the view that music arouses emotion, but at the expense of a connection between emotion and ethical life.

Meyer himself, however, came to recognize that music often does provoke emotionally charged reflection on such "ethical" matters as the nature of human striving, evil, maturity, and the meaning of life. In "On Value and Greatness in Music," originally published in 1959 (three years after *Emotion and Meaning in Music*), Meyer not only acknowledged this dimension of association in connection with music, but tied its probability to "musical greatness." Meyer suggests in this essay that musical uncertainties themselves can stimulate affect by means of association. In great music (an unexplicated category that Meyer assumes we can consider through our own examples), we associate musical uncertainties with the profound uncertainties of life:

> When we talk of greatness, we are dealing with a quality of experience which transcends the syntactical. We are considering another order of value in which self-awareness and individualization arise out of the cosmic uncertainties that pervade human existence: man's sense of the inadequacy of reason in a capricious and inscrutable universe; his feeling of terrible isolation in a callous and indifferent, if not hostile, nature; and his awareness of his own insignificance and impotence in the face of the magnitude and power of creation. . . . These ultimate uncertainties—and at the same time ultimate realities—of which great music makes us aware result not from syntactical relationships alone, but from the interaction of these with the associative aspects of music. This interaction, at once shaping and characterizing musical experience, gives rise to a profound wonderment—tender yet awful—at the mystery of existence. And in the very act of sensing this mystery, we attain a new level of consciousness, of individualization.

By reminding us of the basic texture of difficulty and insecurity in which our projects take place, great music provokes ethical reflection on the meaning of life and suitably serious and elevated emotions. That Meyer considers our response to be "ethical" in the sense of developing character is indicated by his further comments that link musical uncertainty with tragic suffering:

> It is because tragic suffering, arising out of the ultimate uncertainties of human existence, is able to individualize and purify our wills that we are of more value than the sparrows. . . . In instances where the individual

is able to master it through understanding . . . , as Job did, suffering may ultimately be good. For though, like medical treatment, it is painful, suffering may lead to a higher level of consciousness and a more sensitive realistic awareness of the nature and meaning of existence. Indeed all maturation, all self-discovery, is in the last analysis more or less painful. And the wonder of great art is this: that through it we can approach this highest level of consciousness and understanding without paying the painful price exacted in real life and without risking the dissolution of the self which real suffering might bring.[43]

Music that moves us in this fashion—music in which structure is of greater interest for the associations it suggests than for its internal tensions and resolutions—is great music. "And the greatest works," Meyer concludes, are "those which embody value of the highest order with the most profound—and I use the word without hesitation—content."[44] Thus, Meyer himself concludes that his account in *Emotion and Meaning in Music* does not tell the entire story of either musical emotion or musical significance. And the book's most striking omission is its failure to discuss the deepest emotion that music can arouse—the emotion that responds to music's reflection of our practical human state.

Recent Expression Theory: Peter Kivy

Peter Kivy has recently developed a philosophical version of expression theory that might be described as the opposite of artistic expressionism.[45] Kivy goes out of his way to avoid any definite connection between expressiveness and the composer's personal feelings. In fact, he dissociates the expressive character of music from the personal feelings of anyone—composer, performer, or listener. Music, Kivy claims, appeals to our minds, not our hearts, and this is true even with respect to emotional expressiveness.

Kivy builds on Alan Tormey's distinction between "expressing something" and "being expressive of something." Music need not be expressing something, such as the feelings of a composer, in order to be expressive *of* something, that is, in order to connote or remind the listener of a particular emotional state. Kivy uses the example of a Saint Bernard's face to explain the distinction. To say that the Saint Bernard's face *expressed* sadness would be to imply that the dog was continuously feeling sad. To say that the dog's face is *expressive of* sadness is to imply merely that it suggests the mood of sadness. Our appropriate response in the latter case is cognitive, not affective. We "recognize" sadness; we do not feel it, and we also do not believe that the dog is feeling it.[46]

How is sadness "suggested" by music? Although concerned with expression, Kivy's theory proposes an isomorphism between the physical manifestations of our emotional life (attitudes of face, body, and voice) and the shape of music. It thus bears a resemblance to imitation/representation theories.[47] Musical contour is the basis for the isomorphism that Kivy discusses. "The similarity of certain musical lines, when sung or played, to inflections of the human speaking voice is obvious and unproblematic." Kivy acknowledges that rhythm often mirrors many aspects of human behavior; but he observes that melodic contour, too, plays an underappreciated role in reflecting behavior:

> But beyond the obvious part that rhythm plays in musical expressiveness . . . there is the way we inevitably describe music in terms of motion: particularly "rising" and "falling." . . . The "rise" in pitch, like the raising of a physical body against gravity, requires, at least in a great many of the most familiar cases, increased energy. And the rise of pitch, both in natural organisms and machines, betokens a rise in energy level.[48]

Nonetheless, Kivy supplements this "contour" theory with a "convention theory," which holds that there are also conventional associations between manifestations of emotional life and music. Although he takes vocal music to be paradigmatic (thus returning to an earlier historical perspective), Kivy believes that convention accounts for much of the emotional content of both vocal and instrumental music:

> The match or mismatch of music to text is to be explained, in part at least, in terms of the conventional musical tags which, since the very beginnings of the modern musical tradition in the West, have been used by composers, sometimes consciously, more often not, as the appropriate accompaniment of the words they have set. . . . it seems to be altogether plausible that if we recognize the appropriateness or inappropriateness of tone to text in part by our recognition of the used and reused musical "tags," with their four-hundred-year-old accretion of emotive associations upon their heads, we recognize, in part, by the same means, the appropriateness or inappropriateness of our emotive descriptions of instrumental compositions.[49]

To a considerable extent the distinction between convention and contour collapses. For Kivy argues that some—probably a large percentage—of conventions were developed on the basis of contour: "It is inviting to suppose that many musical features expressive by convention were once more than that: were once heard as resembling identifiable expressive behavior, or at least ingredients in such structures. I am inclined to believe it is the case."[50] One example of this phenomenon is the conventional association of the minor triad with "dark" emotion. Kivy traces this convention to an earlier period of Western music in which the minor third was considered relatively unstable. The minor triad in this period was thus considered an inappropriate resting point—and the "restlessness" of the chord came to be conventionally associated with "restless" human behavior in response to disturbing emotion.

Kivy, like Langer and Meyer, emphasizes structure in his correlation of music and emotion. Certain structural features of music correspond to (and thus are reminiscent of) structural features of emotional behavior; and even the correspondences between music and emotion that we recognize as matters of convention are in many cases based on an original structural similarity between music and some emotional behavior. But unlike Langer and Meyer, Kivy gives context considerable importance in his theory. He parts company with most of his contemporaries and recent predecessors by returning to the paradigm of texted music. He thus gives prominence to textual cues, which provide links between music and specific, everyday emotions. Kivy also strikes a balance between identifying a structural basis for much musical expressiveness and recognizing the preeminent importance of contextual custom in many specific cases.

Because of his sensitivity to the importance of associational and contextual factors, Kivy avoids vulnerability to the objection, directed by Vernon Howard toward isomorphism theories, that similarity between things does not imply that one is a sign of another.[51] This argument has force against theories that stress structural isomorphism and "symbolic" or "semiotic" significance in music. Kivy relies on the human tendency to be reminded of one thing by another, a tendency long ago pointed out by Aristotle in the *Poetics*. Kivy is therefore not locked into any claim about one-way symbolism.

Kivy foresees and preemptively answers Howard's objection by claiming that we tend to endow everything we perceive with the qualities of animate life. Our thinking about the world is pervasively anthropomorphic. And in the case of a phenomenon such as music, which continuously exemplifies dynamic features and contours that are reminiscent of emotional behavior, it is particularly natural that we should interpret it as a reminder of features of emotive life.[52] Although a stickler might demand an account of "nature" or "naturalness" at this point, Kivy's claim that we tend to form anthropomorphic associations with music, as with everything else, does not strike me as seriously controversial.

If Kivy is so concerned with the role of context, why do I consider him here, with Langer and Meyer, as a musical aesthetician in the tradition of Hanslick? I do so because Kivy reveals an intellectualist bias in his treatment of music. Kivy celebrates his intellectualism by branding himself a "cognitivist."[53] As a cognitivist, he contends that expression in music is properly a matter of intellectual recognition, not of emotional empathy. This position militates against the idea that music is a means of affective communication, one of the bases on which the claim that music has an ethical dimension might rest. In addition, Kivy's contextual concessions extend only as far as is compatible with treating the musical structure as fundamental to the musical work. And Kivy is an atomistic structuralist in both his contour and his convention theories of musical meaning.[54] Emotion is linked to the structural detail, whether assessed as a particular "contour" or as a "musical tag." Therefore, despite my admiration for Kivy's efforts to acknowledge the social and contextual dimension of musical expression I find certain difficulties arising in connection with his perspective.

Problems with Cognitivism: The Saint Bernard and the Clenched Fist

Central to Kivy's "cognitivism" is the distinction between "expressive of" and "expressing." This distinction, however, breaks down when one observes the disparity between the paradigms Kivy chooses to explicate the distinction and many cases one confronts in music.

Kivy acknowledges that the concept "expressive of" is parasitic on "expressing." A thing, P, can be expressive of another, Q, only if P is appropriate for expressing Q. A particular piece or passage of music, therefore, can be expressive of emotion H only because its sounds would be appropriate for expressing H:

> We see sadness in the Saint Bernard's face in that we see the face as appropriate to the expression of sadness. And we see it as appropriate to the expression of sadness because we see it as a face, and see its features as structurally similar to the features of our own faces when we express our own sadness. We hear sadness in the opening phrases of the *Lamento d'Arianna* in that we hear the musical sounds as appropriate to the expression of sadness. And we hear them as appropriate to the expression

of sadness (in part) because we hear them as human utterances, and perceive the features of these utterances as structurally similar to our own voices when we express our own sadness in speech.[55]

This final statement is important. Music is appropriate to emotional expressiveness because we perceive it as human utterance. But in hearing music as human utterance, we have made it disanalogous to the Saint Bernard's face. We see the Saint Bernard's face, on Kivy's account, as expressive of sadness because it bears an expression that would be an appropriate expression of sadness on a human face. We do not see it as expressing sadness, because we do not believe that the dog has either the intention of expressing anything, or necessarily the relevant emotional state.

Music, however, is an intentional human act and one that aims at communication. (At least, insofar as music is performed for other listeners besides the individual musician, I do not see why we should *not* consider it a form of communication.) But if this is so, there is little bite in the distinction Kivy draws between "intending to express" and "intending to be expressive" through music. If a composer intends to write music that is expressive of particular human emotions, is he not "expressing" those emotions in some sense, conveying acquaintance, not just with the fact that humans have such feelings, but with the nature of these emotions himself? Kivy himself points out that any vehicle suitable for being "expressive of" feeling must also be appropriate as an expression of feeling. But what more besides the composer's intentional presentation of musical passages appropriate as expressions of emotion do we need for them to constitute actual expressions?

As a prerequisite for saying that music "expresses" emotion, Kivy insists, we would need evidence that the composer experienced and desired to air the experience of the relevant emotions. But, even on Kivy's view, a composer may utilize a musical utterance that we recognize as an emotive expression. Kivy would accept this possibility; he would simply not call this "expressing." But how does the composer convey such emotional material without emotional sensitivity and experience? I see no reason not to call what the composer does in this case "expressing," whether he expresses emotion that he has felt, emotion that he has empathetically attributed to others, or emotion that he now experiences in response to the structure that he himself has created. I do not see why we must be able to trace a simple, uncomplicated connection between a composer's emotional state (past or present) and the expressive character of a musical passage in order to call it an expression of emotion.

Dewey suggests more positive reasons why musical works with expressive contents ought properly to be called "expressions." He argues convincingly that all human emotional expression is mediated and formulated by intellect. Kivy's "paradigm of emotive expression," the clenched fist, is expressive to the extent that it symbolizes and somewhat diffuses aggressive desire.[56] In this respect, it is an intellectually controlled gesture, albeit a simple one. Fine art, in Dewey's view, builds on the same sort of everyday emotional motivations as does the clenched fist. But art transforms the expression of these motivations, making use of complicated, intelligently designed formulation. Expression is thus not incompatible with intellectually controlled communication; as fine art most conspicuously demonstrates, expression depends on intellectual control.

In light of Kivy's paradigm of the clenched fist, it appears that he takes expression to be emotive behavior that is little mediated by intellectual formulation. After all, the clenched fist easily gives way to violence on further provocation. But this seems an inappropriate paradigm. For one thing, the clenched fist is an inordinately simple gesture. With the fist, one communicates essentially nothing else besides hostile emotion. But not all instances of emotive expression are like this. A pat on the back as an expression of affection might communicate caring emotion; but the emotional picture might be more complicated. The pat on the back might also convey frustration with language as a communicative vehicle; or it might indicate that the person making the gesture feels no qualm about invading the recipient's personal space. It may indicate a patronizing feeling along with an affectionate one.

The clenched fist as a paradigm for emotional expression is too simplistic. And its simplicity conceals the relevance that any *particular* context may have to emotional expression. The clenched fist is so conventionalized and transportable that any observer could recognize the force of its meaning. But, to return to my alternative example, the pat on the back might be an expression of any number of things in any range of combination. One would have to know a lot about the particular context of its occurrence to determine what the pat on the back expressed.

When we compare this distinction to a musical situation, we discover that Kivy has chosen his example well for the purpose of exploring the expressive content of autonomous musical works. If one assumes that the work retains its identity in all significant respects from one occurrence (whether score or performance) to another, it makes sense to consider musical passages (understood structurally) as gestures of conventional significance much like that of the clenched fist. Expression in such gestures is understood by the intellect; it is a matter of knowing how to read expressive "signs." And the fact that Kivy refers to musical *works* in his examples suggests that he does link emotional expressiveness with features of music that can be transported from context to context.

But this means that Kivy, too, short-changes context in favor of the autonomous musical work. His acknowledgment of context amounts to a recognition of the extensive roles of convention and textual cues in interpreting musical signs; but the "signs" themselves are understood largely as autonomous structures. What Kivy ignores is the concrete context of the listening experience, in which the listener holistically responds as a human being (not simply as an intellect) to the living occasion in which music is performed and celebrated.

Moreover, as Dewey's analysis suggests, Kivy's bifurcation between recognizing and feeling music's emotional content is a false and overly simplistic dichotomy. Our intellect is involved in the formulation and comprehension of emotional expressions. But our intellectual recognition of a musical expression of emotion does not preclude the music's communication of the emotion itself along with cognitive "meaning." A major difference between the clenched fist and a passage of music is that the cognitive significance of the fist is often a provocation to activity or to actively disposed emotion, while music typically invites one to empathy. The clenched fist can be said to "communicate emotion" only in a nebulous way. When a clenched fist is directed at me, I do not share in an experience with its possessor. I am more likely to respond with anger at the owner of the fist (as opposed to sharing the anger directed at myself). Or I may respond with disgust or pity for the fist's owner. But in either case, to refer to "emotional communication" is to refer to something more like the transmission of an electric charge than the production of a shared experience.

In the case of much music, by contrast, the listener is invited to join in a shared emotional experience.[57] The suggestion of affect by music is usually received by the listener with openness and willingness to entertain it. To speak of "emotional communication" here suggests more than a phenomenon on a par with an electrical charge. In this case, it implies not only a recognition of emotional gestures, but a willingness to respond with empathy.

Of course, the details of emotional response will vary from listener to listener. In response to the overture to *Tristan und Isolde*, an empathetic listener might experience sympathetic longing. This longing might also touch a deep chord in his or her personal emotional experience, or it might simply provoke sympathy with those who long or with human beings in general, all of whom are capable of longing. Each of these possibilities would occasion a different kind of emotional stance on the part of the listener, a stance that might be altered by succeeding musical events, which evoke different kinds of responses. Or a listener might feel each of these stances to a certain extent, shifting his or her affective response quickly and continuously, much as one shifts one's intellectual attention while listening to interesting new music. All of these possibilities are consistent with emotional receptivity to music; and in each case I think it would be fair to describe the situation as a case of emotional communication.

I should point out that I agree with Kivy that not all music aspires to emotional expression. Kivy argues that even when it does not, one's emotions may be engaged while listening to music. I agree with this point as well. However, I disagree with Kivy's characterization of the nature of the listener's possible emotional engagement, because his account rules out sympathetic response. I turn now to Kivy's defense of emotional arousal in connection with music.

Expression and Arousal (or Context Made Too Simple)

In his recent essay "How Music Moves," Kivy points out that he does not believe that our emotions are disengaged while we listen. Although claiming that expression in music is a cognitive matter, not a transmission of emotion, Kivy endorses the view that music (at least good music) arouses emotion in the listener. His endorsement of an arousal position modifies the connotations of his self-characterization as a "cognitivist." But more important for our purposes, his analysis reveals a tendency to emphasize musical structure to such an extent that important contextual considerations are forgotten.

Kivy emphasizes that good music does move us. We are moved by the beauty of music; and in this condition, we are certainly experiencing emotion. But our emotion is a (rather awed) response to beauty, not an experience of the everyday emotions that the music itself expresses.[58]

Kivy's chief defense of the claim that we are not "saddened" or in other ways provoked to common emotional states by music is an argument that we cannot explain the arousal of such emotions by music with "a perfectly ordinary explanation." A perfectly ordinary explanation is the sort that we expect in connection with other experiences of emotional arousal, one that would tell us at what or whom the emotion is directed, how the emotion was aroused, and why it is this and not some other specific emotion. As an example of an ordinary emotion with an ordinary explanation, Kivy describes the case of anger at a particular person (Uncle Charlie) over a particular incident that one analyzes in a particular way (Uncle Charlie once again blames his wife for his failure in business, a claim that is perceived by his nephew as "a self-serving falsehood").[59]

I agree with Kivy that we do not usually have a comparable explanation for experiencing a particular emotion in connection with a piece of music. But Kivy's comparison is loaded. Recent Western aesthetics has insisted that we describe music in such a way that the situational details that would normally serve for "a perfectly ordinary explanation" of emotion are omitted as a matter of principle. A particular performer's vehemence in bowing his or her cello might contribute markedly to my emotional "take" while listening to music. I might empathize with a sense of vehemence toward living and acting, or I might feel disfavor toward such a display because it seems an unmusical demand for attention. But any such situational perspective on emotion experienced in response to music is treated as irrelevant in Kivy's discussion. Before concluding that music does not admit of "ordinary explanations" for emotional arousal, we should at least consider music as an ordinary, situated phenomenon. But that is not what Kivy or other recent Western aestheticians typically do.

Another problem with Kivy's approach in demanding "a perfectly ordinary explanation" for musically aroused emotion is that his paradigm of such an explanation is a case in which a very specific emotional term is adequate to describe a person's affective state. Kivy does not consider a case in which emotional response is an entire texture, although this situation is surely common in everyday life.

Had Uncle Charlie himself discussed his career problems in a more complicated and sensitive fashion, his nephew might still have had an emotional response to his comments. But it might well be a complicated response that involved a kind of medley of emotions. Would the nephew be able to offer "a perfectly ordinary explanation" of his emotional response to Uncle Charlie in this case? That may depend on his temperament (on his tendency to introspection, on his tendency to have a dominant emotion at any given point, or on his tendency to have diffused emotional reactions) as well as on his analytical abilities. I suspect, too, that a third party's willingness to accept the nephew's analysis as an apt explanation would be less straightforward the more complicated the analysis became.

I am convinced that our emotional responses to music are typically complex and textured. "A perfectly ordinary explanation" such as an explanation of anger at a person who has just offended one is not the kind of explanation that would do justice to emotion experienced in connection with music.

One whole dimension of emotional response, which I suggested above, is an active engagement in empathy with any expressive content that one understands in the music. When this dimension is engaged, arousal and expression operate in tandem. In this case, the distinction that Kivy makes between "recognizing the expression" and "being moved by the music" differentiates aspects of a unified experience in which the emotional content is effectively the same. I may recognize my emotion, as a listener, as a "vicarious" emotion, one that I am entertaining but not situationally immersed in outside the listening context. But at the moment of listening, this recognition need not occur to me. At best, it would seem to clarify what I expect to be my condition when I have finished listening to music.

"Being moved by the music" can thus involve being moved to empathize with musical expression of emotion.[60] It can also involve the kind of arousal that Kivy describes—the condition of being stirred to awe or excitement by the beauty of the music. And as Kivy observes, this arousal can be a response to "sheer beauty of the sound as it unfolds in its ebb and flow" as well as a more studied awareness of structural fineness.

In addition, however, the emotional condition experienced by the listener is also a function of myriad contextual details, the constellation of particulars that makes the musical moment I am now experiencing uniquely an experience of *this* musical moment. The uniqueness of the experienced musical moment is, in particular, what recent musical aesthetics has lost sight of. But the experience of the unique musical present is the center both of a vital dimension of emotional experience and of music's link to the bedrock of ethical and spiritual life.

Emotional "Mirroring" in Musical Experience

That I consider music to be an "emotional" vehicle of some sort is probably obvious by now. But so far I have not subscribed to any of the standard theories that we have considered. The reason is that I think all of them aptly reflect "emotional" roles that music often plays. I now proceed to explain why. In doing so, I also lay the groundwork for an argument that music's affective character has ethical repercussions.

Parallel Emotion in Music

Theoretically, imitation, arousal, and expression theory make very different claims about music's relation to emotion. And as we have seen, certain theorists oppose one theory to another. Kivy, for instance, opposes expression theory to arousal theory. I want to suggest, however, that these theoretical viewpoints are not mutually exclusive. When one recognizes the importance of contextual cues in musical experience, each view can be seen to provide an apt reflection of certain musical possibilities.

A basic type of contextual cue that is usually unacknowledged in philosophical discussion of music and emotion is the set of culturally learned expectations regarding what it is to have a musical experience. Meyer is the commendable exception, for he describes as relevant to the listener's experience certain "preparatory sets" that "arise as a result of our beliefs as to the nature of the musical experience" and that "are not specific to any particular musical style or form." Meyer emphasizes physiological and motor adjustments that arise as "products of the belief and expectation that we are going to have an affective aesthetic experience." But he also acknowledges certain mental attitudes that arise whenever we assume the stance of listening to what we take to be music.[61] Among these, I am convinced, are expectations about how music will make us feel.

If we recognize the role of these expectations in our experience as listeners, arousal theory becomes quite plausible. The critic of arousal theory attacks its claim that music evokes emotions with the insinuating question "How?" What both critic and arousal theorist usually ignore is that, typically, the listener is already experiencing emotion as the music begins. He or she expects something.

In our society, one might expect any of a number of things. Much depends on the style, the performance situation, and one's self-identification as a member of (or as alienated from) a particular audience.[62] I might expect to be startled or impressed by the ingenuity of the music's construction; or to be supported and reinforced in my mood, perhaps a religious or patriotic one; or to be drawn into a crowd experience by the very real sense that a whole mob of strangers is pulsating to the same rhythm in the same open disposition as myself. The fact that I usually know certain basic things about the musical style and the context *before* I begin listening, even in this musically multifarious society, means that most of the time I am already keyed into a particular emotional tone in the very act of preparing to listen to music.

If one recognizes this emotional preparation, one will not expect arousal theory to explain how a musical structure can move the listener as if *ex nihilo*. The listener, in the typical case of actual listening, is already emotionally in gear. In order to arouse at least some kind of emotion, therefore, music need only further develop or enhance what is nascently already there.

But there is more to the story of emotion and music. Most of us at least often feel that a musically aroused emotion is not fully specified by performance situation and general style. We find that the "dynamic qualities" of

Hanslick's account suggest certain features of emotional experience and behavior, and that these enable us to associate the music with fairly specific emotions or moods. We do not have to be told, for instance, that the fourth movement of Beethoven's Ninth Symphony begins in a "tragic" mood. The tensions and relationships of the tonally moving forms are sufficient to suggest a tragic state of mind. For those of us who have heard the symphony a number of times, the indisputable (and textually cued) joyousness of the finale so contrasts with the movement's beginning that the initial tragic tension is particularly striking.

Hanslick's insight that music's dynamic qualities provide the basis for many emotional associations is important. My quarrel is not with Hanslick's point but with his relegation of all other factors that suggest emotion to aesthetic unimportance. In fact, a full account even of such associations as Hanslick allows requires recognition of the importance of the listener's emotional preparatory set. We find musical dynamic qualities reminiscent of the dynamics of emotion in large part because we expect to.

Besides the general expectation that the experience of music will involve emotion, most listeners, at least in our society, have another expectation as well. Our typical presumption (at least if we are not assuming the role of "philosopher") is that music is made as a communicative act that expresses something about inner experience, often humanly felt emotion. On the basis of this expectation, we approach music from a stance of willingness to entertain sympathetically its emotional content. We are open to undergoing, through empathy, a course of emotional experience that parallels the one we recognize in the music.

Davies defends the appropriateness of our emotionally "mirroring" the emotions suggested by the "behavior" of music. He compares the suggestions of emotion in music with emotion-characteristics in a person's "behavior, bearing, facial expression and so forth."[63] Such behavior need not correspond to felt emotion, but felt emotion typically is expressed through such "emotion-characteristics in appearance." Usually, we respond empathetically to such emotion-characteristics. We feel vicariously cheered when we observe someone smiling or walking with an exuberant gait. Occasionally, we take such emotion-characteristics as an emotion-object for our own quite different emotion. For instance, we may be offended by a grin that strikes us as sarcastic. But in most cases, we do not emotionally react to the emotion-characteristics with a different emotion but instead find ourselves mirroring the emotion suggested by those characteristics.

The case is similar in music, Davies argues. We typically feel the emotion that the behavioral features of music suggest. Moreover, such mirroring strikes us as appropriate. Davies argues that such emotional mirroring is more fundamental than more complicated emotional reactions to music (although the latter may be appropriate in some cases):

> The mirroring response may not, in *the full context of the work,* be appropriate, for the work may provide reasons for over-ruling the mirroring response. Similarly, if a section can be heard as presenting the aspects of several different emotion-characteristics, the subsequent course of the music may provide reasons why we should hear the section as presenting one rather than the other emotion-characteristic and therefore why one of the possible mirroring emotional responses is inappropriate. . . . The crucial point though is this: However sophisticated an aesthetic response to the expressiveness of a musical work may be, the mirroring response is ontologically prior to the more sensitive and sophisticated response and to be disregarded it must be over-ruled.[64]

Through its behavior music *can* remind us of emotion experienced in other connections. In this respect, imitation theory provides insight into a possibility that is often actualized in music. Davies provides a plausible account of why emotional arousal is not only compatible with musical imitation of emotional behavior, but the paradigm response to it. Our typical response to emotion-characteristics that we recognize in music is to *feel* the emotion we recognize. We also take the presence of emotion-characteristics in music to be an "expression" of emotion, at least in the sense that the emotion is understood as essential to the meaning of a piece or passage of music and as evident to composer, performer, and listener alike.

Davies's model of emotional "mirroring" or parallelism affirms certain insights of each of the three standard theories of the emotion–music connection. In this sense, I think it correctly reflects our impression of emotion in musical experience. We expect to be emotionally moved when we begin listening to music. Dynamic features of music remind us of emotional behavior, and thus of the emotions we take the behavior to represent. In most cases we "entertain" the emotions we find represented, and we take them to be "expressions," in that we take them to be intentionally communicated to us.[65]

Need We Articulate Musical Emotion?

At this point, someone might object that we are being too vague about *which* emotions we recognize and entertain while listening to music. Hanslick considered dynamic features insufficient to establish specific emotional content. Isn't Hanslick correct in claiming that we cannot explicate precisely which emotions are the content of any particular passage of music?

The answer is yes. But this does not constitute a problem. Hanslick is concerned that we have no established criterion for determining the specific emotion suggested by music because he sees this as evidence that our recognition of emotion in music is arbitrary. But this is an unwarranted conclusion.

To see why, let us compare the situation of one's ascertaining a friend's emotional state during a sympathetic conversation with the emotional communication involved in music. Obviously, the fact that conversation is conducted in language while musical communication is not represents an important difference. But I believe that one's interpretation of conversationally expressed emotion and one's own response are in several ways comparable to one's empathetic appreciation of musically expressed emotion. I assume that one's interpretation of a friend's comments depends on behavioral cues and that these are crucial to one's sense of the friend's affective condition. Thus, the fact that language is employed in conversation does not imply that language is the sole medium of communication. I also assume that one can be generally "in touch" or "not in touch" with the emotional state of one's friend. What interests me in either case is whether the ability to specify the emotions communicated is necessary for understanding and empathizing appropriately.

Our inability to explicate a friend's precise emotions does not indicate our lack of empathy. We might have great difficulty articulating the friend's emotional state and yet still have some understanding of it. And if we are concerned to respond in an appropriate practical way, labeling the emotion is both unnecessary and possibly distracting. A summary term for the friend's condition might well be deceptively clear, for actual emotional states often involve admixtures of other emotions.

Definition of precise emotions is similarly unnecessary in the case of music's emotional communication. I am cheered by seeing someone walk by with a cheerful gait, whether or not I label my emotional response. Similarly, we respond emotionally to dynamic features of music that are reminiscent of emotional behavior whether or not we consciously reflect on the matter.

Emotional empathy in other cases of human communication tends to arise developmentally. When we converse with a friend, we do not usually take every new statement as an atomistic expression of emotional content, which may or may not relate to what has just been said. We seek to relate the emotional suggestions made throughout the conversation. Of course, we are open to the possibility that new statements will change our understanding of the emotional expression. But we generally aspire to an overall "take" on the friend's emotional situation.

The musical case is similar. As Davies observes, the overall context of a musical work can modify or clarify the emotional tone of the music. We do not need to specify one-to-one linkages between musical events and emotions to discern the emotional character of the music. Atomistic analysis of the sort that Hanslick seems to be seeking is not a precondition for understanding the emotional content of the music.[66] We can even miss some expressive events entirely and still have a sense of the emotional tone. Of course, we may discover that new developments in the music lead us to revise our first impression of the emotional content. But again, we do not need to label to have a "nuanced" emotional response. Analysis and labeling may enhance our enjoyment (particularly if we are of an intellectual bent), but they are not preconditions for appropriate emotional empathy.

Emotional empathy, in the case of a friend conversing about emotion or in that of music, admits of a whole range of depth. I might attend to details that modify my understanding of the friend's emotion, or I might be satisfied to determine that the friend is or is not "doing all right." I have communicated more fully in the former case; but I have not "gone wrong" if I settle for the latter. And there is a range of possibilities between these two extremes.

In music, similarly, I might have sufficient musical experience and available attention to appreciate a remarkable degree of detail in both structure and performance—and in connection with both I might undergo a rich and nuanced empathetic emotional experience. (Appreciating nuance may or may not depend, in a particular case, on paying equal attention to all of the musical events that pass by; but I do not think that it is the same as atomistic monitoring.) On the other hand, I might be driving through tense traffic while listening to Mozart's *Jupiter* Symphony on the radio and be thankful to recognize that it is joyful even under these conditions. I see nothing problematic about the fact that sometimes I can appreciate more than I can at other times, or that more musical experience is likely to develop my capacity for appreciation and at the same time expand my interest in musical vocabulary. Even under adverse circumstances, when my emotional responsiveness to music is minimal, I may still recognize emotion-characteristics in music and feel emotion in response. (Presumably such experiences are the reason why so many people believe that music can be "uplifting.")

These considerations are relevant to an understanding of musical intersubjectivity. Intersubjective musical experience does not depend on listeners' sharing a response down to the last detail. Different listeners can interpret the emotional content somewhat differently and still share music's emotional character in a significant way.

Some accounts, however, might still be judged wrong as intersubjective claims. For example, a person might erroneously claim that a peppy march sounds melancholy. Considered as purely self-referential, such accounts may still make a kind of sense. While ill, I might find lilting music annoying, even depressing. Some depressed people can find a beautiful, sunny day offensive. One's empirical response to art, as aestheticians since Hume have noted, may be aberrant because of one's particular circumstances. But the dynamic features of music and certain features of performance and its effects that listeners commonly recognize do provide a basis for claiming that the emotional character is intersubjective and not arbitrary.

Hanslick's contention that music does not express or arouse specific (that is, nameable) emotions does not pose a problem for the "mirroring" theory. One does not need a label to respond to emotionally characteristic behavior. In addition, if one includes musical context as essential to the music, contextual cues can contribute to and refine one's sense of the emotion expressed by music.

We need not be able to articulate which emotions music moves us to experience in order to claim that we *feel* them and that we sense that we *share* them. I doubt that our vocabulary of emotional terms is rich enough to specify our precise emotions in most situations, musical or not. But precise terminology is not necessary for the experience or communication of emotion, as examination of how we discover a friend's emotion is likely to demonstrate.

Discussion of emotion in connection with music does have value, however. One of Hanslick's mistakes was to consider analytical precision the only valuable aim of such discussion. And he went on to conclude, with this singular aim in mind, that nonemotional terminology could replace the vocabulary of affect. In the next section I argue that Hanslick missed the value of "emotion talk" in connection with music. Such talk does not attempt and fail at the precision that Hanslick desires. Instead, it facilitates a feature of musical experience that Hanslick ignores: the sense that one shares a moving experience with others.

Why Talk of Music?

One reason Hanslick and his intellectual descendants give for dismissing the affective aspect of music is that one can discuss music more intelligently without it. While acknowledging the aptness of some emotional terms as applied to music, Hanslick urged philosophers to shun them in favor of more precise, technical description. He also considered reliance on the language of feeling to be often symptomatic of pathological (and hence unintelligent) listening. That aestheticians continue to oppose technical and affective language is indicated by Meyer's suggestion that the choice between these vocabularies is a consequence of personal temperament and training.

The underlying assumption in such discussions is that emotion talk and technical talk aim to do the same thing. Only if this is presupposed does it make sense to claim that technical description characterizes music more competently than discussion that employs emotional terms. But this assumption is faulty. Affective discussions of music and technical discussions are referring to quite different things.

Discussions that focus on affect are concerned explicitly with musical *experience*. Technical discussions are much more concerned with the structure of the musical work and with the techniques used in producing the work's auditory component. While concern with such matters may be integral to the production of musical experience, one's concern while involved in the experience may extend to other matters. One might want to comment on how one *feels* (in a broad sense) in response to the music. Among the features of an experience that are more "felt" than analyzed are one's sense that one is significantly coexperiencing something along with other listeners, and the recognition that a performer is really engaged with the music. These are matters of significance to listeners, matters that often move them to comment; but a technical vocabulary does little to reflect such things.

For such matters, we typically employ metaphors and metaphorical figures of speech. When the jazz aficionado remarks to a fellow listener, "Now they're cooking!" for example, he is saying something significant about his experience and expressing his confidence that the experience is shared. This type of remark is not fully translatable into a technical musical vocabulary. A technical vocabulary might note certain technical conditions that underlie a performer's achievement—the complexity that he or she is able to control, for instance—but the control itself, as the listener senses it, is not a phenomenon that admits of precise technical description. And because technical terminology focuses on "objective" features of music such as structural detail and physical techniques of performance, it has few resources for conveying the nature of what listeners experience in the act of engaged listening to a performance.

Feld argues that the construction and use of metaphors in immediate response to musical performance is an indication of engaged listening and of the coexperience of music. During the course of his fieldwork among the

Kaluli tribe of Papua, New Guinea, Feld observed that the Kaluli had two detailed vocabularies for music talk, one a technical system that referred to such matters as intervals, contours, and performance techniques, and the other a vocabulary of metaphors expressing evaluations of a performance in terms of the achievement of various esteemed effects—including successful transmission of an experience to listeners. By attending to such metaphors, Feld argues, we are enabled to track the course of a group musical experience.

Generalizing to the broader spectrum of musical experience, Feld insists that such nontechnical metaphorical vocabularies are not indications of verbal incompetence. Instead, they point to shared features of musical experience that we all, in practice, recognize:

> When people say "it's different from . . .", "it's a kind of . . .", "it sort of reminds me of . . .", and things of this sort, they are creating discourse organization that has locational, categorical, and associational features. When they say, "Well, if I had to name it . . . I mean . . . on some level, . . . for me at least, . . . you know, I really can't say but do you know what I mean? . . ." they are not just tongue-tied, inarticulate, or unable to speak. They are caught in a moment of interpretive time, trying to force awareness to words. They are telling us how much they assume that we understand *exactly* what they are experiencing. In fact, we *do* understand exactly what they are experiencing. We take it as socially typical that people can talk this way about music, stringing together expressives, and we assume that this confirms what we are all supposed to know: that at some level, one just cannot say with words what music says without them.

But the fact that language and music are not mutually translatable does not imply that the proliferation of metaphoric talk is superfluous. To the contrary, the language of metaphor supplements technical vocabulary in the effort to comprehensively discuss the phenomenon of music:

> I would stress that the significant feature of musical communication is not that it is untranslatable and irreducible to the verbal mode, but that its generality and multiplicity of possible messages and interpretations brings out a special kind of feelingful activity and engagement on the part of the listener.[67]

Conceived in this fashion, metaphorical discourse about music is not valued or devalued on the basis of its relative precision by comparison with technical discourse. Instead, technical discourse is valued along with metaphorical discourse as one more mode for enhancing participants' meaningful engagement with music. If the aim of musical aesthetics is similarly conceived as the enhancement of meaningful engagement with music—and this is the conception with which I am operating—then emotive discourse about music, even if imprecise, is of significant concern to the field. And because it is concerned with different features of musical experience than discourse conducted in technical vocabulary, emotive discourse is irreducibly important in a comprehensive philosophical understanding of the phenomena of music.

Conclusion

The meaningful engagement of listeners with music and with one another is most often described and expressed in emotional terms. Philosophy's recognition of the role of such engagement in musical experience depends, therefore, on an acknowledgment of the reality and importance of the emotional dimension of music that listeners typically experience and often express. Western philosophy would do well to regain its earlier insight that music is a profoundly emotional phenomenon. If it did so, it would recognize that the felt sense of engagement basic to musical experience is related to our ethical capacities and orientations.

5 ‖: The Ethical Aspects of Music: Music as Influence and Educator

I remember from my childhood—I could not have been more than seven or eight years of age at the time—witnessing a performance by a traveling theatrical troupe that came to a little town called Shakargarh, now in Pakistan. . . . the music that belonged to the performance apart, what stands out in my mind is the sound of suppressed sobbing that came from the audience. The situation in the play must have been of unbearable grief, arising from some kind of irreversible separation, and several members of the audience seemed to be choked with feeling, silent tears flowing, mouths dry, a lump in their throats that evidently refused to go away. The performance had obviously led to a certain melting of the heart. I remember seeing with a sense of bewilderment grown men wiping tears silently from their eyes and holding their heads between their hands—trying to suppress emotions, anxious not to display them—covering the lower parts of their faces in the coarse cotton sheets that served as wraps around their shoulders in the slight chill of the evening. The spectators seemed to be a rustic, uncouth group of people, but evidently they responded to the performance and were deeply moved by it. Today I would say, recalling that evening, that they were experiencing an aesthetic emotion occasioned by the performance. —B. N. Goswamy, "Rasa"

Music is, first of all, an experience. Celebration calls for music in every culture known to anthropology. People make music to mark the most important events and turning points in their lives. Music is a vital part of most marriages, ceremonies of initiation, and commemorations of important events in the lives of individuals and of civic and religious communities. Describing the range of human uses of music, Merriam observes, "There is probably no other human cultural activity which is so all-pervasive and which reaches into, shapes, and often controls so much of human behavior."[1] What American birthday party would be complete without an often cacophonous rendition of "Happy Birthday to You"? And what American shopping mall would forgo the opportunity to immerse its shoppers in musical gestures toward the "Christmas spirit" as soon as Thanksgiving is past (or even before)?

The seeming universality of "humanly organized sounds" used to heighten and inspire the signal features and events of human and cultural life is a prima facie reason for taking music seriously as an ethical medium. As Donald Ferguson observes,

> It is wholly unimaginable that the huge musical public whose growth the history of music chronicles could ever have been assembled solely through the admiration for an art which, however fascinating as art, bore no reference whatever to the experiences that drive men to fight and love and worship.[2]

But for reasons that we have discussed in the previous chapters, Western aesthetics has become skeptical of the easy connection that most of the world makes between music and ethical life. In particular, the field's tendency to treat music as an autonomous structural object and to minimize concern with the holistic character of musical experience (which depends significantly on context) has obscured the experiential bases for recognizing music's symbolic and motivational roles with respect to ethical living.

In this chapter, I consider three aspects common to typical musical experience that provide bases for considering music relevant to ethics.[3] Musically associated affect figures in all three, but I distinguish (1) music's psychophysiological power to influence the listener's outlook, (2) its ability to develop capacities of value to ethical living, and (3) its capacity to serve in metaphoric and symbolic roles that can assist our ethical reflection. Each of these characteristics of experienced music is linked in a significant way to features of our ethically experienced lives.

Historically, the world's philosophical traditions have advanced a number of arguments in support of the idea that music is linked to ethical experience. These arguments tend to fall into one of three categories: (1) music has physiological or psychological *effects* that have benign ethical influence on outlook and behavior; (2) music develops *capacities* that assist our ethical outlook or our ability to behave ethically; or (3) music makes *revelations* that are ethically valuable to us.

The three aspects of music that I consider provide grounds for recognizing some merit in each of these general approaches to the music–ethics connection. I show, first, that music's psychophysiological character can influence our sense of ourselves as ethical agents and can encourage the belief that the harmonious interplay of our human powers is desirable, even gratifying. Second, music, through its engagement of our affective and (more narrowly) intellectual natures, can develop in us capacities of value in ethical comportment and attitude. And, third, music's role as a symbolic object suits it to the purpose of making revelations of ethical value. I draw upon historical defenses of the music–ethics connection, at least some of which raise possibilities that deserve further consideration in connection with our own musical experience.

A discussion of this sort would be incomplete without a recognition of the many historical claims that music can have pernicious effects on morality. I conclude with a consideration of this alternative perspective on the music–ethics connection. While some of these arguments deserve serious reflection, I maintain that they do not tell against the arguments that I enlist in support of music's positive ethical functions.

The Psychophysiological Influence of Music

Let a man be stimulated by poetry, established by the rules of propriety, and perfected by music.—Confucius, *Analects*

That music can influence outlook and behavior is a commonplace belief in many societies. So powerful is this conviction that several traditions consider musical education instrumental for social harmony. Chou Tun-yi explains the Confucian view: "As the sound of music is calm, the heart of the listener becomes peaceful, and as the words of the music are good, those who sing them will admire them. The result will be that customs are transformed and mores are changed."[4]

The ancient Greek views discussed earlier coincide strikingly with Confucian ideas. While Plato considered music's ability to influence behavior a power for both good and ill, he considered musical inspiration of desirable states of mind to be valuable, even essential, to the education of character:

Omissions and the failure of beauty in things badly made or grown would be most quickly perceived by one who was properly educated in music, and so, feeling distaste rightly, he would praise beautiful things and take delight in them and receive them into his soul to foster its growth and become himself beautiful and good.[5]

Aristotle similarly stressed the role of music in moral education:

> Music has a power of forming the character. . . . There seems to be in
> us a sort of affinity to musical modes and rhythms, which makes some
> philosophers say that the soul is a tuning, others, that it possesses tuning.[6]

But the power of music to insinuate moods and motivations is not obviously an ethical boon. Besides the common objection that certain kinds of music incite morally undesirable behavior, the physical means by which music achieves its influence has struck some thinkers as morally suspect.[7]

Hanslick, as we have observed, takes this tack. Although I am convinced that music's physical character suits it to beneficially influence our ethical life, I think Hanslick's objection should be addressed. His argument rests on the assumption that physical influence detracts from other kinds of impact. In exposing this assumption, we remove a major obstacle to the recognition that music has an ethical dimension.

Hanslick attacks defenders of music's "moral effects" for focusing on the "pathological" aspects of music. The most common Western defense of music as an ethical influence has been that music induces feelings or emotions that are conducive to good moral conduct. It is this traditional defense that Hanslick challenges.

Hanslick's attack is built on well-trodden ethical ground. Moral life, he assumes, depends on the free moral choice of the ethical agent. But if music genuinely does affect the listener as a "crude natural force" (the claim Hanslick sees its moral defenders as making), it is a potential obstruction to moral choice. This danger, Hanslick contends, is yet another argument for intellectual appreciation of music. Sufficient moral and intellectual cultivation enable the listener to focus on the formal features of the music and thereby avoid "unconscious" influence.[8]

Hanslick's dichotomy between intellect and body is decisive in his disparagement of what he caricatures as musically induced "morality." Following Kant, Hanslick considers the ethical ideal to be the intellect's control over emotion and body (or, in Kantian terms, the inclinations). This model represents, within the Western philosophical tradition, the extreme case of intellectualism in ethics. Even Plato, whose ethical model similarly urges the subordination of the rest of our nature to reason, emphasizes the harmonious *cooperation* among the aspects of the soul. Kant and Hanslick, on the other hand, emphasize intellectual *control*. For Hanslick, as a consequence, good behavior won by means of neurophysiological stimulation is of no moral worth whatever.

Hanslick does not often resist the temptation to caricature, and his discussion of music's alleged moral effects is not one of the rare occasions. His caricature is simplistic in the manner of all caricatures. But it is also wrong-headed. Hanslick is wrong in supposing that defenders of music's moral effects are extolling "mindless" mood transformation through neurophysiological stimulation.

The philosophical defenders of music's benign influence on ethical outlook, in fact, do not give such short shrift to the intellect's involvement in the process. Even someone as skeptical of the body's role in musical experience as Augustine observed that music gains admission to the intellect by means of the senses. And Aristotle, one of the most important influences on Western thought about music, believed that music's relaxation of the body was not at the expense of intellectual satisfaction.

Aristotle considered music's ability to relax the listener one of its most important merits:

> All men agree that music is one of the pleasantest things, whether with or without song. . . . Hence and with good reason it is introduced into social gatherings and entertainments, because it makes the hearts of men glad. . . . For innocent pleasures are not only in harmony with the perfect end of life, but they also provide relaxation. And whereas men rarely attain the end, but often rest by the way and amuse themselves, not only with a view to a further end, but also for the pleasure's sake, it may be well at times to let them find a refreshment in music.

But Aristotle also observed that music occasions intellectual enjoyment. In the *Politics* he considers which of its apparent beneficial effects—education, amusement, or intellectual enjoyment—music actually achieves, and concludes that it simultaneously accomplishes all three.

> Music is pursued, not only as an alleviation of past toil, but also as providing recreation. And who can say whether, having this use, it may not also have a nobler one? In addition to this common pleasure, felt and shared in by all. . . , may it not have also some influence over the character and the soul? It must have such an influence if characters are affected by it. And that they are so affected is proved in many ways.[9]

Music can, according to Aristotle, engage the mind in contemplation (although not of a disinterested sort); but this contemplation is enhanced by practical, bodily based knowledge of how music is performed. "It is difficult, if not impossible, for those who do not perform to be good judges of the performance of others." Moreover, Aristotle argues that learning the physical techniques of musical performance is intrinsically worthwhile:

Besides, children should have something to do, and the rattle of Archytas, which people give to their children in order to amuse them and prevent them from breaking anything in the house, was a capital invention, for a young thing cannot be quiet. The rattle is a toy suited to the infant mind, and education is a rattle or toy for children of a larger growth.[10]

Physical relaxation, intellectual contemplation, and mental amusement over physical effects are all, according to Aristotle, pleasures wrought by music. Contemplation is a pleasure in its own right—and, indeed, a higher pleasure than physical enjoyment—but it is not divorced from physical effects. The recuperation of one's entire system attends contemplation; and intellectual comprehension of music is inadequate without a degree of "physical" experience in the form of music-making.

Aristotle's endorsement of musical recreation suggests another reason Hanslick's analysis is fallacious. The human being who enjoys music is not (as the Kantian model would have it) a tenuous duality of intellect and neurophysiology. The listener is a complex union of many elements, each of which is involved in the experience of music. Because music addresses and provides simultaneous satisfaction to the various components that make up the person, it provokes a harmonious integration of the entire multi-faceted human being. The physical appeal of music is an essential element in the larger picture of music's impact on the listener as a complex being. Music's physiological influence is a component—and a necessary one—in its broader engagement of the entire human being.

Friedrich Nietzsche appeals to our awareness of music's multidimensional character when he describes the influence of the Dionysian dithyramb: "We need a new world of symbols; and the entire symbolism of the body is called into play, not the mere symbolism of the lips, face, and speech but the whole pantomime of dancing, forcing every member into rhythmic movement." Nietzsche suggests that our more tranquil experience of music in the concert hall requires a concerted repression of this need to respond with the whole body, but he adds "at least relatively, for to a certain degree all rhythm still appeals to our muscles."[11] The physiological appeal of music remains profound, Nietzsche tells us. But this appeal and our desire to respond with our bodies are not evidence that music's impact is "merely pathological." Instead, we feel compelled to throw our entire bodies into our responding because we find them ready symbols for our entire beings.

One traditional concern of ethics has been the proper interaction of the various aspects of the person. The harmonious interplay of reason, emotion, and appetite was, for Plato as well as for Aristotle, the spiritual ideal for the individual. Inner harmony of this sort was also a precondition for harmonious interpersonal behavior. For only the person in harmony with him- or herself had the self-control necessary for cooperative interaction with others. Plato, Aristotle, and the tradition that succeeded them have often sought the origins of ethical living in the harmonizing of the human being's various powers. The fact that musical experience involves an integration of the human being's vital powers already suggests that musical experience has potential value for ethical living. Feeling myself to be a harmony, I am disposed to behavior as a harmonious, centered being.

This is the first of my reasons for claiming that music's psychophysiological effects can exert a positive ethical influence. In listening to music, we feel that our powers are attuned. And this feeling, I believe, is tremendously helpful in enabling us to behave as coordinated ethical agents. Minimally, it encourages our belief that the various aspects of our being *can* operate harmoniously. In many cases, too, music demonstrates that such harmonious operation can be satisfying to *all* of these aspects.

Plato and Aristotle considered music's harmonious integration of the human faculties to be premised on music's own harmoniousness. But much contemporary music is not harmonious in this fashion. In my view, music that is neither harmonious, soothing, nor reassuring can still provoke harmonious integration of the listener's faculties. For the interplay of these faculties is inherent in the activity of assimilating virtually any music (provided that it is sufficiently interesting to inspire engaged listening).

Music addresses the various aspects of the person even when it does not please all of them. Cacophonous music, for instance, addresses the body as well as the mind, even though it produces physical tensions and perhaps discomfort. Some contemporary music attacks the traditional notion of the work as a well-ordered whole. But the faculties jointly enlisted in response to it do not follow the "example" of the music; they themselves operate as a well-ordered unity. Certainly, when music does present the harmonious interaction of distinct elements, it can serve as a symbol of harmony on other levels, both within the individual and within society. But it need not do so in order to incite the harmonious functioning of the listener's capacities.

By engaging our faculties in harmonious activity, music causes us to see ourselves in a certain way. Musical experience affords a kind of self-awareness. That we link music to human personhood is suggested even by scenes in comedy. Consider, for example, the movie portrayal of the incompetent singer (Geena Davis as Muriel Pritchett) in *The Accidental Tourist*.[12] Macon (played by William Hurt) finds the singing moving because he takes it to represent the entire woman that he is beginning to love. It would be unthinkable to interrupt the singer—the only appropriate role for the listener is silent appreciation. Significantly, the intimacy of overhearing singing is almost embarrassing. Singing, here, is taken to represent the person to a depth that is semisacred.

Or again, consider Bugs Bunny's confrontations with a rehearsing operatic voice. Bugs encounters it as an uncontrollable force of nature. The singing appears to be a presence with which Bugs is not entitled to interfere. He does make abortive efforts to make it stop, but these come off as slapstick violence. The comedy in this situation depends on our sense that it is almost an ethical violation to interfere with singing, that singing is the expression of the singer's very soul.

Listening, as Aristotle suggests, involves an integration of the components of one's own being. It engages and makes us aware of the elements that compose the kind of beings that we are. Musical experience is not simple physical stimulation; it necessarily involves our psychic responses. We encounter music as engaged and embodied *selves*.

Music and the Sense of Self

Music's impact on self-conception is rarely considered. To say that music makes one self-aware is uncommon. And, in the view of our philosophical tradition, this is not even a compliment. Listeners who hear music and "think of themselves" are targets for accusations of "pathological listening" or "self-indulgence." Music, if it pertains to selfhood at all, would seem aimed at self-transcendence more than self-awareness. Whether escapists or spiritual aspirants, people listen in order to forget themselves and their personal problems.

Music does afford both self-awareness and self-transcendence. But more basically, it gives the listener a prereflective sense of *being* a self. Music gives us a sense of fully "being there," with our faculties fully engaged.

Consider the tone-deaf person who sings along with the radio. What is going on here? Is the person self-deceived about his or her talent? Does the person aim to impress an audience? Is such singing in any sense a "presentation" for someone else? I think the person is doing none of these things. Instead, singing along with the radio is a way of "joining in," of "being there too." Joining the music is a means of situating oneself in the world. But if this is so, music-making must be intimately tied to one's sense of self.

Music facilitates a sense of human selfhood, even when one is not making music or singing along oneself, but is engaged in listening. In this connection, the distinction between music-making and engaged listening is not very important. We experience *ourselves* as musical, simply by virtue of appreciative listening. Scruton makes this point when he refers to the listener's "inner dancing."[13]

Many facets of the experience of human selfhood become apparent through music. We can approach these by asking: As a being who experiences music, what am I? In our answers, we again see that the "physical" character of musical experience is not a matter of passively received stimulation. Instead, it is the basis of an awareness of what kind of beings we are.

In the first place, as a listener I am a *temporal* being. I am able to experience and enjoy music because I perceive along the dimension of time. In listening, I also discover myself to be capable of temporal projection. In most musics of a familiar style, I expect certain things and am satisfied when they occur. The music of my tradition (as well as many others) plays with tension and relaxation and thereby brings to my attention the possibility of temporal change. I find myself to be part of a world in which transformation occurs. Music reminds me that I exist in a world in which change is possible and that I myself am changing.

Listening to music also makes me aware that I am an *embodied* being. In many instances, music inspires me to tap my toes or even dance. That I can most easily join in music-making by singing suggests that the body itself is the primary musical instrument. In some traditions, music's relationship to the human voice and respiration is seen as the basis for music's power over listeners, and perhaps the rest of the environment as well. Indian music theory, for instance, considers vocal sound to have causal power, as Rowell explains:

> In a word, sound makes things happen. This notion provides some of the most powerful generating ideas in the musical tradition: that respiration is the model for all music (including instrumental music, and consequently all Indian instrumental traditions are based upon the vocal style); that vocal sound arises from, and thus represents an extension of, inner reality; that music is continuous flow; and that sound emerges from an inner reservoir and needs only to be tapped to be released.[14]

If one considers song to be the fundamental kind of music, one automatically links music to embodied physical life. Through the voice, the body itself becomes the paradigmatic instrument. Sparshott observes that song is also a reflection of psychic life and of the fact that psychic life is joined to the life of the body:

"Voice" in nature is psychic sound, issuing from near the vital center, the heart; it has pitch, tune (*melos,* the quality of lyric, singable perhaps), and phrasing (*dialekton,* the kind of articulation that languages have). Voice includes all animal cries as well as musical performances; articulate speech is a further differentiation of it.[15]

The self who listens and feels related to music is, accordingly, also a *vital* self. Music, simultaneously engaging our physical, emotional, and intellectual receptivities, makes us feel fully alive. The dynamism of music, moreover, reminds us of our own dynamism. We tend to approach music as a reflection of both physical and mental life. Music can represent animate behavior, as many composers have deliberately demonstrated. As Arthur Schopenhauer suggests, we tend to hear the movements of melody as the movements of the conscious human will:

> Melody . . . relates the most secret history of the intellectually enlightened will, portrays every agitation, every effort, every movement of the will, everything which the faculty of reason summarizes under the wide and negative concept of feeling, and which cannot be further taken up into the abstractions of reason.[16]

As we have observed, the typical listener approaches music in a receptive frame of mind. One is open to music, and to the emotional experience that music may bring with it. In this sense, the listener finds him- or herself in the condition of the *receptive* and *nondefensive* self. And although this condition does not always obtain, the experience of oneself as receptive is a kind of self-discovery. One becomes aware of oneself as a being who can relate to the world nondefensively (a realization that even by Kantian standards is of moral value).

Obviously, there are instances of music that have inspired defensive reactions. The rioting audience of the first performance of Stravinsky's *Rite of Spring,* for instance, might be described as defensive and angry. But such reactions actually demonstrate that listening involves a receptive stance. Could the audience have felt so assaulted had they not exposed themselves in an emotional, psychical way? No. Only because the listeners were psychically open could they be vulnerable to the sense of shock that preceded the riot. And could they still be listening once they began to riot? Again, the answer is no, at least insofar as "listening" involves at least minimal attention and interest in what musical event will occur next.[17]

The claim that the listener is receptive, however, does not imply that the listener is entirely passive. The listener is active in a number of ways. In the first place, the attentive listener is absorbed. This does not mean that the listener is necessarily having a disinterested, contemplative experience of the sort that Kant and Hanslick admire, or that absorption in music minimizes physical or emotional response. Foot-tapping or swaying to rhythm might be provoked by music that engages only background awareness; but they might also be symptoms of great involvement in the music. And it is involvement that is at stake in the listener's "absorption."

To some extent, I suspect that Hanslick had absorption in mind as a characteristic of "musical" listening, and that this is why he rails against "pathological" enjoyment of music. I find his contempt for most listeners misplaced, misguided, and snobbish; but Hanslick is surely right that one is not really "with" the music if one does not engage the range of one's powers in response to it.[18] And while one can engage one's responsive powers to varying degrees, one "listens" only when one has assumed a stance in which one is to some degree mentally and physically prepared to respond. Even in the concert hall, we breathe with the music when it really engages us. This is the condition that I am calling "absorption."

In the situation of engaged listening, one usually mirrors emotion, in the fashion that Davies describes. But when one does this, one relates to the music not only as an *emotional* being, but also as oneself an *expressive* being. Donald Callen suggests that in experiencing emotion while listening to music, we are internally "singing along":

> The Schubert opens with an image of anger expressed first in an *assaulting leap,* then in *evenly delivered sharp jabs.* But the anger is momentarily sorrowful, displayed in a *soft whimper,* then *a pointed cry fading to a quiet sigh.* These are activities with which we can identify as we inwardly sing along with and move with the music, and through identifying with the expressions of anger and sorrow we are able to identify with the emotions themselves.[19]

But if "inner singing" (or "inner dancing," as Scruton would have it) is a natural correlate of engaged listening, the listener is apparently involved in a kind of inner act of expressiveness as well.[20]

In many cases, one's sense of self as expressive has specific emotional associations. One may feel expressive as a prayerful being while listening to religious or otherwise "spiritual" music (some of Bach's toccatas and fugues come to mind), or when listening to music in a context that is understood as religious. When listening to lively or ecstatic music, one may feel disposed to express delight, celebration, or play, either in conjunction with or shortly after listening. If one considers the range of one's listening experiences, I suspect one will discover oneself a being with a varied emotional gamut, ranging from depressed to playful to reverent. Through listening one discovers oneself to be capable of a wide range of emotional conditions.

We have already observed that one experiences oneself, while listening, as a being whose powers are coordinated and harmoniously functioning. This condition impresses us with our ability to function as unified beings. Music also gives one an intuition of one's self as engaged with and responsive to a larger world. Concern for something beyond oneself, a prerequisite for ethically good living, is already present in the self-conception that we discover in our musical experience. And this is my second reason for claiming that the psychophysiological impact of music is ethically beneficial. In music, we discover ourselves to be social and socially concerned beings.

Sparshott indicates that music elicits our feelings of affinity for others when he suggests that music enhances our self-esteem:

> Even if we cannot say why it should, the recognition of the fine arts (including music) as important branches of human endeavor rests on the observed fact that they are capable of awe inspiring feats. If an explanation is wanted, we can say that our cognitive powers are those that form the focus of our self-esteem as human beings, that the powers exercised in listening are among such powers, and that objects experienced as challenging those powers in certain ways will appear superhuman and thus inspire awe.[21]

We feel awe for human capabilities, Sparshott claims, because human beings can not only conceive such intricate coordination, but also produce it.

Sparshott emphasizes the cognitive capacities involved in our experience of such music. But I think that the self-esteem he describes rests at least as much on our sense of being coordinated beings. Just as we take satisfaction in our own coordination while dancing (and what else could explain, for instance, the lingering appeal of outmoded dances like the waltz?), most of us take pride when we simultaneously attend to the music and physically thrill to its unfolding. Thus, I think that Sparshott is too narrow when he describes our cognitive powers as forming "the focus of our self-esteem." While the cognitive powers are certainly integral to this focus, we feel self-esteem in connection with the harmonious interaction of the range of our powers, cognitive and noncognitive alike.

Sparshott's remark, however, points to a further aspect of the self that experiences music. For when he observes that we take pride in music because beings like us produce it, he calls our attention to the fact that we normally identify with other human beings when we listen to music. As a listener, one discovers oneself to be a *social* being. One discovers that as a self, one is part of a world that includes others.

Music as a Social Phenomenon

The thought that musical listening is a social phenomenon may seem out of date. In contemporary American society, it is only in the aberrant case that one experiences music in a live, group format. Our primary mode of musical production is recording technology (whether broadcast or personally employed). And through our use of such technology, our culture has become both predominantly passive and individualistic with respect to music.[22] Passivity is encouraged by the fact that, although music is an accompaniment of the typical waking day, much of it is inflicted on us by someone else (a boss, a store manager, or a restaurant owner, for example). And while we choose our own radio stations when we drive, we still rely on stations and disc jockeys to tell us what is worth hearing.

Other features of our everyday experience encourage the impression that music is a matter of individual consumption. The availability of recorded music has made possible the development of a historically novel use of music: individual self-assertion, often in aggressive opposition to others. Such assertions are common in all walks of life. The person who accompanies his or her walking with a boom-box, the driver who blasts his radio station into the surrounding countryside, and the undergraduate who positions stereo speakers in a dormitory window are aggressively foisting their tastes on others. Each is using music for asocial, if not antisocial, ends. And most of us have been irritated at one time or another by the similarly asocial Walkman phenomenon, which enables people to appear in the midst of public bustle with their auditory capacities channeled into an entirely different world. Bloom casts the teenager with the Walkman as an icon of declining Western culture. I think he overstates the point; but the Walkman-wired cyclist I recently saw tying a shoe in front of oncoming traffic surely represents some kind of communicative breakdown.

With such conspicuous uses of music to tune out the immediate social environment, it is no wonder that many Americans besides philosophers do not consider music a particularly communal phenomenon. And yet it is not so many years since Woodstock, which reminded at least one generation that music can create a community, even if a short-lived one.[23] Events like Woodstock, even the well-attended local concert (of whatever musical discourse), make it obvious that a communal dimension of music is still evident to Americans who seek it out.

Furthermore, although our society's appropriation of music disguises its social dimension, this dimension remains inevitably a part of our awareness when we experience music. Music is, by its very nature, a social activity. Even the music heard through the earphones of a Walkman sounds like it comes from external reality. In fact it does come from outside the individual listener. A social relationship between those who produce it and the listener still occurs, albeit a highly mediated one. But in addition, I believe that most listeners experience music, even that which comes to them through earphones, as a kind of communication between themselves and other human beings.

When one identifies with the gait and emotion suggested by music, one senses that one is joining an experience that others share. Even such intimate expressions of the longing individual soul as one hears in Bach's partitas for solo violin admit the listener into a communion of one soul with another. If only in a semiconscious way, one is aware of music as a shared experience—and of its potential to be shared by other listeners as well.

Usually it is not perversity or showing off when, in our society, the owner of records, tapes, or compact discs wants to play them for friends and acquaintances. The typical motivation is to share an experience. And when music is used to encourage a particular mood in guests, the host or hostess is also immersing him- or herself in a musical experience with them. Again, when one hears music that inspires foot-tapping or the desire to dance, one is at least quasi-consciously motivated to put one's entire body into a context of social celebration.

Music is perhaps the most open medium of socially shared experience available in our culture. Contemporary American society has an impoverished range of social rituals, and most are linked to specific group memberships. Even worship services and baseball games typically involve reinforced awareness that one supports one doctrine or team as opposed to others. But although music can be employed to urge solidarity within a faction, it is almost uniquely suited to incite a sense of community among people who have little else in common besides appreciating it.

Merriam stresses the value of music for effecting a sense of communal solidarity:

> Music . . . provides a rallying point around which the members of society gather to engage in activities which require the cooperation and coordination of the group. Not all music is thus performed, of course, but every society has occasions signalled by music which draws its members together and reminds them of their unity. . . . Music is clearly indispens-

able to the proper promulgation of the activities that constitute a society;
it is a universal human behavior—without it, it is questionable that man
could truly be called man, with all that implies.[24]

Even music's effectiveness in reinforcing the solidarity of a particular faction or social subgroup presupposes its more open-ended capacity to create
a sense of community. Within such a subgroup of listeners, the shared experience of music is an effective means of minimizing the importance of
personal differences. Music gives each listener a sense of full involvement
as a self *and* a sense of other individuals sharing in this intense experience.
A. R. Radcliffe-Brown describes this response to music in his description of
the Andamanese dance:

> The pleasure that the dancer feels irradiates itself over everything around
> him and he is filled with geniality and good-will towards his companions.
> The sharing with others of an intense pleasure, or rather the sharing in a
> collective expression of pleasure, must ever incline us to such expansive
> feelings.[25]

Like any shared profound experience, listening to stirring music, which
touches one's sense of what one is, has a socially binding effect on those
who share the listening experience. The personal differences that divide the
members of the audience seem less serious than this shared intense experience. And this is true whether the audience is construed as an open or
closed group.

In one sense, art in general can serve this role of community bonding.
But in our society music is the most likely vehicle for communal aesthetic
experience. With the exception of public monuments, the visual arts, even
when publically available, are usually housed in particular museums. One
must make a concerted effort to visit museums; and those who do tend
to be the well-educated and the economically well-off (who have both the
motivation and the money needed to reach them). The activity of touring
a museum, moreover, most often emphasizes individual autonomy. Even
when one wanders around a gallery with friends, one typically observes at
one's own leisure, interacting with the others only intermittently.

Music, by contrast, dictates the experiential pacing of all its listeners.
It engages our primitive sense of being temporal beings; and this temporal
dimension is a basis for experiencing music as social. When several individuals listen to music, musical events draw them along simultaneously.
And in our society, despite the dearth of social musical occasions, recording
technology has made musical audiences remarkably large and open-ended

in contrast with the relative few who view art exhibited in museums. Publically broadcast music is pervasive, and at least some music (that popular enough to be a common background or radio-transmitted presence) reaches a wide range of our society's members.

If one is not annoyed by the volume or particular music sounding from a nearby boom-box, one can become part of a happenstance musical audience just by virtue of one's occupance of a sidewalk or subway platform. One might or might not appreciate a particular instance of publically available music. But sometimes one does, and this can be a magical moment. I remember a singer with a particularly beautiful voice singing a ballad and accompanying himself on guitar on a Boston subway platform. Although he may have been drunk, as his appearance suggested, the singing turned the diverse crowd of travelers (many of whom had the posture of wariness common in the subway) into a short-lived community. Everyone seemed attentive to the music. One listener, at some distance from the singer, "joined" the performance by slowly and evenly flinging coins in the direction of the musician's hat, placed on the platform for this purpose. The train came, and the scene dissolved.

Phenomenologist Alfred Schutz observes that music of any variety can engender a sense of community, because all music conjoins individuals in a shared experience of time:

> There is in principle no difference between the performance of a modern orchestra or chorus and people sitting around a campfire and singing to the strumming of a guitar or a congregation singing hymns under the leadership of the organ. And there is no difference in principle between the performance of a string quartet and the improvisations at a jam session of accomplished jazz players. . . . The social relationship is founded upon the partaking in common of different dimensions of time simultaneously lived through by the participants.

Schutz analyzes these "different dimensions of time" in terms of subjective and objective senses of temporality. Both subjectively and objectively, listeners are together carried step by step (or "polythetically," in Schutz's terminology) through a common sequence of experience. Schutz describes the (nonimprovisational) performance situation:

> On the one hand, there is the inner time in which the flux of musical events unfolds, a dimension in which each performer re-creates in polythetic steps the musical thought of the (possibly anonymous) composer and by which he is also connected to the listener. On the other

hand, making music together is an event in outer time, presupposing also a face-to-face relationship, that is, a community of space, and it is this dimension which unifies the fluxes of inner time and warrants their synchronization into a vivid present.[26]

Zuckerkandl also argues that musical experience gives the listener a sense of belonging to a larger, social world. Like Schutz, he sees music as involving a primitive awareness of our existential circumstances. Music, according to Zuckerkandl, serves as a means of encounter with a world outside ourselves. "Hearing a tone includes a sensation of 'without.' "[27]

But the world that we encounter through music is not only external—it is the living, social world. Hearing is the sense that makes us most aware of other animate beings. And we experience music as the sound of animate existence *par excellence*: "Among the various experiences of our senses, tone is the only one that belongs exclusively to life. . . . Living beings, out of themselves, add tone to the physical world that confronts them; it is the gift of life to nonliving nature." Music provides a bridge between the self of the listener and this larger world of life. In music, one participates in social being. Music "carries" us outward; "tones lead us away with them." And where they lead is a social community in which we ourselves are active members, and in which differences between individuals seem to collapse.[28]

Merriam argues that music is uniquely capable of facilitating a sense of human community:

Not many elements of culture afford the opportunity for emotional expression, entertain, communicate, and so forth, to the extent allowed in music. Further, music is in a sense a summatory activity for the expression of values, a means whereby the heart of the psychology of a culture is exposed without many of the protective mechanisms which surround other cultural activities. . . . And its own existence provides a·normal and solid activity which assures the members of society that the world continues in its proper path. We may . . . cite the remark of a Sia Indian to Leslie White: "My friend, without songs you cannot do anything."[29]

Music makes us feel ourselves to be connected with our larger social context. Because we respond to music physically, this connection is visceral as well as emotional. It is valuable to ethical living, for it extends one's sense of immediate concern beyond one's private person. It extends the range of one's identity by dissolving one's sense of a barrier between oneself and the rest of humanity.[30]

Ethics minimally requires that one concern oneself with others besides oneself. John Stuart Mill argues that "society between human beings . . . is manifestly impossible on any other footing than that the interests of all are to be consulted." The most positive development for human interaction, he concludes, would be for the individual to become increasingly incapable of considering his or her own interests in opposition to those of others:

> In the comparatively early state of human advancement in which we now live, a person cannot, indeed, feel that entireness of sympathy with all others which would make any real discordance in the general direction of their conduct in life impossible, but already a person in whom the social feeling is at all developed cannot bring himself to think of the rest of his fellow creatures as struggling rivals with him for the means of happiness, whom he must desire to see defeated in their object in order that he may succeed in his. The deeply rooted conception which every individual even now has of himself as a social being tends to make him feel it one of his natural wants that there should be harmony between his feelings and aims and those of his fellow creatures. If differences of opinion and of mental culture make it impossible for him to share many of their actual feelings—perhaps make him denounce and defy those feelings—he still needs to be conscious that his real aim and theirs do not conflict.[31]

That this view is not confined to utilitarian ethics is suggested by the fact that Schopenhauer, who was largely influenced by Kant, expresses a similar outlook:

> The egoist feels himself surrounded by strange and hostile phenomena, and all his hope rests on his own well-being. The good person lives in a world of friendly phenomena; the well-being of any of these is his own well-being.[32]

And Kant himself suggests that a world in which everyone would consider others' well-being is a kind of moral ideal.

I conclude, contra Hanslick, that the physical engagement that we experience in listening to music is a humanizing influence. Because music addresses our bodies as well as our minds, it makes us experience ourselves as beings whose aspects can operate harmoniously. Feeling our various powers in attunement, we are supported in seeing our tradition's ethical model of the internally harmonious being as a possibility within our grasp. More immediately, music's appeal to our physical nature gives us a very immediate sense of enjoyably sharing our world with others. This sense of sharing is ethically beneficial in that it makes it difficult to consider others' experience alien to our own. In fact, we feel that others' living experience is in this case actually our own. When this occurs, our concerns cannot really seem to us a purely private matter. We rejoice beyond ourselves in musical experience. I cannot think of a better basis for ethical concern.

Music's Affective Development of Ethical Capacities

The styles of musical pieces are different, but it is the same feeling of love [that they promote].
—Yo Ki (Record of Music)

The psychophysical orientation induced by listening to music promotes dispositions that are ethically desirable. Music facilitates a sense of oneself as a harmonious, nonconflicted vital being and a sense of intimate connection with the larger human world, both of which characterize "the good human being" on almost any ethical model.

But music does not only facilitate attitudes toward oneself that are valuable to living well in a social world. It also actively exercises and strengthens certain abilities that are involved in ethical action and thought. The typical stance in musical listening involves a sense of sharing life with others. While listening, therefore, we perceive others as compatriots whose immediate interests coincide with our own. But music also refines our ability to approach others empathetically in contexts outside musical experience. In this section I discuss three ways in which music trains our capacity for empathy.

(1) *Music develops our ability to approach others in a nondefensive, noncompetitive fashion.* That this orientation is produced during musical experience has already been suggested. Our listening stance is a receptive one, and it facilitates identification with others. We experience a kind of empathy, for we typically identify with the makers of music and, broadly, with the music's audience in general.

But the more interesting question is whether our adoption of a nondefensive, noncompetitive stance in listening has an impact on our orientation outside the listening context. I am convinced that it does. Music disposes us to consider the empathetic stance intrinsically desirable because it gives us an immediate experience of empathy as a source of pleasure. Enjoyment of music involves the experience of taking satisfaction in a state of mind in which one does not oppose oneself to other human beings.

Friedrich Schiller aptly noted, in the stylized letters of his *On the Aesthetic*

Education of Man, that aesthetic experience is uniquely suited to convincing human beings that it is in their own interest to live in harmony with others. In aesthetic experience, one's own gratification is experienced as compatible with, even simultaneous with, the gratification of others. And because aesthetic experience is intrinsically delightful, and the sharing of it even more so, the person who undergoes it discovers satisfaction in the noncompetitive stance:

> Though need may drive Man into society, and Reason implant social principles in him, Beauty alone can confer on him a *social character*. Taste alone brings harmony into society, because it establishes harmony in the individual. All other forms of perception divide a man, because they are exclusively based either on the sensuous or on the intellectual part of his being; only the perception of the Beautiful makes something whole of him, because both his natures must accord with it. All other forms of communication divide society, because they relate exclusively either to the private sensibility or to the private skillfulness of its individual members, that is, to what distinguishes between one man and another; only the communication of the Beautiful unites society, because it relates to what is common to them all.[33]

Aesthetic experience, according to Schiller, inspires a sense of concord with the rest of the social world. It also reveals the inherent delight of sharing enjoyment.

Schiller's account describes what happens in our enjoyment of music. If one can assume that a perceived source of pleasure is a motivation, then we can safely call music a motivation to emotional openness—and this stance is, precisely, a stance of empathy. The openness we assume in listening also accustoms us to the idea (and the feeling) that others' pursuits are not necessarily in competition with our own. We immediately experience that the free activity and enjoyment of others are not necessarily threatening to ourselves. Through listening, we find that others' pursuit of their own satisfaction is sometimes combinable with our own, and that we enjoy our own satisfactions more when this happens.

In this way, music undercuts the view, often suggested by our less happy interactions with other people, that one best serves one's own well-being through a suspicious and begrudging attitude toward everyone else. Although music cannot prevent the recurrence of situations in which individual goals conflict, it suggests the desirability of formulating our aims in such a way that mutual satisfaction is conceivable. We cannot doubt, in light of our musical experience, that mutual satisfaction is sometimes possible.

And the fact that we enjoy the community that music occasions reminds us that mutual satisfaction is even more enjoyable than satisfaction won at someone else's expense.

Because music does not present itself as accessible only to one or a few individuals, our musical enjoyment is noncompetitive. Our musical pleasure avoids the tense character of enjoyment won through contest with another. We can enjoy music in a state of serenity. This condition is sufficiently fulfilling that one who experiences it is bound to prefer it. Schiller is surely right in thinking that the person who has been aesthetically moved to such an experience will be disposed to seek it again, in everyday as well as more narrowly aesthetic life.

(2) *Music affords a ground for empathy with particular others, even those who are momentarily irritating.* Music creates intimacy. The foundations of intimacy are laid by music's physical appeal. Music engages one in some degree of immediate bodily response (if only, as Nietzsche puts it, "in the muscles"). This engagement is immediate and personal, and yet others are similarly touched in an immediate, physical way. Sigmund Freud claims that our egos are embodied egos, and this strikes me as hard to contest. But whether or not Freud is right, music, as a physical medium, incites feelings of intimacy as does a kiss or a shared meal. Music heightens our awareness that we share the very, particular world that each of us is now in contact with.

Perhaps, as a physical medium, music incites no greater intimacy than does a kiss of greeting. There is, no doubt, something unusual about the musical arousal of intimacy with an undefined group of other people—and this point is not unrelated to the "daemonic" power of music, often cited as a ground for ethical criticism. Recordings and radio broadcasts, moreover, create a less immediate sense of community, and thus one's sense of intimate involvement with others is also less than in the case of live performance.

Nonetheless, there is something important and valuable, from an ethical point of view, about the unusual intimacy forged by music. One's sense of a shared world, which is identified with what one immediately encounters, is independent of one's particular personal circumstances and the particular kinds of relationships that one has toward other members of the audience. As a consequence, our sense of intimate sharing can counterbalance the impression we often have that particular others represent annoying obstacles to our specific practical goals.

Suppose I am angry at a particular individual. I obsess about my fury for days, fanning it to a blaze. I await the opportunity to tell this individual off. But I am intercepted. Just before encountering the person, I hear one of

Josquin's motets, or Simon and Garfunkel's "Scarborough Fair/Canticle," or the latest Peter Gabriel album on the radio. (I assume here that the music elicits my enjoyment.) My fury is blunted. Perhaps I am still enjoying the sense of unimpeded movement that the music stirs in my muscles. At any rate, I feel less captivated by my anger. My nemesis has hit a lucky moment. No use fighting today! (The Wile E. Coyote part of me hopes, later in the day, that a better chance will arise tomorrow.)

Is this a plausible scenario? I think it is. Of course, I have chosen my musical examples somewhat cautiously. Certain music is well suited to fueling anger—Lou Reed's "Leave Me Alone" comes to mind. But most of us, on reflection, can probably recall many cases in which musical enjoyment left us with a sense of peace toward the world and others. Music has, in these cases, assisted our ability to deal with others in our immediate environment.

One might consider it gratuitous that I feel greater peace with particular persons as a result of being moved to peace with the social world at large. But I do not find this remarkable in any but a metaphysical sense. My disagreement with Kant's aesthetics begins with his demand for "complete" disinterestedness. Indeed, one does miss the point of much art if one takes its subject matter too personally. But one can, for instance, concurrently appreciate the "universal" lines of a plot and recognize its relationship to "plots" in one's own personal life. And this conjunction can be ethically edifying. I can read a novel in which the protagonist has a point of view akin to that of a person whose point of view drives me crazy. I think I am best affected, from an ethical point of view, if I can be detached enough to comprehend the "universal" dimension of the story but can also recognize that this protagonist, with whom I identify, is not so different from the friend with whom I am annoyed. Literature, when experienced in this way, can have the ethical impact of reminding me that I (a person who can empathize with the protagonist's state of mind) am not so different from the problematic friend who is actually in that state.

Music, too, can provoke empathy that overcomes the constraints of positional human roles. Salieri, in Peter Shaffer's play *Amadeus*, describes Susanna's aria in act 4 of Mozart's *Marriage of Figaro* as "the voice of pure forgiveness."[34] I doubt I am the only person who both heard the universal point being made and reflected with new optimism on personal relationships in which forgiveness was, at that moment, an issue.

I have no doubt that among the motivations behind music's employment in religious contexts is a recognition of its power to stir us in a context that is removed from our roles. One listens to music, not as lover, lawyer, or mother, but as a human being, and one relates to other listeners as human beings like oneself. This kinship is not grounded on the relatively contingent fact of occupying roles that are similar to or linked with those of other individuals. Instead it is built on sharing the freedom of imagination that enables one to feel empathy with the "movements" of tones, and the simultaneous bodily response to stimuli that one receives without inhibition.

I cannot but believe that practically motivated annoyance or even ill will toward particular individuals would be mitigated by a vision of them sharing the experience we have in our most engaged musical listening. In the spirit of such ethical strategies as the categorical imperative or Jeremy Bentham's hedonistic calculus, I suggest that we would do well to recognize other human beings as beings who can also be stirred by music. Kant might not approve of this tactic as a means of enlisting our inclinations; but I think that this technique, sincerely practiced, would be a motivation to good will (in a colloquial, if not Kantian, sense).[35]

(3) *Music cultivates appreciation.* Ethical experience is too rarely associated with delight. Perhaps this is one reason music seems so distant from ethics. But it is also a symptom of the negative approach to experience incorporated in the typical Western view of ethics. Ethics, understood as "morality," is thought to concern what we ought not do.

A good life devoid of joy, however, is a contradiction in terms. While *joy* is a proper term for an emotion that cannot be continuously experienced, *joie de vivre*—joy in life—can be an attitude that structures one's approach to experience generally. *Joie de vivre* is fortified by the experience of particular joys, but it can serve as an enduring basis for ethically significant action.

Music, often a vehicle for expressing *joie de vivre,* can transmit this condition to listeners. But music that we enjoy with conscious attention also engages our appreciation of whatever nuances we discover in it. In a double sense, the Confucian thinker Hsün Tzu is right when he claims that "music is joy."[36] We find its expressions of joy contagious, and we experience particular joys in appreciating its details (whether it expresses joy or not).

The second of these senses of musical "joy" is the one I mean to emphasize here. My point is that a particular kind of empathy is awakened by shared appreciation. This is not merely a reiteration of my previous point. For "appreciation" is not equivalent to "any kind of enjoyment." "Appreciation," as I am using the term, is a particular response to some highly valued thing or person, and it is characterized by one's imaginatively assuming a perspective that is unusually unegoistic.

In the typical case of appreciation, the perspective imaginatively adopted is that of another person. When one "appreciates" a comment another makes, one is imaginatively noting the entire perspective that motivates it. When one "appreciates" another person, one identifies sufficiently to celebrate that person's being. "I really appreciate my brother" would suggest this sense of being personally gratified that another exists. When one "appreciates" a person's behavior, one assumes that person's perspective in one's estimate of the behavior's value. If I recognize the difficulty the individual, as the particular character he or she is, may have had in doing a particular thing, I feel great appreciation. Appreciation is an extremely undistanced stance toward another. In appreciation, I abandon my defenses and imaginatively assume another's internal outlook, with all its inherent vulnerabilities.

This discussion may seem unrelated to the situation of appreciating music. But musical appreciation is a special case of the more basic scenario I am describing. The basic case of appreciation is appreciation of another person. When one appreciates a thing (or music), one tends to appreciate it as the product and expression of a person. Appreciation of the universe or nature is not far removed from a religious sense of gratitude to (a personified) God. In listening to Bach's music, one appreciates Bach, or "human effort" as it is manifest in Bach, or the Creator to whom one attributes the possibility of Bach's existence.

Too often, "appreciation," applied to the musical case, has been equated with recognition of musical talent. I think this is a misuse of the term. Recognition of talent does not require empathy; it is perfectly compatible with envy and resentment. (Consider Salieri as portrayed in Shaffer's *Amadeus*.) Concern with the level of talent displayed in a musical performance can preempt appreciation of certain kinds of music. I have heard listeners complain, "I could do that!" as an explanation for why they were not enjoying something.

Appreciation is something quite different. It more fundamentally involves one's inward attitude and one's orientation toward what is outside one. It is impossible to appreciate without a willingness to identify. I appreciate music or a feature of music with an imaginative "inner singing." I envision the world from the perspective that I associate with the making of this music.

Appreciating music involves something like reverence for the persons one associates with it (however specifically or generally one might focus this feeling, and whether or not one consciously reflects upon it). This reverence is, I believe, ethically valuable, for reverence is a contagious and expansive emotion. No doubt there are people who so compartmentalize their emotional lives that they can revere Mozart's music and treat other people with contempt. But the fact that most of us feel that there is a contradiction involved here shows that we expect reverence to pervade a person's whole orientation. It strikes us as ironical when someone employs violence to defend "reverence for life" or "reverence for God." The reason is that reverence involves an internal state that is incompatible with a hostile or defense-prone posture. In becoming reverent, I put aside my usual opposition of self and the rest of the world; and if I kick the dog after listening to Mozart, this suggests that I have not actually made the transformation that reverence involves.[37]

Of course, in claiming that music can inspire reverence, I am considering our most moving experiences of music. Such experiences are a part of our musical experience, and therefore I feel it legitimate to regard their effects as among the benefits that music confers. But what about less momentous kinds of musical appreciation? Is everyday musical appreciation ethically beneficial as well?

Yes. In the previous section, we observed that the sociability of musical experience can overcome a sense of irritation with others. But, more positively, musical appreciation also encourages an appreciation of others. A particular, nondefensive intimacy is forged with another person who shares aesthetic experience with me. A friend points to the play of sunlight on a skyscraper, or to the momentary configuration of the moon and the planet Venus, and says, "Look!" so that I can appreciate, too. I do appreciate the beautiful configuration indicated, again in a somewhat anthropomorphic way. If not inspired to religious emotion, I take joy in the seemingly intentional design assumed by the heavenly bodies, or in nature's interaction with buildings formed by human design.

But I also appreciate my friend. I am grateful that the friend chose to share something delightful with me. I admire my friend for being able to assume the stance of aesthetic admiration so easily, in the midst of a practical situation (like conversing about something unrelated while walking down the sidewalk). I recognize my friend's freedom of imagination, and I happily imagine something of the friend's inner life. I feel joy in what I imagine; my friend, I think, must be inwardly rich, having such an eye for aesthetic flashes of joy. I idealize my friend, to some degree, as a result of this experience. I inwardly celebrate the fact that I know this person. I let down my defenses and feel comfortable treating that person's concerns as my own.

Musical opportunities for such moments abound in our society. Although recording technology has been criticized with some justification for privatizing musical experience, it has made access to and appropriation of a tremendous amount of music possible for most members of our society. With a record, compact disc, or tape and the appropriate equipment for playing it, one person can easily point appreciatively to an aspect of music and say, "Listen!" Because music is more available to more people than virtually any other artform, it is probably the most common vehicle for shared aesthetic experience in our society.

Because music typically involves multiple features on which one can focus, recording technology has also enabled listeners to appreciate different facets of the same performance and to appreciate to deeper degrees on repeated occasions of listening. Recordings, in this respect, have also facilitated the kind of listening that Hanslick glorifies. Shared intellectual appreciation of musical forms, I submit, can itself be a boon to empathy and thus be ethically valuable. The fact that much music offers a wealth of facets of intellectual interest makes it especially suitable for shared appreciation of nuances—and thus a likely medium for the magic moments I have been discussing.

The fact that moments of aesthetic sharing have nurtured many friendships in my own experience suggests to me that such moments enhance interpersonal interaction beyond the experience itself. One values another person more for being sensitive to aesthetic experience. One becomes momentarily attuned to the other person's inner life. One realizes that, however self-defensive or self-advancing that person may seem to be, he or she remains vulnerable to being moved. Such vulnerability is precious for its contribution to the person's own life, but it is also a precondition for openness toward others. For this reason, I tend to think of my friend as a *good* person when I recognize his or her ability to appreciate aesthetically.

Obviously, episodes of idealizing a friend can be part of an ethically undesirable plot. All too often an idealized person whose behavior violates one's idealistic vision becomes the object of vicious resentment. But seeing a person in a beautiful light at times is, I think, part and parcel of real friendship. It is also of ethical value. To see someone as worthy of appreciation is already to empathize. And to empathize is to have begun to assume an ethical perspective on others.

6 ‖ : The Ethical Aspects of Music: Music as Metaphor, Symbol, and Model

> *I am concerned primarily with what music is. . . . If we know what it is, we might be able to use and develop it in all kinds of ways that have not yet been imagined.*
> —John Blacking, *How Musical Is Man?*

The structuralist interpretation of music has obscured the experiential basis for recognizing an ethical dimension to music. But a different kind of attention to musical pattern and structure can itself be of value to ethics. Formal features of music can be seen as analogous to patterns observable in ethical experience. If we pursue these analogies, music can suggest metaphors and models of relevance to our ethical lives.

The development of metaphors in connection with musical experience extends beyond the appropriation of emotional terms in describing it. As Feld notes, "Metaphors are the human achievement of instantaneous recognition that things are simultaneously alike and unlike."[1] And once metaphor is accepted as a legitimate outgrowth of musical experience, it is a short step to recognizing that the experience is in many ways "like" features of ethical life.

Music, I suggest, can metaphorically illuminate ethical life in three ways. First, music can assist our thinking about tensions in ethical experience. Second, it can illuminate our own values by manifesting those of others. Finally, it can offer models for desirable modes of social interaction.

Temporal Models of Tension and Resolution

In listening to most music with comprehension, we follow the temporal course of tensions as they unfold and are (in most instances) resolved. This experience gives us practice in a technique that is ethically invaluable but rarely mentioned in discussions of ethics: the technique of mentally appropriating and attending to tensions in process.

Musical experience, from an analytic point of view, can be considered a mode of thinking tensions through. Or more aptly, from an experiential standpoint, it can be described as *enjoying* tension. The role of tension in most musical experience has been observed by many philosophers. Langer, in developing her theory of music as an "image of time," claims that music can play this role in part because it parallels the kind of buildup and resolution of tension that constitutes our experience of time:

> The phenomena that fill time are *tensions*—physical, emotional, or intellectual. Time exists for us because we undergo tensions and their resolutions. Their peculiar building-up, and their ways of breaking or diminishing or merging into longer and greater tensions, make for a vast variety of temporal forms. . . . The direct experience of passage . . . is the model for the virtual time created in music. There we have its image, completely articulated and pure; every kind of tension transformed into musical tension.[2]

Meyer, as we have seen, similarly points to the importance of musical tensions for an assessment of musical value:

> It would seem that . . . value has something to do with the activation of a musical impulse having tendencies toward a more or less definite goal and with the temporary resistance or inhibition of these tendencies.[3]

Tension and the expectation of its resolution are so basic to music that Norman Cazden defines consonance and dissonance in terms of these factors:

> In musical harmony the critical determinant of consonance or dissonance is expectation of movement. This is defined as the relation of resolution. A consonant interval is one which sounds stable and complete in itself, which does not produce a feeling of necessary movement to other tones. . . . Pleasantness or disagreeableness of the interval is not directly involved.[4]

Cazden's last point is important. Musical tension is not unpleasant: it is essential to the development of our expectation of the musical goal. Moreover, the entire cycle of tension's development and resolution occasions our enjoyment.[5]

Music's appropriation of tension can inform our understanding of everyday experience. Ferguson observes that only if we restrict our focus to music as structure will we fail to recognize that music's tensions and motions resemble the motivations and activity of our consciously directed behavior:

> The body of music—physically no more than a substance of tone and rhythm—may be so constructed as to manifest, in its tensions and motions, compulsions beyond those which function for structure—compulsions which so far resemble the drives which actuate the human body that the musical body *becomes* human—becomes Buffon's *l'homme même*. Is not this metaphor? Is there not here a palpable transfer of the behavior-patterns of the body of tone into the behavior-patterns of the human body—even of those which enact the farthest reaches of its consciousness?

Although he does not elaborate, Ferguson observes that music's metaphorical suggestion of emotion and motivation by means of its play of tensions resembles the pattern of motivations in ethical experience:

> Indeed, our ultimate understanding of our fellows and ourselves, although we describe it in apparently objective terms of kinetic or potential action, is primarily conceived in terms of emotion. For emotion, mingled in consciousness with the intellection which directs it, becomes motive, which stands to conduct as simple sensation-stimulus stands to motor reaction. Our final assessment of conduct may thus be made largely in terms of motive.[6]

If the tensions involved in everyday life are analogous to the tensions involved in music, musical enjoyment should incite us to rethink our approach to ethical decision-making. The dominant approach of philosophical ethics emphasizes final resolution over the appreciation of tensions in process. But this is to treat the tensions of everyday life as negatively problematic, not even as means to an end. The possibility that tension itself is an ingredient of a good life has been suggested by thinkers like Jean-Paul Sartre, but this suggestion has not been taken seriously by mainstream Anglo-American ethics. Tension is seen as something to be rejected, reduced, or, ideally, eliminated. The resolution of a moral dilemma is considered most ideal when it affords escape from tension and absolves the ethicist or agent from any need for further thought.

The fact that most of us do think further after reaching an abstract resolution to a moral dilemma suggests that this kind of solution does not practically strike most of us as adequate. John Stuart Mill comes closer to our real criteria for assessing our situations when he notes that if by happiness be meant a continuity of highly pleasurable excitement, it is evident enough that this is impossible. A state of exalted pleasure lasts only moments or in some cases, and with some intermissions, hours or days, and is the occasional brilliant flash of enjoyment, not its permanent and steady flame. Of this the philosophers who have taught that happiness is the end of life were as fully aware as those who taunt them. The happiness which they meant was not a life of rapture, but moments of such, in an existence made up of few and transitory pains, many and various pleasures, with a decided predominance of the active over the passive, and having as the foundation of the whole not to expect more from life than it is capable of bestowing. A life thus composed, to those who have been fortunate enough to obtain it, has always appeared worthy of the name of happiness.[7]

This is to say, I think convincingly, that we are content with our lives only when they are dynamic contexts in which tensions and resolutions both have their place. A good life, on this view, involves creative appropriation, even cultivation, of tension, counterbalanced by intermittent periods of relative relaxation.

The well-handled maintenance of tensions is ethically desirable, for it is essential to living a balanced, happy life. But our analytical intelligence has most often been trained to utilize static models. Unfortunately, static models applied to complicated ethical situations tend either to promote unrealistic expectations or to arouse the belief that one's situation is hopeless. Music is uniquely suited to overcoming the limitations of our static analyses. It gives us practice in an alternative method, engaging us in thought that is temporally extended and tolerant of the currents of tension. And music presents tensions, not as obstructions, but as themselves vehicles to the achievement of resolution.

Zuckerkandl observes that the temporal image that music provides is testimony that the flowing tensions of our lives may be arranged in a satisfying order. Music can foster confidence and hope:

> All fundamental opposition to music . . . is rooted in the same concern: that music may hold the threat of chaos; that it may undermine the foundation upon which order rests. . . . Behind these and related interpretations lies a time-honored dogma—the dogma that order is possible only in the enduring, the immutably fixed, the substantial. . . . But what if music presents us with this very thing—the unprecedented spectacle of an order in what is wholly flux, of a building without matter? Music,

which can even stamp order upon the flowing, which can even wrest great edifices from the immaterial, is anything but a power incompatible with order, a dissolvent power. . . . Order, liberated from all relation to things, *pure order,* bodiless, detached, and free, not as a mere concept, not as a dream, but as a vision beheld—it is to music that we owe our awareness that such a thing can exist.[8]

One type of ordering that our ethical models tend to ignore is the cyclical order of human experience on many levels. Aristotle stressed the importance of relaxation after exertion. But such temporal observations have been underdeveloped in Western thought. We tend to think them banal, preferring instead to rely on models that promise insight into stable structures in our experience. But this reliance often creates more confusion than security. For instance, I might know that a sense of collapse is common after a major life change like moving. But I look for structural problems to account for my sense of uneasiness after moving, thereby nurturing my own discouragement. To dismiss the influence of either psychic or meteorological seasons is to oversimplify one's experience and often to uglify it as well.

It is a commonplace that many Eastern philosophical traditions emphasize temporality to a degree unknown in Western philosophy. Perhaps this explains the prominence in Eastern thought of musical metaphors for spiritual life. Indian musical theory, for instance, treats music as both a reflection of spiritual life and a kind of yogic technique for attaining detachment from emotional disturbance (the basic yogic goal). The Confucian tradition, too, praises music for its ability to illuminate the changes fundamental to inner life. Music serves "to go to the very root [of our feelings] and know the changes [which they undergo]." The twelve tones of the pitch pipes are correlated with the *yin* and *yang* principles, which are utilized in the hexagrams of the *I Ching* (Book of Changes) to represent the changing aspects of nature and human life. In this way, music is linked to the hexagrams and to the calendar and is treated as a representation of the cyclical transitions of life.[9]

Exploration of music's depiction of the flowering and resolution of tension can assist our thinking about our ethical lives. The precise results to be achieved are difficult to indicate, however. The difficulty is similar to that involved in describing the difference between confident and unconfident behavior. What is at issue is the possibility of graceful navigation within a texture of external and internal tensions—and the achievement of this possibility depends on inner balance and sensitivity to the movements of whatever one is balancing against.

Music can, in my experience, be a source of insight regarding balance. Learning to hear passing dissonances in counterpoint, for instance, made me more attentive to (and thus in greater control of) subtle dissonances arising in other areas of experience. (The most conspicuous example is writing.) More generally, the "inner dancing" involved in listening naturally suggests "moving well" in life. Similarly, the organic development of a theme evident in symphonic music, or the culmination of tension toward climax in a jazz solo, are images of motional possibilities that are akin to configurations that arise in practical life. Suppose I am filled with tension: the controlled and delayed release one hears in some of Ravi Shankar's music suggests the possibility of a graceful resolution. Suppose I am exasperated by a schedule that so fragments my projects that I doubt the possibility of bringing any to fruition. The symphonic development of a theme brings to mind the possibility that I can take a longer view of my relationship to any particular project, that perhaps I am making progress even when my particular hours of effort seem ungratifying. Or when a project is moving comfortably forward, music of admirable complexity can suggest the possibility of organization on multiple, often subtle levels.

Of course, such crudely described ideas for streamlining our working day are not the quintessence of what music has to offer ethical reflection. I think music's more important intimations along these lines are quite subtle. What I have in mind resembles the kind of discovery Eugen Herrigel reports in his chronicle of learning archery with a Zen master. Herrigel complained to the master about his difficulty in shooting at the right moment:

> "When I have drawn the bow, the moment comes when I feel: unless the shot comes at once I shan't be able to endure the tension. And what happens then? Merely that I get out of breath. So I must loose the shot whether I want to or not, because I can't wait for it any longer."
>
> "You have described only too well," replied the Master, "where the difficulty lies. Do you know why you cannot wait for the shot and why you get out of breath before it has come? The right shot at the right moment does not come because you do not let go of yourself. You do not wait for fulfillment, but brace yourself for failure. So long as that is so, you have no choice but to call forth something yourself that ought to happen independently of you, and so long as you call it forth your hand will not open in the right way—like the hand of a child. Your hand does not burst open like the skin of a ripe fruit."[10]

Ethics is aimed at living at ease with one's environment. The Aristotelian good life, the Christian kingdom of heaven, even Kant's image of

the kingdom of ends, are all visions of conditions in which external constraint is irrelevant to moral goodness. The ethical ideal is to move freely
and gracefully in harmony with the world. "Thinking wants to be learned
like dancing, *as* a kind of dancing," Nietzsche tells us.[11] Musical images of
graceful, flowing movement can be the teachers of this dancing thought.

Illumination of Our Basic Values

According to anthropologists, the same societal values
are expressed in aesthetics as in ethics. Edmund Leach observes: "Logically,
aesthetics and ethics are identical. If we are to understand the ethical rules
of a society, it is aesthetics that we must study."[12] Radcliffe-Brown makes a
similar point:

> A social system . . . has a certain kind of unity, which we may speak of
> as a functional unity. We may define it as a condition in which all parts
> of the social system work together with a sufficient degree of harmony or
> internal consistency, i.e., without producing persistent conflicts which
> can neither be resolved nor regulated.[13]

What this suggests is that our music not only reveals ethical possibilities,
but also reflects our society's actual ethical values. Recent ethnomusicological studies support this idea. John Shepherd correlates several stages of
Western musical style with reigning conceptions of the proper social order
and with orientations toward activity in time. Western industrial society's
obsession with progress is reflected, according to Shepherd, in tonal music:

> Perhaps the vital characteristic of tonality is its sense of *magnetic pull*
> towards the key-note, and it is this sense which provides the quintessen-
> tial articulation of the concept of progress. . . . Tonal music is, above all,
> the music of explicitly sequential cause and effect. . . . The analysis of
> tonal music, for example, often concerns itself with 'showing' how the
> final satisfying effect of stating the tonic chord is 'due' to previously cre-
> ated harmonic tension. It is probably no accident, in this respect, that
> completed and satisfying harmonic passages are frequently referred to as
> 'harmonic progressions.'[14]

Rose Subotnik argues that contemporary composition of absolute music
reflects the societal "ideal of radical autonomy" by aiming at radically individual internal structure. "To be contemporary, a composition must be able
to vouch for its own integrity as a structure *sui generis;* it must discour-
age efforts to understand it as an example, no matter how excellent, of a

preexisting kind." At the same time this music's inaccessibility reflects the fundamental contradiction involved "in the illusion that total self-definition is possible in society at all." Susan McClary has even argued that Western music reflects a particular orientation toward sexuality, an orientation that is decidedly masculine.[15]

Musical reflection of a societal way of life is, according to Scruton, fundamental to the significance music has for its audience:

> If response is to be significant to the person who feels it, it must bear some relation to his life as a whole: it must be part not only of his enjoyment, but also of his *concern*. . . . The audience must . . . be able to hear musical relations, musical development and musical style in terms of values and interests that govern its life as a whole. It must, therefore, be familiar with such musical experiences as the following: hearing a rhythm as a dance, as a march, as a summons to arms; hearing a stretch of counterpoint as a unity of concurrent movements, moving towards a common stasis; hearing energy, languor, hesitation and resolution; hearing a chord as a question, an answer, a quiescence; hearing a melody as a character, a declaration, a common resolve; hearing a passage as songlike, hymnlike, recitativelike, and so on.

The result of this interpenetration of musical significance and living concerns is that "the excitement of music becomes, in an immediate and intuitive way, the excitement of life itself."[16]

We can hear the pulse of our society's concerns by listening to the music it produces. In the words of Jacques Attali, "Music is more than an object of study: it is a way of perceiving the world." Moreover, it can hint at the limitations inherent in our society's way of organizing experience:

> Music is prophecy. Its styles and economic organization are ahead of the rest of society because it explores, much faster than material reality can, the entire range of possibilities in a given code. It makes audible the new world that will gradually become visible, that will impose itself and regulate the order of things.[17]

Our music gives us a vision of ourselves. In this sense, it can help us to understand what we actually value and where our values are leading us.

Music's intimate connection with societal values strikes Scruton as a ground for defending a rather ethnocentric attitude toward music. Music assumes its important role within a culture's life, he argues, only if it is located within a specific community within which a vocabulary of gestures and references is understood:

The true musical audience is an audience of amateurs for whom music is an integral part of everyday life, and also a recreation (a recreation of the self and of the community upon which the self is predicated). This audience recognizes character, emotion and thought in music, partly because it put it there, in cruder form. The composer refines the raw material that is offered to him by the music of the marketplace—the material of dance rhythms, hymn tunes, plainsong, partsong, and improvisation—and then passes it back in transmuted form.[18]

Perhaps Scruton is right in claiming that membership in a particular community is an irreplaceable precondition for a certain level of detail in musical communication. But he overstates the case. He leaves little room for the possibility of learning to understand another culture's music. Yehudi Menuhin has called Ali Akbar Khan the world's greatest living musician. Are we to assume that Menuhin does not know what he is talking about? Scruton's discussion seems to say so.

Scruton also ignores the insight into one's own way of life that can result from acquaintance with the music of other societies. The music of another society, by reflecting values that contrast with our own, can make our values more apparent to us. Or it can demonstrate the possibility of other attitudes toward being a human, social being, attitudes that might encourage us to reconsider our own. Recognizing one's own values is not always easy without a contrasting foil. Another culture's music can serve as such a foil. And few occasions for self-examination are so agreeable.

One need not know the details of another culture's music to gain some sense of the way in which its values might differ from our own. Lomax has developed a scheme of categorizing various musics in terms of a small number of basic variables, a method that he terms "cantometrics." The variables of interest to cantometrics include

> the phenomena described by European music notation—melody, rhythm, harmony, interval size, etc.—but it looks beyond these European basics at many other factors present in and (as far as we could tell by intensive listening) generic to the song style of other areas. These factors include the size and social structure of the music-making group; the location and role of leadership in the music-making group; the type and the degree of integration in the music-making group; the type and the degree of melodic, rhythm, and vocal embellishment in a sung performance; and the qualities of the singing voice normally effected by the chosen singers in a culture.

Whether a particular music exhibits these variables is recognizable after very brief exposure to the style. Lomax observes: "Music-making is one of the most strictly patterned forms of human behavior. Its modes of communication are so limited that even a casual listener can distinguish quickly the best performers and identify the pieces in an idiom of whose technique and content he knows nothing."[19]

This may be an exaggeration, but the variables that Lomax considers are easily recognized. He uses them to construct "cantometric profiles," which he correlates with modes of social organization. The parallels, he observes, are striking. For example, he observes that Pygmy singing style, which emphasizes group participation and enjoyment in group production of counterpoint and involves a shift of leadership from one singer to another, reflects the cooperative cultural style of Pygmy social interaction. The idiosyncratic yodeling style of Pygmy singing, which "in the estimation of laryngologists, is produced by the voice in its most relaxed state," also reflects cultural conditions: "This extraordinary degree of vocal relaxation, which occurs rarely in the world as an over-all vocal style, seems to be a psycho-physiological set, which symbolizes openness, nonrepressiveness, and an unconstructed approach to the communication of emotion."[20] Recognizing these characteristics of Pygmy social interaction and style of living, we are likely to notice that our own society has different characteristics and that ours are not the only human possibilities.

Listening to the music of other cultures also gives us more immediate insight into our own social nature. Because the listener typically identifies with the act of music-making, listening involves an imaginative projection of oneself into the matrix of social interaction that is heard in the music. In this respect, music yields intuitions of what it is like to interact with other human beings in particular configurations that may or may not resemble those of one's usual musical experience.

When I listen to Michael (Babatunde) Olatunji's "Flirtation Dance," for example, I project myself into a situation in which a group composed of all members of one sex flirtatiously confronts all members of the other sex. Such group confrontation of the two sexes differs strikingly from any situation that I have practically encountered in my own society, where flirtation is extremely individualistic. In my society, instead, any imagined group confrontation between the sexes is almost always portrayed as a battle. David Byrne's "Women vs. Men," which depicts a war with trivial motives but no end in sight, is a musical reflection of this idea.[21]

I think that in both cases, listener self-projection sheds light on social experience. Of course, I probably cannot fully get inside the mindset that conditions Nigerian experience. But consideration of alternative ways of relating to other human beings assists one's understanding of the way one actually does interact with others. What about our society makes the situation to which Olatunji's music belongs so unimaginable for us? Could the "Women vs. Men" mindset be modified by considering the whole conjunction of social male–female attractions as jubilant and something worth celebrating with dance? Precisely because Olatunji's music suggests situations foreign to my own experience, I find my imagination stirred to seek answers to such questions as "Who are the people making this music?" and "Who am I?"

More fundamentally, the open-ended sociability of music puts us in touch with what is common to human beings across societies. The capacity to feel and to respond to musical stimuli is not limited to a particular group of people. By reminding us of our common human makeup, music serves a universal human function. Music locates us first within the human community, and only second and in some cases within our particular society.

Music—both our own and that of other societies—clarifies our place in the world by allowing us to explore different human ways of encountering it. The musics of different societies focus on different features of that place and underscore different ways of understanding it. One society may focus, in its construction and appropriation of music, on human beings' relationship to the supernatural, as Nettl suggests. In another society, one may engage with music as an individual with a certain social role to fulfill. Our classical tradition, by encouraging "disinterested" listening, may obscure this function of music. But it, too, gives us a sense of who we are in the world—most commonly a sense of ourselves as capable of empathy with the range of human emotional experience, unimpeded by personal motive.[22]

Understanding one's place within the world—and particularly within the social world—is important to ethical living. Ethics concerns thought-mediated behavior, and a large extent of the mediation that thought provides is shaped by one's sense of self in relation to others. Music's contribution to this sense makes it ethically important. This role of music also helps make the ideal of harmonious living with others seem both coherent and delightful.

Models of Desirable Social Interaction

Among the values a society's music reflects are its preferred modes of social interaction. But what music mirrors need not be considered unalterable, as Attali reminds us. Becoming clear about our actual values can assist our efforts to reformulate them. Or it can remind us that we have values that are only imperfectly embodied in our lives.

Music can assist both of these recognitions. But if we combine the observations of the previous two sections, we can see another way in which music can assist our efforts to transform our situation. Music can suggest desirable modes of social interaction as well as desirable individual ideals. Music's intimations regarding the nature of tensions can illuminate the tensions we find in our social arena and suggest possible scenarios for their resolution.

An example may indicate what I have in mind. I suggest that the treatment of the jazz solo in progressive jazz offers a model for the interaction of racial groups, a model that avoids certain pitfalls inherent in more extreme approaches to our racial problems.

Extremist Models of Race Relations

In a speech in Detroit in 1966, Stokely Carmichael said:

> They tell us, and see behind me stands ministers of the Bible, and they will bear me out, that Jesus Christ said, and He's the only man who said, "Only through me shall ye enter into the kingdom of heaven." But what white people say to us with integration is that only through me shall you have better things, that's what they say when they talk about integration.[23]

Integration became a heated and ubiquitous term in political and social rhetoric in the United States in the years that followed the birth of the civil rights movement. Integration of some sort was the implicit aim of the civil rights legislation that was passed to remedy *de jure* discrimination on the basis of race. But legal remedies, important as they were, could not eliminate many entrenched patterns of *de facto,* practical racial discrimination as it existed in America. And so the word *integration,* however incendiary, was used to allude to a wide range of dreams and nightmares by the diverse and diversely motivated people who used it. The use of the term itself reflected the conflicting perspectives that the people who used it brought to the question of how and to what extent blacks should be assimilated into the larger society.

And this was true even among those who were totally behind the civil rights movement. Separatists like Carmichael opposed any effort to assimilate blacks into establishment structures that whites had invented and continued to control. "I don't fight anybody to sit next to him. I don't want to sit next to them. I just want them to get the barriers out of my way. . . . I just want them to get off my back."[24] The rhetoric of more moderate leaders of the civil rights movement, however, evoked images of something that approached total assimilation into a colorblind society. Dr. Martin Luther King, Jr.'s, "I Have a Dream" speech provides an instance of such rhetoric:

> I have a dream that my four little children will one day live in a nation where they will not be judged by the color of their skin but by the content of their character. . . . I have a dream that one day down in Alabama with its vicious racists . . . one day right there in Alabama little black boys and little black girls will be able to join hands with little white boys and little white girls as sisters and brothers.[25]

Rhetorical discussion of the ideal interaction between ethnic groups in the United States is again becoming a prominent concern of the press. And little astuteness is required, on consideration of the social interactions of various minority groups with the white majority in the United States, to recognize that relations between races remain problematic and deserve thoughtful attention.

The speeches I have cited suggest two extreme answers to the question of what should be sought in the area of race relations. One might propose a separatist solution of the sort that Carmichael endorsed. Well-publicized proponents of this solution are no longer as plentiful as they once were, perhaps because the concept of separatism is unworkably extreme: in the United States, there will inevitably be some forms of interaction between blacks and whites, for instance; the realistic issue concerns the nature of these forms of interaction. But another serious problem with a separatist solution to the problem of race relations, even if it were a more vociferously supported position, is that it seems to encourage racist outlooks. In the speech quoted above, Carmichael, for instance, says: "I'm going to tell you what a white liberal is. You talking about a white college kid joining hands with a black man in the ghetto, that college kid is fighting for the right to wear a beard and smoke pot, and we fighting for our lives."[26] Criticism of the insensitivity of so-called white liberals is no doubt sometimes apt, but rhetoric of this sort is itself racist, for it suggests that motivations can be determined conclusively on the basis of race.

An alternative extreme view proposes complete assimilation of minority group members into the institutions of the white majority. But why should minority group members want to give up their cultural identity in order to win acceptance as participants in structures designed by white people? Carmichael is right in suggesting that this conception, too, is implicitly racist.

If these extreme views are both objectionable because they are racist, it appears that some different notion of the interaction of racial groups is called for. The general form of a third alternative would seem to be some notion of interaction that allows for a separate cultural identity on the part of minority groups, while recognizing these groups as integral components of the larger society and respecting members of these groups as humanly equal to members of the majority group. Such a formula might be criticized as fundamentally incoherent. But this is a discussion in which music can help us. Taking a cue from ethnomusicological studies that see music as a reflection of actual social relations, I suggest that we can also use music as a means of intuiting possibilities.[27] Specifically, my suggestion is that the structure of progressive jazz music that employs extended jazz solos provides a model of interaction between smaller and larger components of a social whole that can be of value in reflections on race relations.

Why recommend music as an approach to such problems? In part, because music provides an indirect approach. In the context of thinking imaginatively about race relations, I suspect that indirect models are more serviceable tools than direct ones. For the direct discussion of problems of race relations is inevitably burdened by bitter emotion and awareness of a discouraging history of hatred between groups. Movement toward improved race relations must, of course, take historically rooted bitterness into account if it is to be effective. But the goal must surely involve freedom from this kind of bitterness; and models that assist the articulation of this goal should themselves be as free as possible from ugly emotional burdens.

A musical model for reflection is free in this regard. And while free from such emotional or pragmatic burdens, music also stimulates the imagination. Dewey suggests that the reordering of human energies always begins with such provocation of the imagination as art can provide:

> The first intimations of wide and large redirections of desire and purpose are of necessity imaginative. Art is a mode of prediction not found in charts and statistics, and it insinuates possibilities of human relations not to be found in rule and precept, admonition and administration.[28]

In musical experience, as we have observed, one is typically moved to imaginative associations with practical life in a context that is almost ideally unthreatening. Such conditions, surely, are desirable for contemplating solutions to problems of race relations.

The Progressive Jazz Solo as Social Model

What characteristics of the progressive jazz solo suit it to the role of insinuating possibilities for interaction between the races? The progressive jazz solo lends itself to this role most fundamentally because the solo instrument exhibits an individual identity that is not absorbed into the texture of the rest of the band or orchestra. Instead, the solo instrument and the ensemble play against one another. At times the solo is involved in a clear interplay with the ensemble; but at other times the soloist seems literally to be doing his own thing, more or less ignoring the musical project that the rest of the group is involved in.

Of course, this impressionistic description of what one hears in the progressive jazz solo is inaccurate as a description of what the performer is doing. What sounds like a wildly individual voice is quite attentive to the movement of the rest of the group in the successful jazz solo, however far afield it may at times seem to be. But the kind of attention the soloist pays to the larger ensemble does not express itself in harmonic subordination of the sort typical of European classical music. On the contrary, extremes of dissonance between the soloist and the group intensify the impression that the soloist represents a highly individual voice that achieves significance precisely through its individuality.

The progressive jazz work often tolerates long stretches of unrelieved dissonance by traditional European standards. Perhaps this explains why many people educated in the music of the European tradition have difficulty understanding progressive jazz. LeRoi Jones (a.k.a. Amiri Baraka) points out, for instance, that John Coltrane's music is most often disparaged by "people, well meaning and/or intelligent as they might be, who simply do not hear the music."[29] The fundamental structural determinant of jazz is rhythmic, not harmonic (a trait which it shares with sub-Saharan African music). One consequence of this is that listeners who are accustomed to orienting themselves musically on the basis of conventional Western harmony often encounter difficulty understanding jazz. Another is that jazz is able to absorb a vast range of harmonic and melodic materials from other, less rhythmically oriented musical traditions. Keil points out:

> The great flexibility or blending capacity of Afro-American musical forms derives primarily from a rhythmic substructure that can incorporate with ease the most diverse melodic and harmonic resources. Indeed, jazzmen are constantly on the prowl for new forms to devour, new sources of nourishment, and as a result the world's music is rapidly becoming jazz.[30]

Metaphorically, one can understand the assimilation by jazz of widely diverse musical materials as similar to a society's assimilation of various components. This would be a rather trivial point of similarity, perhaps, were it not for the positive value that progressive jazz places on the attainment of a strong individuality in the solo voice, which, despite its independent presence, nevertheless finds a home in the musical matrix of the piece. The aesthetic value of a jazz work is heightened, in fact, by the successful attempt to maintain coherence while allowing for a vitally unique individual presence. Leroy Ostransky asserts, "Arranged jazz is only as important as the solos it frames, and unless it does frame one significant solo, at least, it is poor jazz." Pioneer soloist Louis Armstrong expresses the importance of the individual presence in jazz succinctly: "Jazz," he says, "is only what you are."[31]

This latter remark reflects a perspective common among jazz performers and listeners—the individuality of the solo performance reflects the nature of individual being in the world. As Jones puts the point, different approaches to jazz represent different ways of viewing the world. And attentive jazz listeners recognize and thrill to the spontaneous originality that is basic to individual being. According to Gary Giddins, what jazz listeners recognize is "not only a way of playing music, but a categorical expression of spontaneity, innovation, resilience, and freedom—in Blaise Cendrar's words, 'a new reason for living.'" If jazz means something, this meaning is as individual in essence as is a reason for living. Jones reports that Coltrane was asked about the significance of the title of his work "Alabama." "Coltrane answered, 'It represents, musically, something that I saw down there translated into music from inside me.' Which is to say, 'listen.'"[32]

The individuality of the solo voice in progressive jazz is essential to our enjoyment as listeners. But this individuality is not divorced from its context, either in the immediate sense of the ensemble or in the more general sense of the musical scene in which the solo appears. The phenomenon of solo improvisation on a pregiven melody demonstrates the solo's involvement with its larger musical context, for it involves individual interpretation and expressive reiteration of musical material that is common.

Jazz improvisation on a pregiven melody invites comparison with individual development in the context of the social world. The pleasure we get in hearing the novel restatement of the well-known melody might be seen as akin to the pleasure we take in discovering that we have made the nearly universal pattern of human growth into maturity our own. Or perhaps, because our satisfaction in the solo voice involves a vicarious identification, it is more kindred to the satisfaction we take in seeing a child to whom we are close engage in universal human activities for the first time, or in seeing a younger relative marry. In such cases, we see a universal human theme re-iterated once again in a new way. A satisfying kind of harmony between the uniqueness of individual experience and the common human pattern that it instantiates is also achieved at focal moments of our own lives. This har-mony is similar to that achieved by improvisation on a familiar theme, and, in general, by jazz solo performance. Jones alludes to this achievement of the jazz solo when he distinguishes between imitation, which he considers to be of little artistic value, and the use of material from outside oneself that is involved in significant jazz:

> Using, or implementing an idea or concept is not necessarily imitation and, of course, the converse is true; imitation is not necessarily use. I will say first that use is proper, as well as *basic*. Use means that some idea or system is employed but in order to reach or understand quite sepa-rate and/or dissimilar systems. Imitation means simply reproduction (of a concept) for its own sake. Someone who sings exactly like Billie Holi-day or someone who plays exactly like Charlie Parker (or as close as they can manage) *produces* nothing. Essentially, there is nothing added to the universe. It is as if these performers stood on a stage and did nothing at all. Ornette Coleman uses Parker only as a hypothesis; his (Coleman's) conclusions are quite separate and unique.[33]

Musical and Social Maturity

It may seem as though we've strayed far from the relationship between jazz and the interaction of racial groups. But in a sense the relationship between minority groups and a majority group is significantly similar to that between the individual and a larger context, musical or otherwise. The significant question that must be answered if a positive vision of desirable interaction between races is to be attained is: How much individual inde-pendence should a minority group have if the goal is to maximize rapport between the races? The suggestion made by jazz that emphasizes the solo is that rapport is not necessarily compromised by extremely strong indi-viduality of expression, and that in fact the results of encouraging vibrant individual expression of this sort can be quite satisfying. Of course rap-port is assumed on some level as soon as the jazz ensemble begins playing; and this is essential to the construction of a musical context that is as flex-ible as the performance of jazz solos requires. Analogously, one might infer that good will among the minority and majority groups who participate in society is an essential precondition for the possibility of their satisfying interaction as strong and distinct social components. But assuming a basic level of good will, the suggestion of the solo is that diversity in unity is not only coherent, but also a dazzling human achievement.

This achievement, in either social relations or jazz, is not possible without tension. The high level of dissonance often involved in the jazz piece indicates a willingness to operate with sustained tension. But Ostransky sees this willingness as fundamental to jazz of high quality. In *The Anatomy of Jazz* he remarks:

> What distinguishes superior creative musicians from the mediocre ones of all periods is the manner in which they create resolutions, and to create resolutions it is necessary to set up irresolutions. . . . Poor and mediocre jazzmen . . . often do not understand that the quality of their jazz will depend not on any resolution, however elaborate, but rather on the inherent intricacy of the irresolution. The answer to two plus two is four, and finding a way to solve this by calculus does not make the problem more profound. The first-rate jazzman sets himself difficult examinations.[34]

What follows is that quality depends on the musician's taking risks when setting up the tensions to be resolved. Instability is tolerated for the sake of attaining a striking resolution between disparate parts, and the brilliance of this achievement depends on tensions being created between the parts in the first place. This recalls Meyer's discussion of greatness in music. Great music strikes us as profound, Meyer contends, because it makes us aware of the fundamental uncertainties of existence; and in this respect it indirectly furthers the listener's project of maturity. Maturity, both individual and cultural, "consists . . . in the willingness to forgo immediate, and perhaps lesser gratification, for the sake of future ultimate gratification."[35] While Meyer's category of "great music" is, I believe, too restrictive (since it excludes music constructed on nonteleological principles), I agree that musically delayed gratification reflects a scenario basic to mature ethical life. Music can help us approach mature appreciation of uncertainty on all levels.

The play of tensions in progressive jazz suits this type of music to Meyer's analysis. Coltrane's "A Love Supreme," for example, which builds toward a postponed and greatly desired climax (often evading release at an obvious point, thereby heightening tension to a maddening pitch), calls to mind the delay with which gratification is often achieved. Enjoyment of such postponement surely does involve a kind of maturity—a willingness to suspend one's demand for immediate satisfaction in favor of a more encompassing resolution. At the same time one might say this music trains one to seek mature approaches to satisfaction. For one discovers in listening to such music that slowly achieved resolution of intricate tensions is more deeply satisfying than quick, superficial satisfaction.

Maturity is surely what is called for in approaching the question of the ideal relation between minority and majority races in any society. Simplistic forms of analysis are more immediately gratifying than complicated ones. But the antidote to racism, itself a mode of interpreting the world oversimplistically, cannot be another simplistic analysis. Successful resolution of the complex problems of race relations must be the outcome of a genuine development of social maturity, and such a development can be assisted by a positive vision of what an improved social configuration might be. The jazz solo, to recall Dewey's expression, insinuates that a nonracist solution to problems of race relations is not only conceptually coherent, but a prospect that is so aesthetically compelling that it could itself represent a new reason for living.

Unethical Music: The Opposition

Coltrane's "A Love Supreme" reveals both the possibility of and the delight involved in musical resolutions of intricate tensions, as well as the possibility of a liberated individual presence subtly cooperating with a distinct ensemble. In this sense, it can be a source of ethical revelation. But the straightforwardly erotic character of my description of Coltrane's work will probably have caught the attention of many readers, particularly those who have heard it. The "love" described in the title is fervent devotional love of God; but Coltrane, like many before and since, incorporates in his devotional music clear allusions to the terrestrial realm of physical love.

The amenability of music to suggestions of human erotic life has been evident to many at least since antiquity. And this often exploited potential of music has been the source of a longstanding counterargument to my thesis. Music, so the complaint runs, can be a negative influence on ethics. It can incite lascivious passions and lower inhibitions. Music, far from an ethical boon, is a positive impetus to immorality.

The idea that music encourages illicit or immoral behavior has recurred throughout the centuries, although in various forms. The belief that licentious music posed a threat to civic organization led Plato and Confucius to recommend censorship. Many religious traditions, particularly Western ones, have felt compelled to respond to the perceived threat music posed to morality or religious devotion. Ancient Judaism, like ancient Greek philosophy, frowned on certain instrumentation, which was considered too lascivious, often because it was connected to ecstatic cults. Augustine and Calvin both insisted on musical simplicity in order to minimize sensuous appeals that might disturb the focus of the worshiping soul. The only music-like production that orthodox Islam encourages is the chanting of the Koran (which, as we have noted, is not even considered music); other modes of music-making are considered sinful.[36] The Quakers ban music from worship altogether. Dancing is still considered sinful by conservative American Baptists.

Hanslick, in a more secular vein, complained that music, when approached pathologically, could lower the listener's level of moral inhibition. A similar complaint has been leveled at particular kinds of music (often types that encourage "pathological" enjoyment). Rock 'n' roll, for example, has recently (as throughout its history) been the target of worried moralists, among them Tipper Gore: "I'm a fairly with-it person, but this stuff is curling my hair."[37] And the fact that notoriously evil men have been notorious music lovers inspires suspicion regarding music's ethical influence. Nero played the violin while Rome burned; Hitler was a Wagner enthusiast (although perhaps more as a propaganda ploy than from love of the music); and Goebbels is said to have wept at a sentimental opera plot during a performance by Jews in a concentration camp.

While these complaints commonly emphasize music's capacity to circumvent certain usual or ethically desirable inhibitions, the focus of these arguments is various. Traditionally, seven common arguments have been offered against music (or some kinds of music) on ethical grounds: (1) music arouses passions that are harmful or difficult to control; (2) music encourages the abandonment of reason; (3) music lowers moral inhibitions; (4) music excites sexual appetite; (5) music glamorizes unethical causes; (6) music encourages emotional support for a questionable status quo; (7) music distracts from more important concerns.

These arguments, although distinguishable, fall into two categories, which I label with Nietzsche's terms *Dionysian* and *Apollonian*. The first four arguments are complaints that (some) music is too "Dionysian"—that it invites chaos and disruption, particularly in the conduct of erotic life. The latter three are more Apollonian complaints. They argue that music fills our conscious mind or encourages our assent to inappropriate ideas. I consider these problems in sequence.

The Dionysian Danger

Goethe tells us that, whatever liberates the spirit without also imparting self-control is disastrous. And doubtless many people in our society have encountered such disasters. For what else could explain the resistance that most Americans (myself included) feel toward the idea of immersion in unbridled Dionysian energies?

There is something to Goethe's observation. Spiritual euphoria does not itself produce a happy life. And this is just as true when the euphoria is produced in a musical context as when it is not. The emotional state that music engenders is not itself wisdom. In light of the fact that I consider musical experience to involve the entire context of the experience, I must admit that in some contexts music can be conducive to aberrant behavior and violence. I concede, too, that some music is more suited to violent and licentious states of mind than other music. Concertgoers have been trampled to death at certain rock concerts, but it is hard to envision a similar fate befalling an audience of English madrigals.

But to admit these things is only to admit the obvious. The very states and characteristics that can blossom in spiritual mastery or can be invaluable in certain circumstances can be calamitous in others. Music's power to lower our defenses can enhance our empathy and sensitivity, but it can also make us more susceptible to influence. No doubt there are true stories of disastrous behavior in which music has played a part. But I think such stories reveal that music, like any potentially positive spiritual influence, also has a flip side.

I am also convinced that such occurrences are much less common than many moralists would have us think. In the first place, music does not occur in a vacuum. One does not usually hear music and become a radically different person. One's measure of self-control, trained to a large degree outside the musical context, is still in effect when one listens. Those who are easily influenced to abandon inhibition while listening to music are probably easily influenced by other media as well.

Second, moralistic suspicion is often based on confusion about what music's influence actually is. The loss of self-awareness that occurs in the best musical experience is often confused with loss of self-control. The "what came over me?" feeling may succeed either state, but the situations are very different. Self-awareness does not always facilitate self-control, as Herrigel's story about his archery lesson suggests. And abdication of self-control is not necessarily a surrender to the unconscious.

Confusion regarding these two different spiritual conditions accounts in part for the fear that music can morally damage the listener. Another confusion is that the abandonment involved in certain kinds of musical experience automatically translates into an abandoned way of life. A common moralistic suspicion is that a taste of ecstatic experience creates an addiction that becomes a sordid lifestyle. The teenager felled by rock addiction is a common enough caricature. Each successive older generation comes up with a new term for the young who have made their music a rebellious lifestyle: beboppers, beatniks, rockers, punks, and so on.

The addiction image is not entirely misguided, although it is too negative. Ecstatic experience does lead those who have it to want more of it— and it is ecstatic experience that is feared in many moralistic disparagements of popular music. But even if ecstasy is psychologically addicting, this does not remotely decide the question of how one might pursue the desire it provokes.

The rock 'n' roll image of the drugged, orgiastic lifestyle offers one answer. And it may seem a momentary ideal to certain rock enthusiasts. But this is hardly a realistic image of a happy life. I doubt many, on examination, really desire the actual effects of a continual drugged orgy. What most who admire this "rock" image find desirable are the alleged thrills that go with it. But the fantasy of a life of continual thrill is essentially a fantasy. And I think most consumers of rock see it that way.

For those who do not, music may not dispel the fantasy of the continual thrill. (One of music's virtues, as I see it, is that it conditions us to thrill to nuance—an ability that might make thrill a more frequent element of our everyday experience.) But experience outside music does not support this fantasy. The project of cramming peak experiences into life is typically self-defeating. Peak experiences arise out of larger cycles of experience, and full satisfaction in one's life depends on appreciating the entirety of the cycle. Admiration of the rock image will not make the quest for the continual "high" more satisfying. Nor will rock music serve as a substitute for more basic contentment with life.

I do not mean to deny that many people are confused by fantasy, and that this is a serious spiritual problem. I have no doubt that many members of our society, lacking control of or even a sense of the cycles of their own lives, miss the celebrational state that arises out of the cycle's own peaking. American obsession with entertainment is, I suspect, an effort to induce the state of celebration without a sense of the waves of experience in which celebration naturally culminates. If rock music points to a problem, I do not think it is the moral laxity of the young. Instead, I think it is the American tendency to pursue blasts of entertainment instead of the temporal arc of fulfilling experience.

But the fact that these problems are common is precisely the reason I believe that music can educate our sensitivity to temporal development and fulfillment. This potential of music can actually mitigate the underlying problem that I think critics are really attacking in rock. Some rock music may not be suited to this task of temporal education; repetitive rhythm, in many cases, suggests more stasis than temporal development. But I believe other rock music is equipped for this purpose. Roxy Music's "More Than This" comes to mind.[38] The lyrics discuss a magic moment of reflection in the midst of time, while the music quietly glides the listener to a sense of expanding fullness.

In one sense, the moralist may be consistent in shunning ecstasy. If one subscribes to the view that ethical living involves conformity to clear-cut rules, the ecstatic state is an obstacle. The ecstatic frame of mind is foreign to rule-bound analysis. But this, I think, is an argument in favor of ecstatic musical experience. The entrenched habit of conceiving one's experience through rules needs psychic compensation. Nietzsche was right in his observation that the modern age represses Dionysus to its peril.

And experiences of ecstasy are themselves valuable to ethical living. If they were not, the ecstatic traditions of many of the world's religions would be absolutely incompatible with the moral visions that seem their constant concomitant.[39] The unusual breakdown of distinction between self and others that occurs during moments of ecstasy is not only compatible with moral vision, however. It may be that some sense of the possibility of such a breakdown is involved in everyday caring for other human beings.

Music is not a moral panacea, but it often contributes positively to moral experience. It cannot provide solutions to all our spiritual problems, but it offers suggestions that might help us think through some of them.

One dimension of our society's experience that is fraught with spiritual problems is sexuality. Because sex is often conceived in terms of gratification, it is not surprising that critics like Bloom condemn the easy "gratification" of rock as condoning sexual abandon. But is rock really contributing to our sexual problems?

Rock 'n' roll images of easy gratification certainly exist. The title "Cheap Thrills" tells virtually all about its lyrical content. But the range of depictions of sexuality in rock is broad. Jefferson Starship's "Miracles" is as romantic and personal an erotic image as one could wish (unless one objects to erotic depictions in general, in which case one is likely to find much art in virtually every medium offensive).[40] Rock music, taken as a category, can be seen as an anthology of poetic moments, many of which deal with sexual subjects. The fact that the lyric voice in much of rock celebrates male sexuality (and often its unruly side) suggests something about our societal situation. But I think this is more a mirror than the origin of sexual attitudes that reign in our society.

Rock ideology is too often confused with rock music. This, I think, is a mistake that Bloom makes. Rock is construed as the vanguard of an ideological cult that teaches that, whatever your parents might have told you, quick gratification is the *summum bonum*. At this historical moment, it is hard to imagine why such an ideological cult would be necessary. Older people and young people alike are bombarded with advertisements that offer a quick fix. Bloom himself argues that eroticism that conjoins spiritual ardor to appetite is infinitely more fulfilling than cheap thrills.[41] But he assumes that young people who listen to rock 'n' roll trust rock ideology more than what their own experience is likely to teach them. He seems to suppose that young people learn "I Want Your Sex"[42] by rote and then proceed to follow the trend.

This scenario is unconvincing. It would be plausible only if young people were genuinely spiritual zombies, in which case there would be little point in discussing education (Bloom's topic). But this is not how young people get their orientation on sex. Hormones and the broader *Zeitgeist* contribute more to their sexual practice than does exposure to the music of, say, Frank Zappa, who is often ironic in portraying human sexual foibles. If sexually explicit rock songs are actually used by young people to fortify their sexual attitudes, it is because the songs reflect attitudes that are already pervasive. And if certain attitudes celebrated in rock appear perverted, concerned listeners should consider what this says about their own attitudes, which cannot be fully divorced from those of the broader culture. Sex is commonly presented in our society as the great solution to problems of self-identity and self-esteem. To blame rock for encouraging such attitudes is to avoid the real questions of why we have the societal sex-dreams that we do, and of what would resolve the spiritual problems that we societally dramatize in the sexual arena.

I agree with Bloom that our cultural imaginations might be fuller than they are. Although our popular music is not so impoverished as he seems to think, perhaps our societal images of erotic yearning are underdeveloped. But even if this is so, popular music is not the cause. Instead, popular music can assist us in unraveling the problems in our erotic lives by bringing them into focus. If some of the erotic images suggested by popular music are disturbing, perhaps they reveal some disturbing features of our erotic inter-actions which deserve ethical reflection. I agree with Bloom that great music of our classical tradition can educate listeners in the satisfaction of sustained yearning and ultimate gratification. But popular music can similarly serve to instruct us, both as to what is desirable and as to what is undesirable in erotic life.

Support for Apollonian Evil

Many of the most adamant recent critics of rock 'n' roll have pointed to depictions in rock videos. The video dimension radically alters the musical experience. A song that might suggest different images on different hearings becomes conjoined with a series of visual images. It is difficult to hear a song in conjunction with a video and fail to think of the video images.[43] Video images, however, can direct whatever passionate response one may have to the music toward very specific characters and their actions. The em-pathy that one typically feels for the music-maker is often undercut by visual images of the performers assuming assaultive poses toward the audience.

Music can be conjoined with messages that are alien to what the music would convey without them, and video is a case in point. The ability of music to fortify whatever message it is combined with has often been a ground for moral criticism. Hitler used music in conjunction with grandi-ose spectacles to inspire his multitudes. Theodor Adorno argues that music is often used, in the modern era, to lull its audience into comfort with an objectionable status quo: "It assists in the achievement of most of today's culture: in preventing people from reflecting on themselves and their world, and in persuading them at the same time that since this world provides such an abundance of enjoyable things it must be in good shape."[44] Politi-cians are astute in using music in propaganda. "God Bless America" played at a political party's national convention makes members feel that patrio-tism and God are on their side. Music appears insidious when one considers these situations. It is easily prostituted, and its tunes dance to the wishes of the powerful.

Again, there is something to be said for such criticisms. Music can do all the things mentioned. To the extent that one can manipulate the musical context, one can utilize music to manipulate affections and empathies. This is news to no one. Use of the phonograph to secure seductions is hardly an unusual technique.

But again, propagandistic or manipulative uses exploit aspects of music that are potentially positive. Music forges solidarity; hence it can congeal bonds between those who define themselves in violent opposition to others.

Music can absorb the listener in appreciation; hence it can momentarily cause one to ignore important concerns. Because pleasure desires its own continuance, the pleased listener will want the situation that arouses pleasure to continue. But if the contextual situation is problematic from an ethical point of view, then music will inspire desire for the continuation of something that should not be perpetuated.

Again, music has inherent limitations. But we can use the broader context of our experience to sort them out. And musical experience itself can be instructive in this effort. If we observe the effect of context on the nature of our experience, we will be better able to discern the ways in which context resonates through music. If we begin, in this way, to recognize the ways that ideologies resonate through music, we will be better able to extricate ourselves from ideological appeals.

A related but different concern (argument 7 in my list of criticisms) is that music distracts us from more important things. Perhaps this is sometimes a real problem. Radio music can disturb concentration on homework or other matters. And certain individuals who are prone to obsession might obsess over music, as over other things. But I think the extent of such problems is small. And apart from a few disturbed individuals, most of us can arrange our musical lives with some control and discretion.

This complaint sometimes masks a more pervasive uneasiness with music, often as a symbol of frivolity. This is the source of dubiousness for certain Christian sects. But this grows out of a conviction that living well should be approached with an attitude of constant seriousness. I believe this attitude is misguided, for it misses the cyclical character of life and the importance of psychic compensation. Stressing the potential of music to reinforce what may already be deficient in one's character (an unwillingness to take serious things seriously, for example), this outlook ignores many other musical possibilities that might refresh one for seriousness or strengthen one's ability to deal with one's life.

Which music may prove of greatest ethical value to the listener is an individual matter. Schiller observes that while aesthetic experience is important in compensating for the excesses of character, one must determine in one's own particular case both one's excesses and the appropriate kinds of antidote. He describes two kinds of influence that beauty can have and lets the reader judge which would be more desirable in his or her own condition:

> Energizing Beauty can no more preserve a man from a certain residue of savagery and harshness than melting Beauty can protect him from a certain degree of softness and enervation. . . . So melting Beauty is essential

for a man under the constraint either of matter or of form; since he has been moved by greatness and strength long before he began to become sensitive to harmony and grace. The need of a man swayed by the indulgence of taste is for energizing Beauty; since in the state of refinement he fritters away only too lightly a strength which he brought over from the state of savagery.[45]

Schiller's point is that one must assess the context of one's own character and psychological needs in order to determine how best to utilize the beautiful. We can translate his point to the musical situation by considering our uses of music to indulge a mood. I can choose, if my record collection is sufficiently extensive, a record that will milk my maudlin mood or flame my state of fury. But to take these as the typical cases of musical enjoyment is to prejudge, with self-fulfilling prophecy, that music cannot be employed with greater discrimination or to more beneficial effect.

Preferring Aristotle's optimistic ethical overview to most offered by the Western tradition, I am convinced that people are naturally disposed to seek their own well-being and that they are educable with respect to the elements involved in well-being and the methods most apt to achieve it. I have been arguing that music can be used in ways that enhance the listener's ability to thrive. Throughout the centuries, some people have used music in a misguided fashion, just as some have misused every human experience, including that of the finest spiritual insight. Music, or any other component of human life, cannot ensure that all such components are organized properly. But it can, in numerous ways, assist the effort to impart balance to one's life and world if one is open, as a listener, to this possibility.

7 ‖ : How Music Can Assist Philosophical Ethics

Perhaps our ethical lives would benefit if we paid more attention to music. But what does this have to do with philosophy? Why should philosophical ethics bother with music, something so seemingly divorced from the practical world? These questions reflect the probable perspective of the dominant camp of philosophical ethics. Its orientation is as unamenable as that of contemporary musical aesthetics to recognizing a relationship between music and ethics. In order to explain what music can contribute to philosophical ethics, therefore, I begin by considering the source of mainstream resistance.

The Reign of the Moral Dilemma

With a few notable exceptions, contemporary ethical thinking has been dominated by a concern with moral dilemmas. Moral discussion has, by and large, focused on the crisis situation and the best means to resolve it. As a consequence, ethical thinking has been viewed as principally applicable to traumatic moments, not as vital to the intelligent direction of the continuum of everyday living. Even those ethical theories that attempt to extend the purview of ethical thought beyond moments of crisis fail to reflect human action adequately in its character as a continuum. Sartre, for instance, although emphasizing the radical freedom we enjoy in even the most banal situation, nevertheless takes the crisis model as a paradigm. By insisting that every moment is a moment of significant choice, he extends ethical focus to include the everyday only at the price of analyzing every moment as a moment of crisis.

Recent discussions of virtue ethics and of the inadequacy of what Edmund Pincoffs has termed "quandary ethics" reflect a need felt by some philosophers to integrate consideration of the ongoing, continuous character of our behavior into models for ethical thinking.[1] The emphasis in such discussions on the gradual nature of moral development has directed attention toward the temporal and dynamic character of the ethical context. Often acknowledging indebtedness to Aristotle, who analyzes virtue as a developmental effort to achieve an ideal "balance" in one's actions, these moral thinkers have stressed the ethical importance of understanding our ideals as vital and evolving, and of sensitivity to our often changing context. In a similar vein, Hubert Dreyfuss has recently suggested that ethics be reformulated with emphasis on preventing moral problems instead of developing techniques for solving them. According to our ethical history,

> ethics consists in knowing the principles on which you're acting and being able to justify those principles. According to Habermas and Kohlberg and Kant, that's ethical maturity. Suppose ethical maturity were being able to act in such a way that you didn't run into ethical problems, and you just knew intuitively how to act in most situations.[2]

This appreciation of the temporal, changing nature of our moral experience has led some virtue ethicists to seek alternatives to the moral dilemma paradigm. Significantly, a number of these philosophers have turned to an artistic model in their effort to provide an account of virtuous living. Alasdair MacIntyre, Martha Nussbaum, and others have suggested that the literary work, which reflects the character of the human moral situation, can serve ethical reflection by directing detailed attention to the complexities and temporal dynamics of particular situations.[3]

The literary work's suitability for this purpose can be defended on a number of grounds. A realistic novel bears an obvious relationship to practical living: the plot is modeled on human action, and great works exhibit complexities that are akin to those faced in real life. The very fact that "plot" is involved calls attention to the developmental character of most human action. This character has often been overlooked by recent moral theory, which typically underplays the extent to which appropriate choice of action depends on the context created by events and choices that precede it. The fictionality of the novel, moreover, liberates our reflection from the prejudices and interests that encumber our responses to actual situations. And it can afford a common focus for various persons who are concerned to reflect about the good life. Finally, as Nussbaum observes, the novel awakens our moral sensibility directly, for in moving us to feel concern for its characters, it "calls forth our 'active sense of life,' which is our moral faculty."[4]

Literary works can and often do reflect the complexity and the irreducible particularities that face us in actual life. Their reflection of the role of temporality in our moral situation, moreover, is a merit often missing in the criteria of moral philosophers. But literary models have limitations that prevent them from being completely adequate as reflections of everyday moral life.

The literary work tends to focus on the dramatic moment and the clear development of particular currents in the characters' lives. Indeed, the aesthetic merit of a literary work has since Aristotle often been judged in terms of its clear portrayal of single lines of action. Details that complicate the lives of the characters are viewed as desirable only when they bear on the focal action of the story. But this kind of focus and clarity, aesthetically desirable as it may be in a novel, is exactly what is lacking in the typical ethical situation. Our daily lives are not, for the most part, series of dramatic plots which, however complicated, dominate our attention throughout their duration. Instead, the circumstances of our lives tax our attention in various unrelated ways at once. The currents prominent at any given moment do not usually maintain our complete attention until they are exhausted. Other currents vie for our thought and energy. And the closure that encapsulates the novelist's story is neither available nor desirable in ours.

The ethical value of vicarious literary experience is akin to the value of actual transformative experiences in our lives. Such experiences invite us to reconsider basic aspects of our ethical orientation in light of those striking situations that we can assess with an unusual degree of clarity. What vicarious literary experience does not in general provide is a reflection of the fragmented texture of experience in which the majority of our ethical choices take place.

Details obscured by a model may yet be relevant to the matter that one intends to survey. In such a case, the obvious move is to consider additional, counterbalancing models. Music's value to philosophical ethics is to remind it of aspects of our ethical experience that are forgotten in other models. In the discussion that follows, I suggest some of the ways in which musical experience can serve as a reminder to ethics. I am convinced that what music has to offer is vitally needed by the field, which tends to forget that human action occurs in a temporal flux and that we require navigational techniques if we are to direct our action intelligently.

Music and Everyday Tensions

Contemporary ethical discussion, like everyday ethical thinking, tends to underplay the ongoing, changing pattern of tensions that moral situations always involve. Of course, in one respect discussion of a moral dilemma always focuses directly on tensions. A moral dilemma itself is a kind of tension; and ethical discussions of moral dilemmas are concerned with how the focal tension of the moral dilemma can be eliminated. But the inevitable result of this focus is distortion of the larger pattern of tensions that are the context of any actual moral dilemma.

Overly simplifying the depiction of tension involved in moral situations, such analyses distort our ethical thinking in important ways. First, they ignore nonfocal tensions, although these are often significant for a balanced assessment of what we ought to do. Second, they also distort our understanding of the focal tensions that the moral dilemma isolates. To isolate a tension by describing it in abstract terms is to make it appear to be an instance of a standard scenario. The particular situation that concerns one, however, may be contextually related to various unmentioned factors that are not reflected in the abstract description. Such factors may have much to do with whether one's analysis is actually appropriate in the particular case.

Besides excessively simplifying the tensions we confront in everyday experience, the contemporary approach to the moral dilemma typically involves treating tension as inherently negative. Mainstream philosophical ethics is committed to satisfaction as a practical ideal.[5] The kind of satisfaction envisaged is an unrealistic goal for practical moral life, however, in which the complete resolution of the serious tensions that lead to dilemmas is rarely a genuine possibility.

Reflection on music suggests that satisfaction need not be construed as a drastic reduction or elimination of tension. Instead, satisfaction can be found in controlled and coordinated manipulation of tension itself. Musical experience also suggests the fallacy involved in making satisfaction our overriding ethical concern. Risk itself has a positive value in both musical and ethical experience.

Tolerance of risk is fundamental to psychic openness—and, as we have seen, such openness is fundamental to the listener's capacity to respond to music. Ethical sensitivity requires vulnerability. In order to be sensitive to another's needs and situation, one must be able to dissolve to some extent one's defenses toward that person.

Nussbaum sees our vulnerability in ethical experience as an additional reason for cherishing human goodness when it actually thrives. Commenting on Pindar's *Nemean*, she notes its striking suggestion "that part of the peculiar beauty of *human* excellence just *is* its vulnerability." But our tradition has not fully appreciated this fact. Nussbaum observes that "aspiration to rational self-sufficiency," an ethical goal we inherit from the Greeks, is a quest to put one's "life, or the most important things in it, under the control of the agent (or of those elements in him with which he identifies himself), removing the element of reliance upon the external and undependable." Kantian ethics, divorcing ethical principle from empirical conditions, also presents invulnerability to situational contingencies as an ethical ideal. This ideal, however, is foreign to our moral experience.

> That I am an agent, but also a plant; that much that I did not make goes towards making me whatever I shall be praised or blamed for being; that I must constantly choose among competing and apparently incommensurable goods and that circumstances may force me to a position in which I cannot help being false to something or doing some wrong; that an event that simply happens to me may, without my consent, alter my life; that it is equally problematic to entrust one's good to friends, lovers, or country and to try to have a good life without them—all these I take to be . . . everyday facts of lived practical reason.[6]

In ethical life we are vulnerable, just as we are in musical experience. Ethical theory should reflect this character of our existence. It should also recognize that risk, in certain contexts, deserves positive celebration.

Risk is taken to be an aesthetic value in the performance of certain kinds of music. For instance, in the improvised sections of south Indian kritis (and in other Indian classical forms of both north and south India), one of the essential conditions of the soloist's success is the maintenance of both the rāga (the scale pattern) and the tāla (the rhythmic pattern) throughout. This is a significant achievement. The tāla might establish a cycle that is quite lengthy by Western standards (often twelve or sixteen beats to the cycle). And in the kriti the structure of the rāga is improvisationally unfolded. The aim is to explore the rāga in a serious fashion, but at the same time to approach the opening beat of a cycle in a musically intelligent way. The risk the performer takes in working out the tension between these two aims is an important factor in what the audience enjoys in performance.[7]

Risk is often considered a positive value in composed music as well. Meyer's theory of musical value is, in a sense, constructed on the observation that we value music when it surprises us, when it does something we had not foreseen.[8] And indeed, we do not favorably evaluate music when we can outguess its every move.

Although vitality is rarely discussed as an ethical value in itself, we clearly assess our own lives on such a basis. We want our lives to have sufficient novelty to be exciting. At the same time, we want our lives to be routine enough that they have a kind of shape. We also expect others to respect the basic shape of our way of life; we demand that they not ask us to do anything to damage it. The tension between exciting novelty and reliable routine is fundamental both to successful living and to successful music.

Taking its cue from music, philosophical ethics should reevaluate its ideals in light of the role that tension plays in a happy human life. It should learn from music that resolution of tension is a gradual temporal process, that this process can be well or ill handled, and that the process itself can be a source of satisfaction.

Divided Attention

One basic feature of the everyday experiential situations in which ethical decisions are made is that our attention is divided. Much music (perhaps paradigmatically that of the Western classical tradition) similarly divides attention. The appreciation of music (for both the music-maker and the listener) involves the intelligent apprehension of a flux of discrete elements in continuously changing tensions with one another. Ethical thinking, to the extent that it concerns the continuous texture of living, involves a similar apprehension of elements in shifting currents of tension. Both involve active recognition of complex patterns in process.

But recognition of pattern is only the beginning of either musical understanding or sound ethical reflection. In addition, both kinds of thinking involve such mental activities as (1) imaginative grasp of similarities and nuances of difference; (2) appreciation of the conditions of balance in the context of an unstable configuration of elements; (3) the achievement of relative focus at any given time by mental assertion of a foreground/background framework of interpretation, a framework that acknowledges the continuing activity of background elements and remains receptive to the shifting of elements from background to foreground; and (4) continuous reconsideration of one's structural understanding up to the present. The more listening experience we have, the better we feel it gets—and part of what makes listening improve is a gain in our attention's fluidity, its ability to shift back and forth without getting lost.

In this respect, philosophical ethics stands to profit from a consideration of how we make sense of musical structure, from observing and analyzing the mental balancing act involved in our best achievements of musical comprehension while listening.[9] What keeps the various streams of attention in balance when we listen to a symphony? How do we make progress in learning to understand music of a different culture? When is our ability to label elements helpful to our comprehension? When is it a hindrance?

When does it assist our sense of where we are in the larger context of the work? What makes the difference?

Ethics aspires to illuminate the good life. But living well requires a sense of where one is in multiple plots. By involving us in a similar and nonvicarious effort to orient ourselves within multiple streams of events, musical experience illuminates the thought processes involved in all temporal orientation. Our whole range of listening achievements (from best to worst) can assist the effort to discover why our thinking about ongoing processes works when it works, and why it breaks down when it doesn't. Musical experience can intimate patterns that play roles in our ethical experience. In answering such questions as those above, it can suggest answers to such ethical questions as: What conditions optimize our distribution of attention to various matters that place practical demands upon us? How do we improve our ability to attend to everything we need to? When is a moral principle or a crystallized insight of benefit to our ethical thinking? When do such rigid ideas blind us? What role do static formulations play in our efforts to navigate our lives in a good way? How do we tell whether they are helping or hurting?

The Role of Analysis and the Folly of Pedantry

Philosophical ethics, in its quest to formulate principles and insights of value to good living, has difficulty recognizing the limitations of its own formulations. Its tendency is to present its findings as universal absolutes, applicable to all situations. Within an ethical theory, the fact that principles and formulated insights themselves *interpret* and carve up the ethical situation is typically ignored. And the shape of such situations is treated as always conformable to static description. That practice belies theory is known to everyone. But theorists often seem comfortable with this disparity, for they rarely address how we might attempt to shorten the gap between the two.

At the very least, music can help alert us to where the gap occurs. Foibles that occur in our attempt to make sense of the musical process parallel certain foibles in our ethical thinking. Almost everyone with sufficient musical training to approach music analytically recognizes that too much analysis can impoverish the experience. This discovery strikes most of us who have made it with some force. When one first acquires various tools of analysis, one usually discovers much more sense in the music. The later discovery that analysis can also cause sense to disintegrate seems paradoxical and rather alarming.

The resolution of the paradox occurs when one realizes the importance of attending to the whole musical matrix—not just to disconnected musical elements. Zuckerkandl emphasizes the role of the musical continuum when he observes:

> Let anyone who is capable of it call to mind the immediately preceding tone of a melody that he is hearing. *The instant he does so, he will have lost the thread of the melody.* . . . Any turning back of consciousness for the purpose of making past tones present immediately annuls the possibility of musical hearing.[10]

Making sense of music requires that one have a sense of where one is within the overall flow.[11] When one loses the flow in the analytical quest to observe elements, one has lost one's bearings in music.

That practical life admits of a parallel problem is confirmed by the cliché character of the adage "He couldn't see the forest for the trees." The ethical version of this problem is described by Schopenhauer as "moral pedantry." "Pedantry," as he analyzes it, is "a form of folly" that

> arises from a man's having little confidence in his own understanding, and therefore not liking to leave things to its discretion, to recognize directly what is right in the particular case. Accordingly, he puts his understanding entirely under the guardianship of his reason, and makes use thereof on all occasions; in other words, he wants always to start from general concepts, rules and maxims, and to stick strictly to these in life, in art, and even in ethical good conduct.

Unfortunately for the pedant,

> the incongruity between the concept and reality soon shows itself, as the former never descends to the particular case, and its universality and rigid definiteness can never accurately apply to reality's fine shades of difference and its innumerable modifications. Therefore the pedant with his general maxims almost always comes off badly in life, and shows himself foolish, absurd, and incompetent.

Schopenhauer specifically criticizes the pedantic effort to resolve all ethical issues by appeal to abstract maxims:

> In many instances the infinitely nice distinctions in the nature of the circumstances necessitate a choice of right, proceeding directly from the character. For the application of merely abstract maxims sometimes gives false results, because they only half apply; sometimes it cannot be

carried out, because such maxims are foreign to the individual character of the person acting, and this can never be entirely hidden; hence inconsistencies follow.

Schopenhauer concludes, "Abstraction consists in thinking away the closer and more detailed definitions, but it is precisely on these that very much depends in practice."[12]

Schopenhauer's criticism would be applicable to anyone who acted consistently on the results of philosophy's techniques of dilemma resolution. In fact, most of us are not pedants in this sense. We may believe it optimal to decide on a purely rational, nonemotive basis, but that is not what we typically do. Nonetheless, Schopenhauer's analysis suggests an innovation in moral thinking that is relevant, I suspect, to most of us. He suggests that we should recognize the value of intuition and emotion in making practical choices. This is also an important recognition for the field of ethics. Far from inciting us to inner dissonance when we act on some other basis than mechanical application of rules, philosophical ethics should remember the moderation in analysis that our musical experience teaches.

The Uniqueness of the Musical Moment

Music makes us all Heracliteans, for it is a commonplace that a piece of music is never the same twice. Performances of a given musical work are never absolutely identical to one another. The differences between one performance and another range from aesthetically crucial differences in overall interpretation of the work to slight deviations in timing that are minimally perceptible to the ear.[13] The fact that two performers working from the same musical score—or a single performer working from the same score on different occasions—can produce such markedly different results, often results of different aesthetic merit, is recognized and remarked upon by virtually everyone who considers the ontology of music.[14]

Our experience as listeners, too, is never repeated, even when we listen to the same recording of the same performance over and over again. We notice different features of the music every time. The structure of the work becomes clearer as we hear it more often, and as the structure becomes clearer, we are able to recognize and make greater sense of nuances of the work as performed. Our other musical experiences, too, affect and change what we notice in a recorded performance. Hearing a different performance of the same work will obviously direct our attention to features of the well-known performance different from those we have previously noticed. But other obviously similar musical experiences will also affect what we are attentive to, thereby changing our impression of a performance that we know well.[15]

Each musical experience is unique. In this respect it parallels our ethical situation. The universal character of most traditional moral ideals ignores the importance and potential value of the uniqueness of the particular situation. Realism in ethics dictates that we take this character into account. The complications and confusions of "learning from experience" arise in large part from our recognition in practice that the present situation is unique, no mere repetition of a previous or recurrent situation. The present ethical situation has its own individuating features which may or may not be decisive for one's manner of dealing with it. Thus, no matter how sincerely one might *want* to employ the lessons of accumulated life, one ends up having to consider whether the differences between this and previous cases are not more important than the similarities. This is the only way to avoid mishaps stemming from inertia of habit or reactionary insistence that one will "never do that again."

Several factors that contribute to the uniqueness of the immediate situation are relevant to balanced ethical decision. The individuality of the person dealing with an ethical situation is importantly relevant to the realistic range of possibilities available for dealing with it. It is also decisive for the way in which possible resolutions of moral tensions can be integrated into the larger texture of that person's life. In addition, the person's current state of maturity and the experiences that intervene between the present situation and previous, apparently similar ones affect the degree to which accumulated experience can appropriately be brought to bear on the present.

But the uniqueness and immediacy of our situation are not only complicating factors in the analysis of ethical problems. They also positively contribute to the sense that our lives have value. The importance of valuing the unique details of one's life is emphasized by both Søren Kierkegaard and Milan Kundera.

Kierkegaard stresses the profoundly personal character of significant choice. Ethical living, he contends, depends on one's choosing a "self." This amounts to making a decision to pursue and accept the responsibilities of one particular life as opposed to all others. One cannot arrive at such a choice by calculation. And it is too intimately personal to be established by "principles" cast in universal terms:

> The ethical individual knows himself, but this knowledge is not a mere contemplation (for with that the individual is determined by his necessity), it is a reflection upon himself which itself is an action, and therefore

I have deliberately preferred to use the expression "choose oneself" instead of know oneself. . . . Only within him has the individual the goal after which he has to strive, and yet he has this goal outside him, inasmuch as he strives after it. For if the individual believes that the universal man is situated outside him, that from without it will come to him, then he is disoriented, then he has an abstract conception and his method is always an abstract annihilation of the original self. Only within him can the individual acquire information about himself.[16]

An appreciation of what is unique to our own character, disposition, and circumstances is essential to structuring our life in a coherent fashion. Such structuring, in turn, is crucial to our sense that our life has significance, that it is not just "one thing after another."

Kundera discusses the means by which one's life assumes structure in *The Unbearable Lightness of Being*. This structuring occurs, according to Kundera, on the basis of aesthetic evaluations that are produced by what he calls "poetic memory": "The brain appears to possess a special area which we might call poetic memory and which records everything that charms or touches us, that makes our lives beautiful." The images that strike the poetic imagination and linger in memory, Kundera's narrator tells us, are decisive in determining whom a person chooses to love, what course of life seems comfortable, and whether or not a major life decision seems retrospectively to be the right one. Such decisions are poetic decisions. "Love begins with a metaphor."[17] One loves a person who moves one to poetic reflection; and one feels secure in a major decision when one finds the life that results to be beautiful, literally filled with images of beauty.

Kundera's notion of poetic memory illuminates the process by which we come to the ethically crucial personal decision of which particular life to live. Our imaginations, often unconsciously, select the objects of our concern and determine when this caring will shape our lives. One loves when one finds a person to be of unique, irreplaceable value. And when one does so, one bears in one's imagination images of that person, images suffused with loveliness.

In a sense, we do not control what our imagination will or will not respond to in this fashion. Kundera is open-minded about what sorts of images can contribute to our sense of meaning in this way. From a third-person perspective, they can be positively quirky. But *that* we respond in such a way is, according to Kundera, crucial to our ability to judge that our life is a good one.

A sense that one's life has aesthetic value is fundamental to one's ability

to affirm it. To find our lives significant, we must find them somehow coherent, and coherence is achieved by the continual caring we feel for the
persons and projects that are most focal in our lives. Poetic images stimulate
our determination of our life's structure. They also establish hope and the
conviction that the particular life chosen remains worth pursuing. Kundera
describes the panic his character Tereza experiences when her husband,
whom she had left in Geneva, perhaps forever, returns to live with her in
Prague. She overcomes her panic when poetic images come to mind:

> But all at once she recalled that just before he had appeared at the door
> of their flat the day before, the church bells had chimed six o'clock. On
> the day they first met, her shift had ended at six. She saw him sitting
> there in front of her on the yellow bench and heard the bells in the belfry
> chime six.
>
> No, it was not superstition, it was a sense of beauty that cured her
> of her depression and imbued her with a new will to live. The birds of
> fortuity had alighted once more on her shoulders. There were tears in her
> eyes, and she was unutterably happy to hear him breathing at her side.[18]

In order to live well, we must believe that this unique life we have is valuable. And this conviction cannot be generated by means of moral principles,
which are formulated to apply to a countless number of possible lives. One's
life is legitimated, according to Kundera, by "a sense of beauty." Following the lead of traditional Western aesthetics, Kundera links this "sense of
beauty" with the notion of aesthetic necessity. This traditional criterion of
aesthetic value holds that a work is ideally arranged when one senses that
the arrangement could not have been otherwise—that one could not have
added or subtracted anything without the effect being destroyed.

Kundera suggests that we evaluate our lives in a similar fashion. It does
not matter whether one rationally recognizes that things might have happened differently. When one is basically content with one's life, one feels
that it is going as it *has* to go, that it could not go otherwise.

Music provides an image of the beauty of the unique, and, in particular,
of a unique track undergone over time. "The musical work" itself suggests
the value of unique configurations. Only because just *these* elements, in this
sequence, combined in precisely this way have been appreciated as of unique
value could a particular work of our classical tradition have attained the
status *of* a work. The work's unique array of tonally moving forms is worth
hearing again and again. Certain classical works are, for many people, precisely the kind of poetic images that Kundera sees as partially constitutive
of a meaningful human life.[19]

But the enduring value of certain musical works is not the only musical reminder of the importance of appreciating uniqueness. A static work of art, seen many times, can do that. Music, however, because it occupies time and intensely directs the experience of time, makes a unique "now" present to the listener.

Ingarden, in describing our experience of a given performance of a work of music, points to the "temporal coloring" that characterizes it. Temporal coloring is a concrete quality that stamps as individual the particular experienced temporal process. It "depends on a complete range of processes and events that occur in that phase and are accessible to the subject of consciousness in direct experience." This coloring also bridges past and present experience. It is "dependent in a particular synthetic way on the temporal coloring of the preceding moment not yet extinguished in the experiencing of the present." In other words, temporal coloring has a certain temporal extension in real time. Ingarden distinguishes discrete temporal colorings within a given work as those that correspond to distinguishable temporal phases. Temporal coloring is always new, and it is the primary reason every musical performance is unique and unrepeatable.[20]

Reflection on ethical experience suggests a similar phenomenon. Our attempts to implement our ethical intentions are most successful when they harmonize stylistically with what might be called the "temporal coloring" of the given point in time. A person who seems always to respond appropriately to the occasion might be described as being sensitive to such coloring. Philosophical ethics should attend to what is involved in the temporal coloring of music and to how one comes to be sensitive to it. What is at stake is the answer to the question: How do we bring a synthetic impression of previous experiences to bear on our sense of the present situation's unique significance?

For too long, philosophical ethics has treated moral decision as comparable to the pedantic employment of an etiquette book. If I want to know how to address a letter to the Pope, I can consult Emily Post. Similarly, mainstream ethics suggests that if I want to do the right thing, I determine the "type" my situation instantiates and apply the appropriate rule. But generating and conforming to ethical principles is as far from ethical sensitivity as living by the rules of an etiquette book is from genuine politeness.[21]

Ethical sensitivity depends on appreciation of the unique as well as the typical. In coming to grips with the difference between the two, philosophical ethics should consider our simultaneous appreciation of the unique and the typical as it occurs in much of our musical experience.

The Aesthetic Character of Living Well

Through listening to music, we develop our musicality. We become, that is, appreciative of music, and we develop our musical understanding. I have been suggesting that ethical sensitivity is a kindred capacity, and one that is assisted by developing a sense of what music is.[22] Good judgment in ethics, like musicality in our approach as listeners, involves a developed capacity for almost immediate assessment and response.

Ethics has long been dominated by negative restrictions that focus on what considerations should limit human action and by emphasis on the crisis situation as the paradigm circumstance in which ethics can provide practical guidance. I propose a more positive approach to ethics, one that emphasizes the actual contents of one's life and the ways in which one might best organize them.

Musical experience, I propose, is an arena from which we might gain ideas for such a positive ethical orientation. What philosophical ethics needs is a model of the ethical situation that allows for an open-minded, imaginative approach to resolving ethical tensions. Such a model is offered by music, and by its nature this model is a kind of aesthetic image.

When we colloquially describe the life of a person we ethically admire, we are unlikely to make comments like "She (or he) is good at solving moral dilemmas" or "He consistently subsumes his situation under the correct moral principles."[23] We are much more likely to say that that person always does what the situation calls for, whether or not the situation involves a paradigmatic ethical puzzle. We admire his or her intuition and finesse in immediate response.

Our language reflects a sense that musical and ethical sensitivity are kindred qualities, for we describe both a musical person and an ethically sensitive person as having "grace." Grace, in a sense, is at the heart of what we have been discussing—and I think the essence of what mainstream ethics has lost sight of. In its deliberations about rational strategy and sets of principles that one can apply with consistency, it has forgotten the goal that I think most of us aspire to: some vision of living life as well as Marcel Marceau moves.[24] Do we not desire to be beings whose every movement is vital and graceful? Do we not wish to be filled with life, equipped for every adventure?

I am not arguing that ethics can be conflated with aesthetics, or that we do not need a field of ethics so long as our sense of aesthetics is sufficiently refined. Ethical guidelines have their place, but their function should not be exaggerated. Guidelines should be viewed as generalized descriptions of perceived ethical constraints; they should not be conceived as absolute determinants with respect to any given situation.

In addition to this negative guidance, our ethical thought should be nurtured with positive insights and aspirations as well, insights regarding harmony and the temporal nature of our ethical lives. Music, I submit, is a forgotten source for such insights. As Plato argues, it can and should be a potent instrument for making our souls graceful.

▌: Notes

Introduction

1. *Yo Ki* (Record of Music), in *The Sacred Books of China*, trans. James Legge, pt. IV: *The Li Ki*, vols. XI–XLVI (Delhi: Motilal Banarsidass, 1968), bk. I, chap. 28, p. 103; Plato, *Republic*, bk. III, 401, as cited in *Philosophies of Art and Beauty: Selected Readings in Aesthetics from Plato to Heidegger*, ed. Albert Hofstadter and Richard Kuhns (Chicago: University of Chicago Press, 1964), p. 28.
2. Allan Bloom, *The Closing of the American Mind* (New York: Simon and Schuster, 1987), p. 73. It is perhaps worth noting that Bloom admires the erotic character of classical music; hence it is not musical reflections of sexuality per se that he deplores, but the specific reflections he finds in rock 'n' roll.
3. Nikita Khrushchev, in a 1963 declaration of his views on music, as quoted in Nicolas Slonimsky, *Music since 1900*, 4th ed. (New York: Scribner, 1971), p. 1379; cited in Arnold Perris, *Music as Propaganda: Art to Persuade, Art to Control* (Westport, Conn.: Greenwood, 1985), p. 67.
4. Bloom, *Closing of the American Mind*, p. 72.
5. Aristotle, *Nicomachean Ethics*, bk. I, chap. 3.
6. See Nelson Goodman, *Languages of Art* (Indianapolis: Hackett, 1976), pp. 117–18, 177–92.
7. Francis Sparshott, "Aesthetics of Music: Limits and Grounds," in *What Is Music? An Introduction to the Philosophy of Music*, ed. Philip Alperson (New York: Haven, 1988), p. 59.
8. John Blacking, *How Musical Is Man?* (Seattle: University of Washington Press, 1973), p. 10. My analysis throughout is strongly influenced by such ethnomusicologists as Blacking, Steven Feld, and Charles Keil. I have also been influenced by a host of phenomenologists concerned with music, among them Alfred Schutz and Victor Zuckerkandl. Although the field of philosophy has been dominated by aesthetic formalism in its analyses of music, these phenomenologists have done much to direct philosophical attention to the experiential dimension of music. While their concern is accurate description and analysis of musical phenomena and not musical aesthetics as such, their accounts, in my opinion, offer a basis for preferring one aesthetic orientation to another, and my discussion here is greatly in their debt.

Chapter 1

1. Bruno Nettl, *The Study of Ethnomusicology: Twenty-nine Issues and Concepts* (Urbana: University of Illinois Press, 1983), p. 16. See *The New Harvard Dictionary of Music*, ed. Don Randel (Cambridge: Harvard University Press, 1986), p. 516.
2. *The Macmillan Encyclopedia of Music and Musicians*, ed. Albert E. Wier (New York: Macmillan, 1938), p. 1234.
3. *Webster's New Twentieth Century Dictionary of the English Language*, ed. Jean L. McKechnie (New York: Simon and Schuster, 1983), p. 1184.
4. Nettl, *Study of Ethnomusicology*, p. 16.
5. Alan P. Merriam, *The Anthropology of Music* (Evanston: Northwestern University Press, 1964), pp. 120–21.
6. See ibid., p. 80, and David P. McAllester, *Enemy Way Music: A Study of Social and Esthetic Values as Seen in Navaho Music* (Cambridge: Peabody Museum of American Archaeology and Ethnology, Harvard University, 1954).
7. Merriam, *Anthropology of Music*, pp. 222–27, 272, and John Blacking, *How Musical Is Man?* (Seattle: University of Washington Press, 1973), pp. 7–9.
8. Francis Sparshott, "Aesthetics of Music: Limits and Grounds," in *What Is Music? An Introduction to the Philosophy of Music*, ed. Philip Alperson (New York: Haven, 1988), p. 43.
9. Jan L. Broeckx, "Works and Plays in Music," in *Contemporary Views on Musical Style and Aesthetics* (Antwerp: Metropolis, 1979), p. 126. Lydia Goehr points out that this notion of the musical work has been with us only since the eighteenth century. See Lydia Goehr, "Being True to the Work," *Journal of Aesthetics and Art Criticism* 47/1 (Winter 1989): 55–67. Goehr notes, for instance, that "Bach did not think centrally in these terms; Beethoven did. Haydn marks the transition" (ibid., p. 56).
10. Broeckx, *Contemporary Views*, pp. 126–27, 131.
11. Nettl, *Study of Ethnomusicology*, p. 20. Philip Gbeho is quoted in R. F. Thompson, *African Art and Motion* (Berkeley and Los Angeles: University of California Press, 1974), p. 242.
12. Charles A. Culver, *Musical Acoustics* (Philadelphia: Blakiston, 1941), pp. 4–5.
13. See Merriam, *Anthropology of Music*, pp. 66–67; Steven Feld, "Aesthetics as Iconicity of Style (uptown title), or (downtown title) 'Lift-Up-Over-Sounding': Getting into the Kaluli Groove," *Yearbook for Traditional Music* 20 (1988): 80; "East Asia," in *New Harvard Dictionary of Music*, p. 257; Kate Bush, "Moving," on *The Kick Inside*, EMI SW-17003. Although current scholarship no longer attributes the Toy Symphony to him, I follow tradition in calling it "Haydn's."
14. Nettl, *Study of Ethnomusicology*, p. 21.

15. Merriam, *Anthropology of Music*, p. 65; Steven Feld, "Sound Structure as Social Structure," *Ethnomusicology* 28/3 (September 1984): 395; Nettl, *Study of Ethnomusicology*, p. 21; Plato, *Phaedrus* 259; Charles Hartshorne, "Metaphysics Contributes to Ornithology," *Theoria to Theory* 13 (1979): 127–28, 131, 133; cf. Friedrich Schiller, *On the Aesthetic Education of Man, in a Series of Letters*, trans. Reginald Snell (New York: Ungar, 1954), p. 133.

16. Nettl, *Study of Ethnomusicology*, pp. 23–24.

17. Cf. Jean Gabbert Harrell, *Soundtracks: A Study of Auditory Perception, Memory and Valuation* (Buffalo: Prometheus, 1986), pp. 19–31.

18. I do not, however, agree with Scruton's insistence that the musical understanding his definition presupposes can be achieved only within a well-defined community. Scruton's claim that any given musical discourse—paradigmatically Western classical music—is properly understood only by a relatively closed community does not leave much room for valuable appreciation of musics of other societies besides one's own. Nor does it account for the vitalization, in this century, of one musical tradition by another.

19. Eduard Hanslick, *On the Musically Beautiful: A Contribution towards the Revision of the Aesthetics of Music*, trans. and ed. Geoffrey Payzant (Indianapolis: Hackett, 1986), p. 48.

20. Jerrold Levinson, "What a Musical Work Is," *Journal of Philosophy* 77/1 (January 1980): 5–6.

21. Lewis Rowell, *Thinking about Music: An Introduction to the Philosophy of Music* (Amherst: University of Massachusetts Press, 1983), pp. 34–36.

22. See "Notation," in *New Harvard Dictionary of Music*, ed. Randel, p. 544, and Donald Jay Grout, *A History of Western Music*, shorter ed., rev. (New York: Norton, 1973), p. 43.

23. Grout, *History of Western Music*, pp. 118–19.

24. Ibid., p. 204.

25. See "Counterpoint," in *New Harvard Dictionary of Music*, pp. 205–6. The exception to my general claim is the suspension in which one tone from the preceding beat is held through the strong beat to produce a dissonance with another voice and is resolved on a weak beat.

26. See Grout, *History of Western Music*, pp. 276–77. For further discussion of harmonic principles, see "Harmony," in *New Harvard Dictionary of Music*, pp. 366–69.

27. "Temperament," in *New Harvard Dictionary of Music*, ed. Randel, p. 837.

28. "The Well-Tempered Clavier," in ibid., p. 932.

29. *Musical Aesthetics: A Historical Reader*, ed. Edward A. Lippman, vol. I: *From Antiquity to the Eighteenth Century* (New York: Pendragon, 1986), p. 121.

30. Hanslick, *On the Musically Beautiful*, p. 29.

31. See ibid., pp. 30–31; see also p. xiv. Hanslick's account of emotion and music is considered in more detail in Chapter 3.

32. Ibid., p. 58.

33. Ibid., p. 59.

34. See Edward Lippman, *A Humanistic Philosophy of Music* (New York: New York University Press, 1977), pp. 31–41, where Lippman defends his decision to describe his humanistic inquiry into music as "philosophy of music" instead of "musical aesthetics."

35. Carl Dahlhaus, *The Esthetics of Music*, trans. William Austin (Cambridge: Cambridge University Press, 1982), p. 24. Dahlhaus also observes that the legacy of this view was still felt in Hanslick's day, and that as a consequence, "even Hanslick felt compelled, when he maintained the primacy of instrumental music, to expound his thesis as a polemic" (ibid., p. 29).

36. See Broeckx, *Contemporary Views*, pp. 134–35; Roman Ingarden, *The Work of Music and the Problem of Its Identity*, trans. Adam Czerniawski, ed. Jean G. Harrell (Berkeley and Los Angeles: University of California Press, 1986), pp. 4–5; Peter Kivy, "Platonism in Music: A Kind of Defense," *Grazer Philosophische Studien* 19 (1983): 123–28.

37. See Richard Wollheim, *Art and Its Objects*, 2d ed. (Cambridge: Cambridge University Press, 1980), pp. 74–84; Nicholas Wolterstorff, *Works and Worlds of Art* (Oxford: Clarendon Press, 1980), p. 62; Kingsley Price, "What Is a Piece of Music?" *British Journal of Aesthetics* 22/9 (Fall 1982): 331–35.

38. The latter problem arises when the score itself is taken to be an incomplete designation of the work's ideal character. Some Platonists attempt to circumvent this problem by considering the score to be definitive of all properties of the work. This strategy has its own problems, which I consider below.

39. Cf. Rita Laplante Raffman, "Ludwig Wittgenstein's Concept of Family Resemblances and Contemporary Music," *Music and Man* 2/1–2 (1976): 117–23.

40. See Levinson, "What a Musical Work Is," pp. 14–19.

41. In this connection, it is interesting that Wolterstorff himself, since writing *Works and Worlds of Art*, has suggested that focusing on the ontological status of "transcendent" works of art results in an impoverished view of music as practiced. See Nicholas Wolterstorff, "The Work of Making a Work of Music," in *What Is Music?* ed. Alperson, pp. 101–29.

42. Price, "What Is a Piece of Music?" p. 334.

43. Such recognitions do not, however, require that one be able to specify any of these elements or that one be consciously reflective about what one is observing. Cf. Edward Cone, "Music and Form," in *What Is Music?* ed. Alperson, pp. 134–35.

44. Roger Sessions, *Questions about Music* (Cambridge: Harvard University Press, 1970), p. 103.

45. Like Platonism, other brands of formalism also underplay the sensuous, perceptual character of musical experience, and thereby ignore both the

nature of what is intellectually apprehended and a whole dimension of what we value in music. This failure is particularly ironic. For while formalism emphasizes contemplation as the appropriate response to form, its account of contemplation is itself impoverished.

46. Victor Zuckerkandl, *Sound and Symbol: Music and the External World*, trans. Willard R. Trask, Bollingen Series XLIV (Princeton: Princeton University Press, 1956).

47. Ibid., pp. 336–48.

48. Ibid., pp. 34–37.

49. Catherine J. Ellis, *Aboriginal Music: Education for Living* (St. Lucia: University of Queensland Press, 1985), pp. 22–23.

50. Blacking, *How Musical Is Man?* p. 104.

51. Nettl, *Study of Ethnomusicology*, p. 60.

52. Alan Lomax, *Folk Song Style and Culture* (Washington, D.C.: American Association for the Advancement of Science, 1968), p. 133.

53. Kivy, James Anderson, Donald Walhout, and Wolterstorff all defend discoverist views as a corollary to Platonism. See Kivy, "Platonism in Music," pp. 118–19; James C. Anderson, "Musical Kinds," *British Journal of Aesthetics* 25/1 (Winter 1985): 43–49; Donald Walhout, "Discovery and Creation in Music," *Journal of Aesthetics and Art Criticism* 45/2 (Winter 1986): 193–95; Wolterstorff, *Works and Worlds of Art*, pp. 62–73. (See also, in connection with Wolterstorff's view, note 41 above.)

54. Walhout, "Discovery and Creation in Music," pp. 194–95; Anderson, "Musical Kinds," pp. 42–49.

55. Levinson, "What a Musical Work Is," p. 9.

56. Kivy, "Platonism in Music," pp. 112–19.

57. Arnold Schönberg, "New Music, Outmoded Music, Style and Idea," in *Style and Idea* (New York: Philosophical Library, 1950), p. 49.

58. Ludwig van Beethoven, as quoted in Ernest Newman, *The Unconscious Beethoven* (New York: Knopf, 1930), pp. 145–46.

59. Cf. Walhout, "Discovery and Creation in Music," p. 193.

60. Renée Cox, "Are Musical Works Discovered?" *Journal of Aesthetics and Art Criticism* 43/4 (Summer 1985): 370.

61. Ibid.

62. Levinson, "What a Musical Work Is," p. 15; Stephen Davies, "Authenticity in Musical Performance," *British Journal of Aesthetics* 27/1 (Winter 1987): 39; Wolterstorff, *Works and Worlds of Art*, p. 64.

63. Broeckx, *Contemporary Views*, p. 139.

64. Kivy, "Platonism in Music," pp. 123–28.

65. See Charles M. H. Keil, "Motion and Feeling through Music," *Journal of Aesthetics and Art Criticism* 24/3 (Spring 1966): 337–50. Feld argues that musical understanding of any style involves "getting into the groove." See Feld, "Aesthetics as Iconicity of Style."

66. *Back to the Future*, directed by Robert Zemeckis, Universal Pictures, 1985.
67. This example of a dramatization of the discoverist's position was suggested to me by Robert C. Solomon.

Chapter 2

1. Kenneth Burke, "On Form," in *Esthetics Contemporary*, ed. Richard Koste-lanetz (Buffalo: Prometheus, 1978), pp. 134–35.
2. See Eduard Hanslick, *On the Musically Beautiful: A Contribution towards the Revision of the Aesthetics of Music*, trans. and ed. Geoffrey Payzant (Indianapolis: Hackett, 1986), p. 80: "Music has no form other than the content." Hanslick goes on, however, to discuss a range of meanings that the terms *form* and *content* may have in connection with music. See ibid., pp. 77–83, for the full discussion.
3. My thanks to several audiences who heard me present some of the following analysis and offered constructive comments and suggestions. These include the philosophy department of California State University–San Bernardino, the philosophy department of the University of Texas at Austin, the philosophy department of Simon Fraser University, the philosophy department of the University of Auckland, and the 1988 meeting of the Australasian Association of Philosophy in Perth, Western Australia.
4. Immanuel Kant, *Critique of Judgment*, trans. Werner S. Pluhar (Indianapolis: Hackett, 1987), pp. 53, 64, 84, 90 (hereafter cited as *CJ*).
5. Immanuel Kant, *Critique of Pure Reason*, trans. Norman Kemp Smith (New York: Macmillan, 1961), p. 112.
6. "Kant's emphasis," observes Dahlhaus, "is a matter of method and logic, not founded in the nature of experience." See Carl Dahlhaus, *The Esthetics of Music*, trans. William Austin (Cambridge: Cambridge University Press, 1982), p. 72.
7. Kant, *CJ*, p. 62.
8. Ibid., pp. 76–77.
9. Ibid., p. 66.
10. Ibid., pp. 70–71.
11. Ibid., p. 159.
12. See ibid., pp. 185–87.
13. Ibid., p. 55.
14. My thanks to Sanford Weimer, M.D., for directing my attention to this fact.
15. My thanks to Professor Thomas K. Seung of the University of Texas at Austin for pointing out the ambivalent role of "sense" in Kant's aesthetics.
16. For the purposes of this discussion, I assume that any musical example well suited to Kant's aesthetic model can be described in terms of "musical works." Kant's third moment, with its demand for purposiveness, implies the closure characteristic of musical works. However, as Lydia Goehr points out, the terminology of "musical works" can and does invade discussions

of much music to which the concept is alien. Cf. Lydia Goehr, "Being True to the Work," *Journal of Aesthetics and Art Criticism* 47/1 (Winter 1989): 57–58.

17. Leonard Meyer even correlates the value (or "greatness") of musical works with the degree of uncertainty regarding resolution that their structure creates. The more musically meaningful resolutions a work's structure allows, the more excellent it is. See Leonard B. Meyer, "Some Remarks on Value and Greatness in Music," in *Music, the Arts, and Ideas: Patterns and Predictions in Twentieth-century Culture* (Chicago: University of Chicago Press, 1967), pp. 27–28.

18. See Aristotle, *Poetics* 1450b. On Beethoven's late string quartets, see Donald Jay Grout, *A History of Western Music*, shorter ed., rev. (New York: Norton, 1973), pp. 360–62.

19. The same complaint can be made against Kant's descendants in the analytic camp, who similarly appeal to the precise lines established by their terminology. And compare Hanslick, *On the Musically Beautiful*, p. 75, where he defends his claim that music does not represent nature against counter-examples (like Haydn's cockcrow in *The Seasons*) by asserting that such imitations have "not musical but poetical significance."

20. See Kant, *CJ*, pp. 225–30.

21. My elaboration of Kant's model may seem, in its mention of quasi-conceptual recognitions, to be at variance with Kant's own insistence that the pure judgment of the beautiful is "without a concept." Kant's account, however, equivocates between claiming that such judgments are independent of any concept and claiming that they are independent of any *determinate* concept. Although this equivocation invites interpretive debate, I assume here that Kant is internally consistent and conclude that when he refers to "concepts," he has "determinate concepts" in mind throughout. This conclusion is also suggested by the fact that he introduces the distinction between "determinate concepts" and "indeterminate concepts" only late in the "Critique of Aesthetic Judgment" and there claims that "a judgment of taste is not based on *determinate* concepts." See ibid., p. 213.

22. On Mbira music, see Paul Berliner, *The Soul of Mbira* (Berkeley and Los Angeles: University of California Press, 1978). Diana Raffman has recently developed a computational model of musical comprehension that corresponds in certain ways to the Kantian account. See Diana Raffman, "Toward a Cognitive Theory of Musical Ineffability," *Review of Metaphysics* 61/4 (June 1988): 685–706. The computational language, however, validates structural characteristics as exclusively important for understanding music. It thus ignores other aspects of music that might be significant for our understanding.

23. Kant, *CJ*, pp. 163–64.

24. Dahlhaus, *Esthetics of Music*, p. 73.

25. Kant, *CJ*, pp. 200–201.
26. Ibid., p. 173.
27. Cf. Herbert M. Schueller, "Immanuel Kant and the Aesthetics of Music," *Journal of Aesthetics and Art Criticism* 14 (1955–56): 218.
28. See Kant, *CJ*, pp. 193–95.
29. Rudolph H. Weingartner, "A Note on Kant's Artistic Interests," *Journal of Aesthetics and Art Criticism* 16 (1957–58): 262.
30. Again, we might question whether recognition of other sensuous features besides timbre might have made Kant less certain that the sensuous and the intersubjective are opposed. Certain rhythmically based features of music, for instance, might be thought to be sensuously appealing to human beings because of the physiology that we commonly possess. Clearly, however, this would be a very different ground for intersubjective experience than the one to which Kant appeals.
31. Schueller, "Immanuel Kant and the Aesthetics of Music," p. 222. See Dahlhaus, *Esthetics of Music*, pp. 29–31.
32. See Kant, *CJ*, p. 199, where he ranks instrumental music as the lowest art. This passage is discussed further below. See also Dahlhaus, *Esthetics of Music*, pp. 31–32. We should not conclude that Kant was merely influenced in this opinion by tradition and his traditionalist contemporaries. Kant was obviously aware of a number of the musical controversies of his era and willing to take stands on them. In arguing that merely agreeable instrumental music falls short of fine art, for example, he addresses the stylistic controversy between the classical and the rococo. Contending that the beauty of a work depends on its form, not its agreeableness or emotional evocativeness, Kant sides with the aesthetic ideal of the classicists.

    Kant's account of music is also informed by the *Affektenlehre*, the German doctrine that took the main aim of music to be the arousal of passions and emotions. By insisting on the primacy of form and the irrelevance of emotional expression to the aesthetic value of music, Kant rejects the dominant German view of music in his century. However, the *Affektenlehre*'s interpretation of music on the model of rhetoric is echoed in Kant's discussion. Kant divides the arts into three groups that correspond to the three elements of word, gesture, and tone in speech. Schueller sees this as an indication that Kant considers music an incomplete form of expression, which can be made complete only in conjunction with language. See Schueller, "Immanuel Kant and the Aesthetics of Music," pp. 223–24.
33. Kant, *CJ*, pp. 193–94. Dahlhaus finds Kant's position on the possibility of a mathematical basis for musical perception ironical. Kant, he argues, fails to recognize a potential grounding for music's universal appeal in his own conception of time. Time, as analyzed in the *Critique of Pure Reason*, is a form of intuition, governing the representation of objects for all human beings. Thus, "temporal proportioning of simple and complex sensations of

tone" should be the same for everyone. A universal mathematical basis for musical experience, which Kant sought but questioned in connection with the vibrations of intervals, can thus be found in the rhythms inherent in music. "While the 'mathematical form' of intervals may be only latent, that of rhythms is manifest." See Dahlhaus, *Esthetics of Music*, p. 33.

34. Kant, *CJ*, p. 228.

35. Kant develops several points of analogy between beauty and morality. See ibid., p. 229.

36. Ibid., pp. 196–97.

37. Ibid., pp. 198–99.

38. Schueller, "Immanuel Kant and the Aesthetics of Music," p. 218.

39. Geoffrey Payzant observes that "we have neither internal nor collateral evidence" that Hanslick was directly influenced by Kant (Hanslick, *On the Musically Beautiful*, pp. xv–xvi). Nonetheless, as Payzant himself argues, Hanslick's orientation resembles Kant's in a number of respects, perhaps owing to his father's familiarity with Kantian aesthetics or to his own awareness of other authors who were directly influenced by Kant (see ibid., pp. xiv–xvi).

40. Ibid., pp. 4, 30, 32.

41. Ibid., pp. 30–31.

42. In light of Hanslick's criticism of emotivist interpretations of music, it is striking that he admits "feeling" as an aspect of music's ideal content. We consider his concessions regarding emotion in the next chapter.

43. Hanslick, *On the Musically Beautiful*, p. 12.

44. Ibid., pp. 28–29.

45. Ibid., pp. 33, 35. Hanslick's obsession with "exactitude" is also evident in another argument: "Even if it were possible for feelings to be represented by music, the degree of beauty in the music would not correspond to the degree of exactitude with which the music represented them" (ibid., p. 21).

46. Ibid., p. 14.

47. Ibid., pp. 58–59.

48. Ibid., p. 3.

49. See Peter Kivy, "Something I've Always Wanted to Know about Hanslick," *Journal of Aesthetics and Art Criticism* 46/3 (Spring 1988): 416–17.

50. Hanslick, *On the Musically Beautiful*, pp. 9, 32.

51. Ibid., pp. 58–59.

52. I wish to thank Steven Feld for the information about Kaluli singing preferences. According to Feld, the Kaluli often sing in the presence of a waterfall, and the resonance that is produced is part of what they enjoy. See Feld, "Sound Structure as Social Structure," *Ethnomusicology* 28/3 (September 1984): 395. For an example of African uses of resonators, see James T. Koetting, "Africa/Ghana," in *Worlds of Music: An Introduction to the Music of the World's Peoples*, ed. Jeff Todd Titon et al. (New York: Macmillan, 1984),

p. 75. A high value is also placed on resonance in Indian music. The sitar, for instance, standardly includes a gourd resonator. See "Acoustics," in *The New Harvard Dictionary of Music*, ed. Don Randel (Cambridge: Harvard University Press, 1986), p. 12, which points out that the soundbox of the Western violin is a kind of resonator. See also "Resonator," in ibid., p. 696. On Javanese music, see Judith and Alton Becker, "A Musical Icon: Power and Meaning in Javanese Gamelan Music," in *The Sign in Music and Literature*, ed. Wendy Steiner (Austin: University of Texas Press, 1981), pp. 203–15.

53. This, I am afraid, is the effect of Scruton's endorsement of the "bourgeois" approach to music. See Roger Scruton, "Musical Understanding and Musical Culture," in *What Is Music? An Introduction to the Philosophy of Music*, ed. Philip Alperson (New York: Haven, 1988), pp. 349–58. Scruton contrasts his sense of *bourgeois* with that of most Marxists: "I am, if any sense attaches to the expression, a 'cultivated bourgeois music lover.' . . . I believe that the spirit of which I partake can and ought to be defended, that it is not, in any relevant sense, the spirit of a mere 'consumer,' and that, if it implies the existence of 'exploitation' (whether or not in the persuasively defined Marxian sense of that term), so much the better for exploitation. . . . it is a sign that we have not yet emerged into the happy era that Sparshott calls 'post-Marxist' that it is still necessary . . . to defend the great self-questioning 'bourgeois' culture from which our major musical achievements (not to speak of all our other achievements) derive." Bourgeois culture has made it possible for us to have the leisure to enjoy music as amateurs and a sense of being part of a cooperative community whose life music reflects and renews. I consider the ethnocentrism implicit in Scruton's discussion in Chapter 6.

54. Hanslick, *On the Musically Beautiful*, pp. 30–31.

55. Obviously, Kant is rather naive about the nature of the musical "recognitions" that his own theory presupposes. But he acknowledges empirical cultural differences in the appreciation of art, although he discusses these in connection with the "representational" arts, not music. In interpreting an artistic "representation," we make reference to concepts regarding what the work is to be, according to Kant. And such concepts, developed in particular contexts, can vary from place to place. Musical conceptions of what a work "is supposed to be" or "involve" do vary from culture to culture; and although Kant does not consider such cultural differences in connection with music, they could be described in terms of the "conceptual mediation" that he considers for the other arts.

56. See Hanslick, *On the Musically Beautiful*, p. 30.

57. Ibid., pp. xv–xvi.

58. Ibid., pp. 32, 58. See Gordon Epperson, *The Musical Symbol: A Study of the Philosophical Theory of Music* (Ames: Iowa State University Press, 1967),

p. 11. See also Dahlhaus, *Esthetics of Music*, pp. 53–54, and Malcolm Budd, *Music and the Emotions: The Philosophical Theories* (London: Routledge and Kegan Paul, 1985), p. 28.

59. See Hanslick, *On the Musically Beautiful*, p. 1. See also Epperson, *The Musical Symbol*, p. 110, and Dahlhaus, *Esthetics of Music*, p. 53. As Hanslick himself notes in the foreword to the eighth edition of *On the Musically Beautiful*, "I protest only against the erroneous involvement of feeling in science" (*On the Musically Beautiful*, p. xxii).

60. Cf. Timothy Binkley's criticism of Susanne Langer's excessive concern for understanding at the expense of imagination, in Timothy Binkley, "Langer's Logical and Ontological Modes," *Journal of Aesthetics and Art Criticism* 28/4 (Summer 1970): 455–64.

61. Steven Feld, "Communication, Music, and Speech about Music," *Yearbook for Traditional Music* 16 (1984): 8.

62. Ibid., p. 8; The Carla Bley Band, "European Tour 1977," ECM Records, 1978, Watts/8, #831-830-2.

63. Feld, "Communication, Music, and Speech about Music," p. 12.

64. Hanslick, *On the Musically Beautiful*, p. 30.

65. Ibid., p. 64.

Chapter 3

1. A similar basis for a connection between music and ethics is elaborated in the music theory of India, but the account of how music suggests emotion and of the relationship of emotion to ethics stands in marked contrast to the accounts generally offered by Western philosophy. See Rowell, *Thinking about Music*, pp. 202–10. See also Pravas Jivan Chaudhury, "The Aesthetic Attitude in Indian Aesthetics," *Journal of Aesthetics and Art Criticism*, Special Supplement (Fall, 1965): 145–49.

2. Plato, *Republic*, bk. III, 399–400, trans. Paul Shorey, in *The Collected Dialogues of Plato*, ed. Edith Hamilton and Huntington Cairns, Bollingen Series LXXI (Princeton: Princeton University Press, 1961), pp. 644–45.

3. Aristotle, *Politics*, bk. VIII, 1340, trans. Benjamin Jowett, in *The Basic Works of Aristotle*, ed. Richard McKeon (New York: Random House, 1941), p. 1311.

4. Socrates, in the *Republic*, expressly demands that music be composed in single modes and uncomplicated rhythms. See Plato, *Republic*, bk. III, 398–400. In addition, when Plato and Aristotle link emotions with specific modes, they are not pinpointing any structural element. A mode determines available pitches but does not dictate melody. A mode cannot properly be described as a structural element—instead it is the tonal matrix that designates the restrictions on elements that can properly be introduced into a melody. A given piece of music (whether described as a structure or not) might not even employ all the tones of a modal scale. Thus a correlation

between an emotion and a mode does not amount to a correlation between a part of a musical structure and an emotion. Cf. Harold Osborne: "The musical scale is part of the musical material which is to be enformed and not an element in the form of a composition." Harold Osborne, *Theory of Beauty* (London: Routledge and Kegan Paul, 1952), pp. 102–3.

5. Plato, however, suggests that the appropriateness of mode to emotion is inherent. See Plato, *Laws*, bk. II, 657. See also *Republic*, bk. III, 402c. For Hanslick's discussion of this matter, see Eduard Hanslick, *On the Musically Beautiful: A Contribution towards the Revision of the Aesthetics of Music*, trans. and ed. Geoffrey Payzant (Indianapolis: Hackett, 1986), p. 63.

6. There was one purely instrumental form in ancient Greek music, but for the most part Greek music consisted of texted vocal melody, either accompanied or unaccompanied. See "Greece," in *The New Harvard Dictionary of Music*, ed. Don Randel (Cambridge: Harvard University Press, 1986), p. 346. On Plato, see Carl Dahlhaus, *The Esthetics of Music*, trans. William Austin (Cambridge: Cambridge University Press, 1982), pp. 20–21. That the textual cue was seen as primary is suggested by the sequence in which Plato discusses the verbal and musical elements of poetry in the *Republic*. The Baroque *Camerata*'s style of opera developed in response to the ancients' subordination of musical elements to verbal ones. See Donald Jay Grout, *A History of Western Music*, shorter ed., rev. (New York: Norton, 1973), pp. 205ff.

7. Aristotle, *Politics*, bk. VIII, 1342a. The states of mind that Plato and Aristotle held music to arouse include a broader range of things than we would typically describe as "emotion." We would be more likely to describe the meanness and insolence that Plato associates with certain rhythms (in *Republic*, bk. III, 400), for instance, as external expressions of character than as emotions.

8. Neither Plato nor Aristotle would have conceived of a musical work constructed of diverse passages of different emotional content. Thus, once one recognized the dominant emotional content of a piece of music, one recognized the emotional content of all its "passages" as well.

Doubt as to whether listeners necessarily concur in their emotional responses to music is a modern problem, linked to modern concern with the private subject. This is an important point, to which we return below; for the modern presupposition that the intersubjectivity of musical experience is suspect unless demonstrated is not the historical or cross-cultural norm.

9. See Dahlhaus, *Esthetics of Music*, pp. 17–18.

10. See Augustine, *De Musica*, in *Philosophies of Art and Beauty: Selected Readings in Aesthetics from Plato to Heidegger*, ed. Albert Hofstadter and Richard Kuhns (Chicago: University of Chicago Press, 1964), pp. 189–90.

11. Augustine, *Confessions*, bk. II, chap. 33, trans. William Watts, cited in

Source Readings in Music History: Antiquity and the Middle Ages, ed. Oliver Strunk (New York: Norton, 1965), p. 74.

12. Ibid.

13. René Descartes, cited in "Aesthetics," in *New Harvard Dictionary of Music*, ed. Randel, p. 15.

14. René Descartes, *Compendium of Music*, trans. Walter Robert (Rome: American Institute of Musicology, 1961), pp. 11–13.

15. Lewis Rowell, *Thinking about Music: An Introduction to the Philosophy of Music* (Amherst: University of Massachusetts Press, 1983), p. 104.

16. See Peter Kivy, *The Corded Shell: Reflections on Musical Expression* (Princeton: Princeton University Press, 1980), p. 35.

17. *Musical Aesthetics: A Historical Reader*, ed. Edward A. Lippman, vol. I: *From Antiquity to the Eighteenth Century* (New York: Pendragon, 1986), p. 121. See Dahlhaus, *Estetics of Music*, pp. 17–18.

18. Charles Batteaux, "Les Beaux arts reduits à un même principe" (1743), in *Musical Aesthetics*, ed. Lippman, vol. I, p. 262.

19. Ibid., pp. 265–66.

20. Ibid., pp. 266–67. Rousseau similarly defended the view that music can imitate emotions because it is a natural emotional language. According to Rousseau, music imitates the "original language" of primeval times. Passionately inflected, this ancestor of both music and modern language survives only vestigially in the latter. The tonal expression of primitive passions remains prominent in our music, however. And this similarity explains why music arouses such powerful emotion in listeners. This theory, which Kivy terms "the 'speech theory' of the origin of music," included among its adherents Richard Wagner and Herbert Spencer as well as Rousseau. See Dahlhaus, *Estetics of Music*, p. 21, and Kivy, *Corded Shell*, pp. 18–26. Edmund Gurney, a relatively recent arousal theorist, also takes this speech theory as his point of departure. See Edmund Gurney, *The Power of Sound* (London: Smith, Elder, 1880), pp. 113–26. See also Malcolm Budd's discussion of Gurney in *Music and the Emotions: The Philosophical Theories* (London: Routledge and Kegan Paul, 1985), pp. 52–75.

21. Most eighteenth-century theorists considered vocal music to be the paradigm case. Even Batteaux believed that vocal music represented the animated utterances of feeling most clearly. But unlike Rousseau, who could make little sense of instrumental music, Batteaux thought that instrumental music, too, could imitate such utterances. Rousseau considered the intersubjective basis of musical imitation to be innately recognized inflections of human speech, inflections that were conspicuous in vocal music. See Dahlhaus, *Estetics of Music*, p. 21. Belief in the objectivity of musical imitations, together with an interest in defending the intelligibility of instrumental music, led Batteaux to defend stylization and idealization in emotional

portrayal despite his "natural language" sentiments. He reconciled these views by claiming that the intersubjective accessibility of music's natural language was enhanced by stylized formulas. See Jean Jacques Rousseau, "Essai sur l'origine des langues" (1753), chap. XII, in *Musical Aesthetics*, ed. Lippman, vol. I, pp. 323–27.

22. See Dahlhaus, *Esthetics of Music*, p. 21.

23. Ibid., p. 22.

24. It may seem odd to say that Hanslick admits that structural defenses of the expressionist theory are legitimate. Certainly Hanslick does not admit that expressionism has any valid defense. But he himself allows that structural features of music—"tonally moving forms"—are reminiscent of emotion and can be utilized by the composer to provoke such reminiscences. These reminiscences do not, however, pinpoint specific emotions. Hanslick interprets expressionist theory as asserting that specific emotions are expressed by music; thus he argues that the emotional reminiscences he acknowledges do not vindicate the expressionist case. As Langer notes, however, Hanslick gives away more than he realizes in allowing that music can suggest emotions to our minds, and can do so through structural features that can be universally recognized by listeners. See Susanne K. Langer, *Philosophy in a New Key: A Study in the Symbolism of Reason, Rite, and Art*, 3d ed. (Cambridge: Harvard University Press, 1957), p. 239.

25. Even when national folk idioms regained popularity in the music of the nineteenth century, this did not reflect a return to interest in contextual ethos; instead, it reflected an internationalistic trend, for the allusions to the folk idioms of various nations were part of a universal musical vocabulary, recognizable to listeners across Europe. See Grout, *History of Western Music*, p. 372.

26. See ibid., p. 368. See also G. W. F. Hegel, *Aesthetics*, trans. T. M. Knox, 2 vols. (Oxford: Oxford University Press, 1975), vol. II, chap. II, and Arthur Schopenhauer, *The World as Will and Representation*, trans. E. F. J. Payne (New York: Dover, 1969), vol. I, p. 261.

27. See Alan David Auerbach, *The Ideas of Richard Wagner: An Examination and Analysis of His Major Aesthetic, Political, Economic, Social, and Religious Thoughts*, rev. ed. (Lanham, Md.: University Press of America, 1988), p. 20.

28. The musical theory of Schopenhauer, who significantly influenced Wagner, might be similarly described.

29. See Auerbach, *Ideas of Richard Wagner*, p. 34.

30. Wagner's doctrine of the composer-priest is relevant to our later discussion of the view that music can be a vehicle for instilling virtue. Wagner is often taken as a counterexample, for his musical talent was thoroughly compatible with what strikes many as personal vice.

31. Richard Wagner, "'Music of the Future,'" in *Three Wagner Essays*, trans. Robert L. Jacobs (London: Eulenburg, 1979), p. 44, and *Opera and Drama*,

in *Richard Wagner's Prose Works*, trans. and ed. William Ashton Ellis, vol. 2, (New York: Broude Brothers, 1893), p. 109.

32. See "Expressionism," in *New Harvard Dictionary of Music*, ed. Randel, pp. 295–96.
33. Hanslick, *On the Musically Beautiful*, pp. xi, xvi.
34. Ibid., p. 10.
35. Ibid., pp. 9, 11.
36. Ibid., pp. 3–5, 7.
37. Ibid., p. 7. Hanslick considers the possible counterargument that physiology might provide a scientific basis for establishing links between music and arousal. He acknowledges the contribution of physiological factors to musically aroused emotion, but he does not believe that a physiological account of musical listening is sufficient to account for the listener's emotions. See ibid., pp. 55–56. The necessary connections that the science of physiology establishes are not the ones that "scientific" aesthetics seeks. Nor are the sensations that physiology investigates sufficiently linked to emotion to provide a scientific interpretation even of "emotional" arousal. Emotions involve the mental representations of objects, and these representations are unavailable to scientific scrutiny.
38. Ibid., p. xxii.
39. Ibid., p. 42.
40. Ibid., p. 37.
41. Ibid., p. 49.
42. Ibid., p. 61.
43. Budd, *Music and the Emotions*, p. 28.
44. Ibid., p. 25.

Chapter 4

1. Peter Kivy, "How Music Moves," in *What Is Music?: An Introduction to the Philosophy of Music*, ed. Philip Alperson (New York: Haven, 1988), p. 153.
2. Susanne K. Langer, *Philosophy in a New Key: A Study in the Symbolism of Reason, Rite, and Art*, 3d ed. (Cambridge: Harvard University Press, 1957), pp. 204–45.
3. Ibid., p. 225.
4. Ibid., pp. 233–35 (emphasis in the original).
5. Ibid., pp. 208, 218–22 (emphasis in the original).
6. On Hanslick, see ibid., pp. 224ff. Langer (ibid., p. 226) discusses evidence for the "usefulness of so-called musical 'dynamics' to describe the forms of mental life." See also her itemization of principles of musical perception derived from Dr. Kurt Huber's experiments, which she considers evidence for music's power to represent feeling by means of perceived dynamics (ibid., pp. 229–31).

7. Ibid., pp. 224–26, 238 (emphasis in the original).
8. Ibid., pp. 222, 240–41 (emphasis in the original).
9. Ibid., p. 243 (emphasis in the original).
10. See Susanne K. Langer, *Feeling and Form: A Theory of Art* (New York: Scribner, 1953), pp. 104–19.
11. See Langer, *Philosophy in a New Key*, pp. 240–44.
12. Malcolm Budd, *Music and the Emotions: The Philosophical Theories* (London: Routledge and Kegan Paul, 1985), pp. 115–16.
13. For a discussion and criticism of Langer's cognitive bias in her approach to music, see Timothy Binkley, "Langer's Logical and Ontological Modes," *Journal of Aesthetics and Art Criticism* 28/4 (Summer 1970): 455–64.
14. See Carl Dahlhaus, *The Esthetics of Music*, trans. William Austin (Cambridge: Cambridge University Press, 1982), p. 19. Kivy also discusses a range of such theories. See Peter Kivy, *The Corded Shell: Reflections on Musical Expression* (Princeton: Princeton University Press, 1980), pp. 35–45. Many versions of this theory are more appropriately classified as arousal theories than as imitation theories. A few, however, observe a similarity between elements of music and the physical condition involved in an emotional experience without insisting that arousal necessarily be involved. Hamburg theorist and composer Johann Mattheson, for example, in *Der vollkommene Capellmeister*, focuses on such similarity when he argues that expanded intervals can best *express* joy. See Hans Lenneberg, "Johann Mattheson on Affect and Rhetoric in Music," *Journal of Music Theory* 2 (1958): 51–52.
15. Deryck Cooke, *The Languages of Music* (London: Oxford University Press, 1959). Cooke himself does not opt for either imitation, arousal, or expression theory. Instead, he embraces all at once, claiming that musical form is the means through which a composer communicates a "general but clearly defined attitude toward existence" to the listener (ibid., p. 212), and that the resemblance between physiologically based emotional states and our responses to musical intervals and rhythms is the basis of the emotional "language" of tonal music.
16. Budd, *Music and the Emotions*, p. 114.
17. Langer, *Philosophy in a New Key*, p. 210.
18. Ibid., p. 212 (emphasis in the original).
19. See, for example, John Dewey, *Art as Experience*, excerpted in *Philosophies of Art and Beauty: Selected Readings in Aesthetics from Plato to Heidegger*, ed. Albert Hofstadter and Richard Kuhns (Chicago: University of Chicago Press, 1964), pp. 586–92.
20. Langer, *Philosophy in a New Key*, p. 222. (emphasis in the original).
21. Edward Bullough, "'Psychical Distance' as a Factor in Art and as an Aesthetic Principle," *British Journal of Psychology* 5 (1912–13): 91.
22. See Leonard B. Meyer, *Emotion and Meaning in Music* (Chicago: University

of Chicago Press, 1956), p. 19 (hereafter cited as *EMM*). Analysis demands historical sensitivity, in Meyer's view. Thus, it would be unfair to claim that he thinks that arousal can be directly read from the score. Moreover, Meyer acknowledges the supreme importance of association in our emotional response to music. This emphasis on association is in tension with the prominence given to the syntactic–structural orientation of his basic theory of music in relation to the emotions, as we see below.

23. Ibid., p. 14.
24. I wish to thank Peter V. Czipott for this point.
25. Meyer, *EMM*, pp. 35, 39.
26. Ibid., p. 40.
27. Ibid., pp. 19, 32–35.
28. Ibid., pp. 31–32.
29. Ibid., pp. 31–32, 35. Obviously, Meyer's theory assumes that musical "works" are the appropriate focus of a theory of music and emotion. One problem with Meyer's qualification regarding stylistic conventions is that such conventions change constantly. "Mastery" of these conventions is thus, of necessity, relative. Meyer simply accepts this consequence of his theory.
30. Meyer acknowledges many factors external to the musical work that modify the listener's sense of expectation with respect to a given progression. See, for example, ibid., pp. 60–73.
31. Ibid., pp. 259–60.
32. Ibid., p. 260.
33. Ibid., p. 262.
34. Ibid.
35. Ibid., pp. 72ff.
36. Ibid., p. 65.
37. See ibid., p. 72. Cf. Joseph Margolis, "On the Semiotics of Music," in *What Is Music?* ed. Alperson, p. 232. Margolis argues that Meyer reverts to a hierarchy of rule over practice.
38. See Meyer, *EMM*, pp. 234, 254.
39. Susan Walton, "Music of the Javanese Gamelan: Aesthetics and Mysticism," paper delivered at the American Society for Aesthetics meeting, Vancouver, October 1988, p. 4. See also Ernst Heins, "Indonesia, II: Instrumental Ensembles," in *The New Grove Dictionary of Music and Musicians*, ed. Stanley Sadie (New York: Macmillan, 1980), vol. 9, pp. 173–78.
40. Walton, "Music of the Javanese Gamelan," pp. 12, 15–16.
41. Meyer, *EMM*, p. 239.
42. See Leonard B. Meyer, "Some Remarks on Value and Greatness in Music," in *Music, the Arts, and Ideas: Patterns and Predictions in Twentieth-Century Culture* (Chicago: University of Chicago Press, 1967), pp. 32–33; *EMM*, p. 239.
43. Meyer, "Value and Greatness," pp. 38–39.

44. Ibid., p. 39.
45. See Kivy, *Corded Shell*. See also Kivy, "How Music Moves."
46. Kivy, *Corded Shell*, pp. 12, 49.
47. Kivy, however, takes pains to distinguish his view from representation views and, in particular, from Langer's theory of isomorphism. See ibid., pp. 60–66.
48. Ibid., pp. 54–55.
49. Ibid., pp. 75–77.
50. Ibid., p. 82.
51. See Anthony Newcomb, "Sound and Feeling," *Critical Inquiry* 10 (June 1984): 618, where Newcomb considers whether Kivy is vulnerable to Howard's objection. Howard's original objection to isomorphic theories is made in Vernon A. Howard, "On Musical Expression," *British Journal of Aesthetics* 11/3 (Summer 1971): 271–73.
52. See Kivy, *Corded Shell*, pp. 57–59.
53. See Kivy, "How Music Moves," p. 149.
54. Cf. Newcomb, "Sound and Feeling," pp. 617–18. Newcomb notes that Kivy interprets music as "gestures in sound." Jenefer Robinson discusses the atomism of Kivy's account in "The Expression and Arousal of Emotion by Music," paper delivered at the American Society for Aesthetics meeting, New York, October 1989.
55. Kivy, *Corded Shell*, pp. 50–51.
56. Ibid., p. 12. See Dewey, *Art as Experience*, excerpted in *Philosophies of Art and Beauty*, ed. Hofstadter and Kuhns, pp. 596–632.
57. Cf. Alfred Schutz, "Making Music Together: A Study in Social Relationship," in *Symbolic Anthropology: A Reader in the Study of Symbols and Meanings*, ed. Janet L. Dolgin, David S. Kemnitzer, and David M. Schneider (New York: Columbia University Press, 1977), pp. 116–19.
58. Kivy, "How Music Moves," pp. 157–58.
59. Ibid., pp. 150–51.
60. See Kendall Walton's discussion of emotion elicited through imaginative introspection in response to music, in Kendall L. Walton, "What Is Abstract about the Art of Music?" *Journal of Aesthetics and Art Criticism* 46/3 (Spring 1988): 351–64.
61. Meyer, *EMM*, pp. 77, 79.
62. See James Bogan, "Finding an Audience," *Pragmatics* 1/2 (1987): 35–65.
63. Stephen Davies, "The Expression of Emotion in Music," *Mind* 89/353 (January 1980): 68. Analyzing musically suggested emotions in terms of emotion-characteristics that resemble those in human behavior, Davies argues that "only those emotions which may be naturally expressed in behavior can be mirrored by emotion-characteristics in appearances, and only these same emotions can be aesthetic emotional responses to the emotions expressed

in music" (ibid., p. 85). The first clause in this passage strikes me as plausible, at least so long as one is concerned only with emotions that are being expressed or represented by the music. However, I would not withhold the term *aesthetic* from emotions that are experienced in connection with particular musical performances and that arise from characteristics of the performances not reflected in the musical structure.

64. Ibid., pp. 83–84.
65. It is well known that a good performer can be "convincing" in conveying emotion that is far removed from his or her actual state of mind. A talented performer can, for example, convey great joy through music even when personally depressed. This phenomenon does not undercut my point, but instead supports it. In such a case, the performer must intend to convey the music's emotional content with an unusual effort of will. When such a performer is convincing, we take the emotion so conveyed to be "sincere," and I think this assessment is not inappropriate.
66. Of course, Hanslick does not say that it is. But he obviously considers specification of detailed links between music and emotion to be the only kind of analysis that would really be intellectually penetrating. I am suggesting here that such an analysis, even if one could be constructed, would not necessarily provide the best access to emotional content, and might even miss the forest for the trees.
67. Steven Feld, "Communication, Music, and Speech about Music," *Yearbook for Traditional Music* 16 (1984): 13–14.

Chapter 5

1. See Bruno Nettl, *The Study of Ethnomusicology: Twenty-nine Issues and Concepts* (Urbana: University of Illinois Press, 1983), p. 149, and Alan P. Merriam, *The Anthropology of Music* (Evanston: Northwestern University Press, 1964), p. 218; see also ibid., p. 216: "It is evident that music is used as accompaniment to or part of almost every human activity."
2. Donald N. Ferguson, *Music as Metaphor: The Elements of Expression* (Westport, Conn.: Greenwood, 1960), p. 5.
3. Again, I am assuming that we are considering "engaged" musical experience, in which the listener is paying attention to the music and in which music is perceived as a pleasant, or at least not abrasive, phenomenon.
4. Chou Tun-yi, "Penetrating the Book of Changes" (*T'ung-shu*), chap. 19, "Music—Part 3," in *A Source Book in Chinese Philosophy*, ed. Wing-tsit Chan (Princeton: Princeton University Press, 1963), p. 473.
5. Plato, *Republic*, bk. III, 401–2, trans. Paul Shorey, in *The Collected Dialogues of Plato*, ed. Edith Hamilton and Huntington Cairns, Bollingen Series LXXI (Princeton: Princeton University Press, 1961), p. 646.

6. Aristotle, *Politics*, bk. VIII, chap. 5, 1340b, trans. Benjamin Jowett, in *The Basic Works of Aristotle*, ed. Richard McKeon (New York: Random House, 1941), p. 1312.

7. Cf. Immanuel Kant, *Groundwork of the Metaphysics of Morals*, trans. H. J. Paton (New York: Harper and Row, 1963).

8. Eduard Hanslick, *On the Musically Beautiful: A Contribution towards the Revision of the Aesthetics of Music*, trans. and ed. Geoffrey Payzant (Indianapolis: Hackett, 1986), p. 61.

9. Aristotle, *Politics*, bk. VIII, chap. 5, 1339b–1340a, trans. Jowett, pp. 1310–11.

10. Ibid., chap. 7, 1340b, trans. Jowett, p. 1313.

11. Friedrich Nietzsche, *The Birth of Tragedy and The Case of Wagner*, trans. Walter Kaufmann (New York: Random House, 1967), p. 40, and *Twilight of the Idols*, in *The Portable Nietzsche*, trans. Walter Kaufmann (New York: Penguin, 1968), p. 520.

12. *The Accidental Tourist*, Warner Brothers, 1988; based on Anne Tyler, *The Accidental Tourist* (New York: Knopf, 1985).

13. Roger Scruton, "Musical Understanding and Musical Culture," in *What Is Music? An Introduction to the Philosophy of Music*, ed. Philip Alperson (New York: Haven, 1988), p. 357.

14. Lewis Rowell, "Thinking Time and Thinking about Time in Indian Music," *Communication and Cognition* 19/2 (1986): 233. See also Stephen M. Slawek, "Popular *Kīrtan* in Benares: Some 'Great' Aspects of a Little Tradition," *Ethnomusicology* 32/2 (Spring/Summer 1988): 82–85.

15. Francis Sparshott, "Aesthetics of Music: Limits and Grounds," in *What Is Music?* ed. Alperson, p. 47.

16. Arthur Schopenhauer, *The World as Will and Representation*, trans. E. F. J. Payne (New York: Dover, 1969), vol. I, p. 259. Jenefer Robinson considers examples of music representing animate behavior in examples of musical mimicry in "Music as a Representational Art," in *What Is Music?* ed. Alperson, pp. 178ff.

17. Spike Lee's film *Do the Right Thing* (A Spike Lee Joint Production, 1989) portrays the use of music as a reinforcement to agressive movements, both in dance and in everyday behavior. This use of music to reinforce aggressive activity or styles of movement is important, and it deserves discussion. I consider it in Chapter 6 in connection with arguments that music can be ethically harmful. For the moment, it should be observed that although such "listening" (to the extent that the "listener" is actually attending to the music) involves the kind of openness to the music's stimulation that I have been discussing, in these cases the listener already knows what type of response the music will call for. The music is selected with its potential for fortifying aggression in mind. This is a very different case from that of the Parisian rioters at the Stravinsky performance, who had no prior expec-

tation of what the music would involve, as their surprise and consequent anger revealed.

18. Rowell notes a wide range of sensuous and formal values that traditionally play a role in the evaluation of Western classical music. See Rowell, *Thinking about Music*, pp. 150–89.

19. Donald Callen, "Transfiguring Emotions in Music," *Grazer Philosophische Studien* 19 (1983): 88.

20. Nietzsche, discussing Friedrich Schiller, comments on the "musical mood" that is productive for the playwright. See Nietzsche, *The Birth of Tragedy*, p. 49. Hanslick himself refers to an "inner singing" as the incentive that moves the gifted composer to write music. See Hanslick, *On the Musically Beautiful*, p. 26.

21. Sparshott, "Aesthetics of Music," p. 75.

22. The passivity that recording technology has made possible strikes William Ivey, director of the Country Music Foundation, as cause for alarm: "With this exposure, this immersion, in recorded music, it comes as little surprise that the audience is jaded, bored, and harder and harder to 'reach.' Music has taken on an almost utilitarian definition: it is *for* something—for relaxing, for stimulating, for dancing, for background. Music in such a context is always something subordinate, something supportive of a mood or activity. As we, the audience, grow more and more at home with music behind our daily routines, our ability to listen hard—to focus our every nerve upon a passage or phrase—has become diminished." See William Ivey, "Recordings and the Audience for the Regional and Ethnic Musics of the United States," in *The Phonograph and Our Musical Life: Proceedings of a Centennial Conference, 7–10 December 1977*, ed. H. Wiley Hitchcock, I.S.A.M. Monograph no. 14 (New York: Institute for Studies in American Music, Brooklyn College of the City University of New York, 1980), p. 10. See also Allan Miller's comments in response to Jane Jarvis, "Notes on Muzak," in ibid., p. 18.

23. Cf. Christopher Small, *Music, Society, Education* (London: Calder, 1977), pp. 170–71.

24. Merriam, *Anthropology of Music*, p. 227.

25. A. R. Radcliffe-Brown, *The Andaman Islanders* (Glencoe, Ill.: Free Press, 1948), p. 252.

26. Alfred Schutz, "Making Music Together: A Study in Social Relationship," in *Symbolic Anthropology: A Reader in the Study of Symbols and Meanings*, ed. Janet L. Dolgin, David S. Kemnitzer, and David M. Schneider (New York: Columbia University Press, 1977), pp. 114, 118.

27. Victor Zuckerkandl, *Sound and Symbol: Music and the External World*, trans. Willard R. Trask, Bollingen Series XLIV (Princeton: Princeton University Press, 1956), p. 274.

28. Ibid., pp. 1, 4, 291.

29. Merriam, *Anthropology of Music*, p. 225.
30. Cf. Peter Singer, *The Expanding Circle: Ethics and Sociobiology* (New York: New American Library, 1981), pp. 111–24.
31. John Stuart Mill, *Utilitarianism*, ed. Oskar Piest (Indianapolis: Bobbs-Merrill, 1957), pp. 40, 42–43.
32. Schopenhauer, *World as Will and Representation*, vol. I, p. 374.
33. Friedrich Schiller, *On the Aesthetic Education of Man*, trans. Reginald Snell (New York: Ungar, 1954), p. 138.
34. *Amadeus*, Saul Zaentz Film Company, 1984; based on Peter Shaffer, *Amadeus* (New York: Harper and Row, 1981).
35. While I focus here on music's ability to suggest our shared humanity, I think that our sensitivity to nonhuman beings is also likely to be enhanced through our listening experience. The delight we take in music, coupled with our tendency to think of it as an encounter with the living world, enables music to incite us to appreciation of the entire animate world.
36. Hsün Tzu, *Basic Writings*, trans. Burton Watson (New York: Columbia University Press, 1964), p. 112. Hsün Tzu puns here, for the same written character is used for the words *yueh* (music) and *lo* (joy).
37. I agree with Schopenhauer's description of aesthetic experience to the extent that he describes it as "ego-less." I disagree, however, with his adoption of the Kantian requirement that aesthetic experience be disinterested (or "will-less," in Schopenhauer's terminology). See Schopenhauer, *World as Will and Representation*, vol. I, pp. 178–81.

Chapter 6

1. Steven Feld, "Communication, Music, and Speech about Music," *Yearbook for Traditional Music* 16 (1984): 14.
2. Susanne K. Langer, *Feeling and Form: A Theory of Art* (New York: Scribner, 1953), pp. 112–13.
3. Leonard B. Meyer, *Music, the Arts, and Ideas: Patterns and Predictions in Twentieth-century Culture* (Chicago: University of Chicago Press, 1967), p. 26.
4. Norman Cazden, "Musical Consonance and Dissonance: A Cultural Criterion," *Journal of Aesthetics and Art Criticism* 4/1 (September 1945): 5.
5. Cf. Friedrich Nietzsche's discussion of musical dissonance in *The Birth of Tragedy and The Case of Wagner*, trans. Walter Kaufmann (New York: Random House, 1967), pp. 141–42. Nietzsche argues that dissonance, far from being unpleasant, is intrinsically pleasurable. At the same time, it induces a longing to transcend it. This dual response provoked by dissonance makes it comparable to what Nietzsche understood as the healthy response to tragedy: "Is it not possible that by calling to our aid the musical relation of dissonance we may meanwhile have made the difficult problem of the

tragic effect much easier? For we now understand what it means to wish to see tragedy and at the same time to long to get beyond all seeing: referring to the artistically employed dissonances, we should have to characterize the corresponding state by saying that we desire to hear and at the same time long to get beyond all hearing."

6. Donald N. Ferguson, *Music as Metaphor: The Elements of Expression* (Westport, Conn.: Greenwood, 1960), pp. 185–86.

7. John Stuart Mill, *Utilitarianism*, ed. Oskar Piest (Indianapolis: Bobbs-Merrill, 1957), p. 17.

8. Victor Zuckerkandl, *Sound and Symbol: Music and the External World*, trans. Willard R. Trask, Bollingen Series XLIV (Princeton: Princeton University Press, 1956), pp. 241–42.

9. See Lewis Rowell, "Thinking Time and Thinking about Time in Indian Music," *Communication and Cognition* 19/2 (1986): 229–40; G. B. Mohna Thampi, " 'Rasa' as Aesthetic Experience," *Journal of Aesthetics and Art Criticism* 24/1 (Fall 1965): 75–80; Pravas Jivan Chaudhury, "The Aesthetic Attitude in Indian Aesthetics," ibid., pp. 145–49; *Yo Ki* (Record of Music), in *The Sacred Books of China*, trans. James Legge, pt. IV: *The Li Ki*, vols XI–XLVI (Delhi: Motilal Banarsidass, 1968), bk. VIII, chap. 2, p. 114; Fung Yu-Lan, *A History of Chinese Philosophy*, trans. Derk Bodde (Princeton: Princeton University Press, 1953), vol. II, p. 118. The Confucians made extensive correlations between musical elements and basic natural principles, aspects of social organization, and human characteristics. For further consideration of the prominence of music in Confucian discussions, see Kathleen Higgins, "Music in Confucian and Neo-Confucian Philosophy," *International Philosophical Quarterly* 20/4 (December 1980): 433–51. Cf. Stephen M. Slawek, "Popular *Kīrtan* in Benares: Some 'Great' Aspects of a Little Tradition," *Ethnomusicology* 32/2 (Spring/Summer 1988): 81–82.

10. Eugen Herrigel, *Zen in the Art of Archery*, trans. R. F. C. Hull (New York: Random House, 1953), p. 34.

11. Friedrich Nietzsche, *Twilight of the Idols*, in *The Portable Nietzsche*, trans. Walter Kaufmann (New York: Penguin, 1968), p. 512.

12. Edmund Leach, *Political Systems of Highland Burma: A Study of Kachin Social Structure* (London: Athlone, 1977), p. 12. See Henry Kingsbury's discussion in *Music, Talent, and Performance: A Conservatory Cultural System* (Philadelphia: Temple University Press, 1988), p. 10.

13. A. R. Radcliffe-Brown, *Structure and Function in Primitive Society* (Glencoe, Ill.: Free Press, 1952), p. 181.

14. John Shepherd, "The Musical Coding of Ideologies," in John Shepherd et al., *Whose Music? A Sociology of Musical Languages* (New Brunswick: Transaction, 1977), pp. 107–8.

15. Rose Rosengard Subotnik, "The Challenge of Contemporary Music," in *What Is Music? An Introduction to the Philosophy of Music*, ed. Philip Alper-

son (New York: Haven, 1988), pp. 372, 390; Susan McClary, in a letter cited by Leo Treitler in his talk "Feminist Criticism and Musicology," presented to the Department of Music, The University of Texas at Austin, March 3, 1989.

16. Roger Scruton, "Musical Understanding and Musical Culture," in *What Is Music?* ed. Alperson, pp. 353–54.

17. Jacques Attali, *Noise: The Political Economy of Music*, trans. Brian Massumi (Minneapolis: University of Minnesota Press, 1985), pp. 4, 11.

18. Scruton, "Musical Understanding and Musical Culture," pp. 356–57.

19. Alan Lomax, "Song Structure and Social Structure," in *Readings in Ethnomusicology*, ed. David P. McAllester (New York: Johnson Reprints, 1971), pp. 227–29.

20. Ibid., pp. 237–40.

21. Michael (Babatunde) Olatunji, "Baba Jinde," on *Olatunji! Drums of Passion*, Columbia, #8210, 1960; David Byrne, "Women vs. Men," on *Rei Momo*, Luka Bop/Sire Record Company, #9-25990-4, 1989.

22. I am thinking here of cases in which music suggests distinct characters. Often such music indicates one character as the protagonist (as in Moussorgsky's *Pictures at an Exhibition*, Berlioz's *Symphonie Fantastique*, and Stravinsky's *Petrushka*). But music that emphasizes multiple voices in contrapuntal relationships (much of Bach's music, for example) engages our empathy in connection with each of the voices (so long as they are distinct). And one might even consider the progressive statements of the theme in the final movement of Beethoven's Ninth Symphony to suggest separate characters (or groups of characters) with whom we sequentially identify. My thanks to Wanda Therese Farah for drawing my attention to some of the ways in which we identify distinctive "behavior" in music with distinctive "characters." She discusses musical characters and behavior in "The Principle of Counterpoint and Its Expression in Music, Dance, and Cinema," Ph.D. dissertation, University of Texas at Austin, 1985.

23. Stokely Carmichael, "Stokely Carmichael Explains Black Power to a Black Audience in Detroit," in *BlackAmerican Literature, 1760–Present*, ed. Ruth Miller (Beverly Hills, Calif.: Macmillan, 1971), p. 690.

24. Ibid., p. 692.

25. Martin Luther King, Jr., March on Washington speech, 28 August 1963, cited in Stephen B. Oates, *Let the Trumpet Sound: The Life of Martin Luther King, Jr.* (New York: Harper & Row, 1982), p. 26.

26. Carmichael, "Stokely Carmichael Explains Black Power," p. 695.

27. Ernst Bloch, like Attali, considers music to be valuable as a means of intuiting future possibilities. See Ernst Bloch, "The Exceeding of Limits and the World of Man at Its Most Richly Intense in Music," in *Essays on the Philosophy of Music*, trans. Peter Palmer (Cambridge: Cambridge University Press, 1985), pp. 195–243.

28. John Dewey, *Art as Experience*, excerpted in *Philosophies of Art and Beauty: Selected Readings in Aesthetics from Plato to Heidegger*, ed. Albert Hofstadter and Richard Kuhns (Chicago: University of Chicago Press, 1976), p. 646.

29. LeRoi Jones, "A Jazz Great: John Coltrane" (1963), in *Black Music* (New York: Morrow, 1967), p. 57.

30. Charles Keil, *Urban Blues* (Chicago: University of Chicago Press, 1966), pp. 33–34.

31. Leroy Ostransky, *The Anatomy of Jazz* (Seattle: University of Washington Press, 1960), p. 77; Gary Giddins, *Riding on a Blue Note: Jazz and American Pop* (New York: Oxford University Press, 1981), p. vii, quoting a liner note by Hughes Panassie.

32. LeRoi Jones, "Jazz and the White Critic" (1963), in *Black Music*, p. 19; Giddins, *Riding on a Blue Note*, p. xii; LeRoi Jones, "Coltrane Live at Birdland" (1964), in *Black Music*, p. 67.

33. LeRoi Jones, "The Jazz Avant-Garde" (1961), in *Black Music*, pp. 72–73.

34. Ostransky, *Anatomy of Jazz*, p. 83.

35. Meyer, *Music, the Arts, and Ideas*, p. 33.

36. See Eric Werner, "If I Speak in the Tongues of Men. . . . St. Paul's Attitude toward Music," in *Three Ages of Musical Thought: Essays on Ethics and Aesthetics* (New York: Da Capo, 1981), pp. 113–18.

    Sufi Qawwali singing is a marked exception to the typical Islamic practice. For a discussion of this ecstatic form of religious music, see Regula Burckhardt Qureshi, "Qawwali: Making the Music Happen in the Sufi Assembly," *Asian Music* 18/2 (Spring/Summer 1987): 118–57.

37. Linda Martin and Kerry Segrave, *Anti-Rock: The Opposition to Rock 'n' Roll* (Hamden, Conn.: Archon, 1988), p. 299. This book chronicles the history of opposition to rock music, usually on moral grounds. In all fairness, I should note that Tipper Gore objects to the lyrics more than to rock's amenity to pathological listening. But many who object to the lyrics also object to rock's mode of appeal, which depends on its heavily rhythmic character.

38. Bryan Ferry, "More Than This," on Roxy Music, *Avalon*, Warner Brothers, #7599-23686-1, 1982.

39. Qawwali music is a striking example.

40. Frank Zappa, "Cheap Thrills," *Cruising with Ruben and the Jets*, MGM/Verve cs D4-74209, 1968; Marty Balin, "Miracles," on Jefferson Starship, *Red Octopus*, Grunt Records (RCA), #BLF1-0099, 1975.

41. Allan Bloom, *The Closing of the American Mind* (New York: Simon and Schuster, 1987), pp. 72, 79–80.

42. George Michael, "I Want Your Sex," on *Faith*, Columbia Records, #0-7464-40867-1, 1987.

43. I wish to thank Richard C. McKim for first bringing this aspect of the video phenomenon to my attention.

44. Theodor W. Adorno, *Introduction to the Sociology of Music*, trans. E. B. Ashton (New York: Continuum, 1976), p. 42. See also Bloom, *Closing of the American Mind*, p. 105.

45. Friedrich Schiller, *On the Aesthetic Education of Man, in a Series of Letters*, trans. Reginald Snell (New York: Ungar, 1954), pp. 83–84.

Chapter 7

1. Edmund L. Pincoffs, *Quandaries and Virtues: Against Reductivism in Ethics* (Lawrence: University Press of Kansas, 1986).

2. Hubert Dreyfuss, "Artificial Intelligence vs. Human Intelligence," paper delivered at the Conference on Philosophy and the Human Future, St. John's College, Cambridge University, August 1989.

3. See, for example, Martha C. Nussbaum, "'Finely Aware and Richly Responsible': Moral Attention and the Moral Task of Literature," *Journal of Philosophy* 82/10 (October 1985): 516–29.

4. Martha C. Nussbaum, *The Fragility of Goodness: Luck and Ethics in Greek Tragedy and Philosophy* (Cambridge: Cambridge University Press, 1986), p. 14, and "'Finely Aware and Richly Responsible,'" p. 527.

5. I wish to thank Karsten Harries for first bringing to my attention the Western philosophical tradition's emphasis on the "ethics of satisfaction."

6. Nussbaum, *Fragility of Goodness*, pp. 2–5.

7. See Harold S. Powers, "India," in *The New Grove Dictionary of Music and Musicians*, ed. Stanley Sadie (New York: Macmillan, 1980), vol. 9, pp. 102–5, 112–13, 117–22.

8. Leonard B. Meyer, *Emotion and Meaning in Music* (Chicago: University of Chicago Press, 1956), pp. 64–73.

9. Thus, even if one restricts "aesthetic appreciation" of music to the intellectual comprehension of "tonally moving forms," one can still find in musical experience parallels to what is involved in navigating our ethical lives.

10. Victor Zuckerkandl, *Sound and Symbol: Music and the External World*, trans. Willard R. Trask, Bollingen Series XLIV (Princeton: Princeton University Press, 1956), p. 231.

11. Even in nonteleological music, the listener makes sense of the music only to the extent that he or she is oriented within it. In some cases, orientation may amount to a recognition that one is experiencing a suggestion of "suspended time." See Lewis Rowell, *Thinking about Music: An Introduction to the Philosophy of Music* (Amherst: University of Massachusetts Press, 1983), pp. 171–72.

12. Arthur Schopenhauer, *The World as Will and Representation*, trans. E. F. J. Payne (New York: Dover, 1969), vol. I, pp. 60–61.

13. Slight deviations of this sort that are mechanically detectable but too slight to be recognized by the ear would, of course, differentiate one performance

from another. But such a high degree of similarity between two performances is an analytic invention; in fact, no two actual performances are so similar to one another.

14. See, for example, Roman Ingarden, *The Work of Music and the Problem of Its Identity*, trans. Adam Czerniawski, ed. Jean G. Harrell (Berkeley and Los Angeles: University of California Press, 1986), pp. 13–14.

15. See Meyer, *Emotion and Meaning in Music*, pp. 77–79.

16. See Søren Kierkegaard, *Either/Or*, vol. II, trans. Walter Lowrie (Princeton: Princeton University Press, 1959), pp. 170ff., 263. While Kierkegaard contrasts ethical choice with "aesthetic" flirtation with one lifestyle after another, he recognizes an aesthetic moment in the life he extols as the only ultimately meaningful life, the "religious" life.

17. Milan Kundera, *The Unbearable Lightness of Being*, trans. Michael Henry Heim (New York: Harper and Row, 1984), pp. 208–9. Cf. Kierkegaard, *Either/Or*, vol. II, p. 145, where Kierkegaard's narrator defends marriage on the ground that erotic memory enhances the eroticism of life.

18. Kundera, *Unbearable Lightness of Being*, pp. 77–78.

19. Cf. ibid., pp. 31–35, where Kundera's narrator explains his notion of aesthetic necessity in one's life by using the image of the final movement of Beethoven's last string quartet. See also ibid., p. 52: "human lives . . . are composed like music. Guided by his sense of beauty, an individual transforms a fortuitous occurrence (Beethoven's music, death under a train) into a motif, which then assumes a permanent place in the composition of the individual's life."

20. Ingarden, *The Work of Music*, pp. 66–67.

21. See Herbert Fingarette, *Confucius: The Secular as Sacred* (New York: Harper and Row, 1972), esp. pp. 9–10, 49–56. Significantly, Fingarette employs a musical model to discuss sincerity in behavior (see ibid., pp. 53–54).

22. Cf. Friedrich Nietzsche, *The Gay Science, with a Prelude of Rhymes and an Appendix of Songs*, trans. Walter Kaufmann (New York: Random House, 1974), sec. 334, p. 262: "*One must learn to love.*—This is what happens to us in music: First one has to *learn* to *hear* a figure and melody at all, to detect and distinguish it, to isolate it and delimit it as a separate life. Then it requires some exertion and good will to *tolerate* it in spite of its strangeness, to be patient with its appearance and expression, and kindhearted about its oddity. Finally there comes a moment when we are *used* to it, when we wait for it, when we sense that we should miss it if it were missing; and now it continues to compel and enchant us relentlessly until we have become its humble and enraptured lovers who desire nothing better from the world than it and only it. But that is what happens to us not only in music. That is how we have *learned to love* all things that we now love. In the end we are always rewarded for our good will, our patience, fairmindedness, and gentleness with what is strange; gradually, it sheds its veil and turns out

to be a new and indescribable beauty. That is its *thanks* for our hospitality. Even those who love themselves will have learned it in this way; for there is no other way. Love, too, has to be learned."

23. Cf. William Gass, "The Case of the Obliging Stranger," *Philosophical Review* 66 (1957): 193–204.

24. My thanks to Dionisio Escobedo for suggesting this idea to me.

Bibliography

Adorno, Theodor W. *Introduction to the Sociology of Music*. Translated by E. B. Ashton. New York: Continuum, 1976.

Alperson, Philip. "'Musical Time' and Music as an 'Art of Time.'" *Journal of Aesthetics and Art Criticism* 38/4 (Summer 1980): 407–17.

————. "On Musical Improvisation." *Journal of Aesthetics and Art Criticism* 41/1 (Fall 1974): 17–29.

————, ed. *What Is Music? An Introduction to the Philosophy of Music*. New York: Haven, 1988.

Ames, Van Meter. "What Is Music?" *Journal of Aesthetics and Art Criticism* 26/2 (Winter 1967): 241–49.

Anderson, James C. "Musical Identity." *Journal of Aesthetics and Art Criticism* 40/3 (Spring 1982): 285–92.

————. "Musical Kinds." *British Journal of Aesthetics* 25/1 (Winter 1985): 43–49.

Apel, Willi, ed. *Harvard Dictionary of Music*. 2d ed., rev. Cambridge: Harvard University Press, 1972.

Aristotle. *The Basic Works of Aristotle*. Edited by Richard McKeon. New York: Random House, 1941.

Attali, Jacques. *Noise: The Political Economy of Music*. Translated by Brian Massumi. Minneapolis: University of Minnesota Press, 1985.

Auerbach, Alan David. *The Ideas of Richard Wagner: An Examination and Analysis of His Major Aesthetic, Political, Economic, Social, and Religious Thoughts*. Rev. ed. Lanham, Md.: University Press of America, 1988.

Backer, Thomas E., and Manson, Eddy Lawrence. "In the Key of Feeling." *Human Behavior* 7/2 (February 1978) 63–69.

Berliner, Paul. *The Soul of Mbira*. Berkeley and Los Angeles: University of California Press, 1978.

Binkley, Timothy. "Langer's Logical and Ontological Modes." *Journal of Aesthetics and Art Criticism* 28/4 (Summer 1970): 455–64.

Blacking, John. *How Musical Is Man?* Seattle: University of Washington Press, 1973.

Bloch, Ernst. *Essays on the Philosophy of Music*. Translated by Peter Palmer. Cambridge: Cambridge University Press, 1985.

Bloom, Allan. *The Closing of the American Mind*. New York: Simon and Schuster, 1987.

Bogan, James. "Finding an Audience." *Pragmatics* 1/2 (1987): 35–65.

Broeckx, Jan L. *Contemporary Views on Musical Style and Aesthetics.* Antwerp: Metropolis, 1979.

Budd, Malcolm. "Motion and Emotion in Music: A Reply." *British Journal of Aesthetics* 27/1 (Winter 1987): 31–34.

————. *Music and the Emotions: The Philosophical Theories.* London: Routledge and Kegan Paul, 1985.

Bullough, Edward. "'Psychical Distance' as a Factor in Art and as an Aesthetic Principle." *British Journal of Psychology* 5 (1912–13): 87–118.

Burke, Kenneth. "On Form." In *Esthetics Contemporary.* Edited by Richard Kostelanetz. Buffalo: Prometheus, 1978.

Busoni, Ferruccio. *The Essence of Music and Other Essays.* Translated by Rosamond Ley. New York: Dover, 1957.

Callen, Donald. "The Sentiment in Musical Sensibility." *Journal of Aesthetics and Art Criticism* 40/4 (Summer 1982): 381–93.

————. "Transfiguring Emotions in Music." *Grazer Philosophische Studien* 19 (1983): 69–91.

Carrier, David. "Interpreting Musical Performances." *The Monist* 66/2 (April 1983): 202–12.

Cazden, Norman. "Musical Consonance and Dissonance: A Cultural Criterion." *Journal of Aesthetics and Art Criticism* 4/1 (September 1945): 3–11.

Chan, Wing-tsit, ed. and trans. *A Source Book in Chinese Philosophy.* Princeton: Princeton University Press, 1963.

Chaudhury, Pravas Jivan. "The Aesthetic Attitude in Indian Aesthetics." *Journal of Aesthetics and Art Criticism* 24/1 (Fall 1965): 145–49.

Clark, Kenneth. *The Nude: A Study in Ideal Form.* Bollingen Series XXXV/2. Princeton: Princeton University Press, 1956.

Clifton, Thomas. "Music as Constituted Object." *Music and Man* 2/1–2 (1976): 73–98.

————. *Music as Heard: A Study in Applied Phenomenology.* New Haven: Yale University Press, 1983.

Cohen, Ted, and Guyer, Paul, eds. *Essays in Kant's Aesthetics.* Chicago: University of Chicago Press, 1982.

Coleman, Francis X. T. *The Harmony of Reason: A Study in Kant's Aesthetics.* Pittsburgh: University of Pittsburgh Press, 1974.

Cone, Edward. "Music and Form." In *What Is Music?* Edited by Philip Alperson. New York: Haven, 1988.

Cooke, Deryck. *The Languages of Music.* London: Oxford University Press, 1959.

Copland, Aaron. *Music and Imagination.* New York: New American Library, 1952.

Cox, Renée. "Are Musical Works Discovered?" *Journal of Aesthetics and Art Criticism* 43/4 (Summer 1985): 367–74.

Crawford, Donald W. *Kant's Aesthetic Theory.* Madison: University of Wisconsin Press, 1974.

Culver, Charles A. *Musical Acoustics*. Philadelphia: Blakiston, 1941.

Dahlhaus, Carl. *The Esthetics of Music*. Translated by William Austin. Cambridge: Cambridge University Press, 1982.

Davies, Stephen. "Authenticity in Musical Performance." *British Journal of Aesthetics* 27/1 (Winter 1987): 39–50.

———. "The Expression of Emotion in Music." *Mind* 89/353 (January 1980): 67–86.

Descartes, René. *Compendium of Music*. Translated by Walter Robert. Rome: American Institute of Musicology, 1961.

Dewey, John. *Art as Experience*. Abridged in *Philosophies of Art and Beauty*. Edited by Albert Hofstadter and Richard Kuhns. Chicago: University of Chicago Press, 1964.

Dipert, Randall R. "Types and Tokens: A Reply to Sharpe." *Mind* 89 (1980): 587–88.

Ellis, Catherine J. *Aboriginal Music: Education for Living*. St. Lucia: University of Queensland Press, 1985.

Epperson, Gordon. *The Musical Symbol: A Study of the Philosophical Theory of Music*. Ames: Iowa State University Press, 1967.

Farah, Wanda Therese. "The Principle of Counterpoint and Its Expression in Music, Dance, and Cinema." Ph.D. dissertation, University of Texas at Austin, 1985.

Feld, Steven. "Aesthetics as Iconicity of Style (uptown title), or (downtown title) 'Lift-Up-Over-Sounding': Getting into the Kaluli Groove." *Yearbook for Traditional Music* 20 (1988): 74–113.

———. "Communication, Music, and Speech about Music." *Yearbook for Traditional Music* 16 (1984): 1–18.

———. "Linguistic Models in Ethnomusicology." *Journal of the Society for Ethnomusicology* 18 (1974): 197–217.

———. *Sound and Sentiment: Birds, Weeping, Poetics, and Song in Kaluli Expression*. Philadelphia: University of Pennsylvania Press, 1982.

———. "Sound Structure as Social Structure." *Ethnomusicology* 28/3 (September 1984): 383–409.

Ferguson, Donald N. *Music as Metaphor: The Elements of Expression*. Westport, Conn.: Greenwood, 1960.

Fingarette, Herbert. *Confucius: The Secular as Sacred*. New York: Harper and Row, 1972.

Finkelstein, Sidney. *How Music Expresses Ideas*. New York: International, 1970.

Gaboury, Placide, S.J. "Electronic Music: The Rift between Artist and Public." *Journal of Aesthetics and Art Criticism* 28/3 (Spring 1970): 345–53.

Gass, William. "The Case of the Obliging Stranger." *Philosophical Review* 66 (1957): 193–204.

Giddins, Gary. *Riding on a Blue Note: Jazz and American Pop*. New York: Oxford University Press, 1981.

Goehr, Lydia. "Being True to the Work." *Journal of Aesthetics and Art Criticism* 47/1 (Winter 1989): 55–67.

Goodman, Nelson. *Languages of Art.* Indianapolis: Hackett, 1976.

Goswamy, B. N. "Rasa: Delight of Reason." In *Essence of Indian Art.* San Francisco: Asian Art Museum of San Francisco, 1986.

Greene, Gordon K. "For Whom and Why Does the Composer Prepare a Score?" *Journal of Aesthetics and Art Criticism* 32/4 (Summer 1974): 503–7.

Grout, Donald Jay. *A History of Western Music.* Shorter ed., rev. New York: Norton, 1973.

Gurney, Edmund. *The Power of Sound.* London: Smith, Elder, 1880.

Guyer, Paul. *Kant and the Claims of Taste.* Cambridge: Harvard University Press, 1979.

Hagberg, Garry. "Music and Imagination." *Philosophy* 61 (October 1986): 513–17.

Hanslick, Eduard. *On the Musically Beautiful: A Contribution towards the Revision of the Aesthetics of Music.* Translated and edited by Geoffrey Payzant. Indianapolis: Hackett, 1986.

Harrell, Jean Gabbert. *Soundtracks: A Study of Auditory Perception, Memory and Valuation.* Buffalo: Prometheus, 1986.

Hartshorne, Charles. "Metaphysics Contributes to Ornithology." *Theoria to Theory* 13 (1979): 127–40.

Hegel, G. W. F. *Aesthetics.* Translated by T. M. Knox. 2 vols. Oxford: Oxford University Press, 1975.

Herrigel, Eugen. *Zen in the Art of Archery.* Translated by R. F. C. Hull. New York: Random House, 1953.

Higgins, Kathleen. "Music in Confucian and Neo-Confucian Philosophy." *International Philosophical Quarterly* 20/4 (December 1980): 433–51.

———. "Nietzsche on Music." *Journal of the History of Ideas* 47/4 (1986): 663–72.

Hitchcock, H. Wiley, ed. *The Phonograph and Our Musical Life: Proceedings of a Centennial Conference, 7–10 December 1977.* I.S.A.M. Monograph no. 14. New York: Institute for Studies in American Music, Brooklyn College of the City University of New York, 1980.

Hutchinson, William. "The Problem of Universals in Music." *Music and Man* 2/3–4 (1978): 235–46.

Ingarden, Roman. *The Work of Music and the Problem of Its Identity.* Translated by Adam Czerniawski. Edited by Jean G. Harrell. Berkeley and Los Angeles: University of California Press, 1986.

Jones, LeRoi. *Black Music.* New York: Morrow, 1967.

Kant, Immanuel. *Critique of Judgment.* Translated by Werner S. Pluhar. Indianapolis: Hackett, 1987.

———. *Critique of Pure Reason.* Translated by Norman Kemp Smith. New York: Macmillan, 1961.

————. *Groundwork of the Metaphysics of Morals*. Translated by H. J. Paton. New York: Harper and Row, 1963.

Keene, Donald. "Japanese Aesthetics." *Philosophy East and West* 19 (July 1969): 297–326.

Keil, Charles M. H. "Motion and Feeling through Music." *Journal of Aesthetics and Art Criticism* 24/3 (Spring 1966): 337–50.

————. "Participatory Discrepancies and the Power of Music." *Cultural Anthropology* 2/3 (August 1987): 275–83.

————. *Tiv Songs*. Chicago: University of Chicago Press, 1979.

————. *Urban Blues*. Chicago: University of Chicago Press, 1966.

Kerman, Joseph. *Contemplating Music: Challenges to Musicology*. Cambridge: Harvard University Press, 1985.

Khatchadourian, Haig. "The Identity of a Work of Music—II." *Music and Man* 2/3–4 (1978): 223–33.

Kierkegaard, Søren. *Either/Or*. Vol. II. Translated by Walter Lowrie. Princeton: Princeton University Press, 1959.

Kingsbury, Henry. *Music, Talent, and Performance: A Conservatory Cultural System*. Philadelphia: Temple University Press, 1988.

Kivy, Peter. *The Corded Shell: Reflections on Musical Expression*. Princeton: Princeton University Press, 1980.

————. "How Music Moves." In *What Is Music?* Edited by Philip Alperson. New York: Haven, 1988.

————. *Osmin's Rage: Philosophical Reflections on Opera, Drama, and Text*. Princeton: Princeton University Press, 1988.

————. "Platonism in Music: A Kind of Defense." *Grazer Philosophische Studien* 19 (1983): 109–29.

————. "Something I've Always Wanted to Know about Hanslick." *Journal of Aesthetics and Art Criticism* 46/3 (Spring 1988): 413–17.

————. *Sound and Semblance: Reflections on Musical Representation*. Princeton: Princeton University Press, 1984.

Krantz, Steven C. "Metaphor in Music." *Journal of Aesthetics and Art Criticism* 45/4 (Summer 1987): 351–59.

Kuhns, Richard. "Music as a Representational Art." *British Journal of Aesthetics* 18/2 (Spring 1978): 120–25.

Kundera, Milan. *The Unbearable Lightness of Being*. Translated by Michael Henry Heim. New York: Harper and Row, 1984.

Langer, Susanne K. *Feeling and Form: A Theory of Art*. New York: Scribner, 1953.

————. *Philosophy in a New Key: A Study in the Symbolism of Reason, Rite, and Art*. 3d ed. Cambridge: Harvard University Press, 1957.

Laszlo, Ervin. "Affect and Expression in Music." *Journal of Aesthetics and Art Criticism* 27/2 (Winter 1968): 131–34.

Leach, Edmund. *Political Systems of Highland Burma: A Study of Kachin Social Structure*. London: Athlone, 1977.

Lee, Vernon. "Varieties of Musical Experience." In *The Problems of Aesthetics*. Edited by Eliseo Vivas and Murray Krieger. New York: Rinehart, 1958.

Legge, James, trans. *Yo Ki* (Record of Music). In *The Sacred Books of China*. Translated by James Legge. P. IV: *The Li Ki*. Vol. XI–XLVI. Delhi: Motilal Banarsidass, 1968.

Lenneberg, Hans. "Johann Mattheson on Affect and Rhetoric in Music." *Journal of Music Theory* 2 (1958): 51–52.

Leppert, Richard, and McClary, Susan, eds. *Music and Society: The Politics of Composition, Performance and Reception*. Cambridge: Cambridge University Press, 1987.

Levinson, Jerrold. "Truth in Music." *Journal of Aesthetics and Art Criticism* 40/2 (Winter 1981): 131–44.

———. "What a Musical Work Is." *Journal of Philosophy* 77/1 (January 1980): 5–28.

Lewis, Richard, ed. *In Praise of Music*. New York: Orion, 1963.

Lippman, Edward A. *A Humanistic Philosophy of Music*. New York: New York University Press, 1977.

———, ed. *Musical Aesthetics: A Historical Reader*. Vol. I: *From Antiquity to the Eighteenth Century*. New York: Pendragon, 1986.

Lomax, Alan. *Folk Song Style and Culture*. Washington, D.C.: American Association for the Advancement of Science, 1968.

———. "Song Structure and Social Structure." In *Readings in Ethnomusicology*. Edited by David P. McAllester. New York: Johnson Reprints, 1971.

McAllester, David P. *Enemy Way Music: A Study of Social and Esthetic Values as Seen in Navaho Music*. Cambridge: Peabody Museum of American Archaeology and Ethnology, Harvard University, 1954.

McKechnie, Jean L., ed. *Webster's New Twentieth Century Dictionary of the English Language*. New York: Simon and Schuster, 1983.

Malm, William P. "On the Nature and Function of Symbolism in Western and Oriental Music." *Philosophy East and West* 19 (July 1969): 235–46.

———. "Practical Approaches to Japanese Music." In *Readings in Ethnomusicology*. Edited by David P. McAllester. New York: Johnson Reprints, 1971.

Margolis, Joseph. "On the Semiotics of Music." In *What Is Music?* Edited by Philip Alperson. New York: Haven, 1988.

Martin, Linda, and Segrave, Kerry. *Anti-Rock: The Opposition to Rock 'n' Roll*. Hamden, Conn.: Archon, 1988.

Maus, Fred Everett. "Music as Drama." *Music Theory Spectrum* 10 (Spring 1988): 56–73.

Meidner, Olga McDonald. "Motion and E-motion in Music." *British Journal of Aesthetics* 25/4 (Autumn 1985): 349–61.

Merriam, Alan P. *The Anthropology of Music*. Evanston: Northwestern University Press, 1964.

Mew, Peter. "The Expression of Emotion in Music." *British Journal of Aesthetics* 25/1 (Winter 1985): 33–42.

Meyer, Leonard B. *Emotion and Meaning in Music*. Chicago: University of Chicago Press, 1956.

————. *Music, the Arts, and Ideas: Patterns and Predictions in Twentieth-century Culture*. Chicago: University of Chicago Press, 1967.

Mill, John Stuart. *Utilitarianism*. Edited by Oskar Piest. Indianapolis: Bobbs-Merrill, 1957.

Miller, Ruth, ed. *BlackAmerican Literature, 1760–Present*. Beverly Hills, Calif.: Macmillan, 1971.

Nettl, Bruno. *The Study of Ethnomusicology: Twenty-nine Issues and Concepts*. Urbana: University of Illinois Press, 1983.

Newcomb, Anthony. "Sound and Feeling." *Critical Inquiry* 10 (June 1984): 614–43.

Newell, Robert. "Music and the Temporal Dilemma." *British Journal of Aesthetics* 18/4 (Fall 1978): 356–67.

Newman, Ernest. *The Unconscious Beethoven*. New York: Knopf, 1930.

Nietzsche, Friedrich. *The Birth of Tragedy and The Case of Wagner*. Translated by Walter Kaufmann. New York: Random House, 1967.

————. *The Gay Science, with a Prelude of Rhymes and an Appendix of Songs*. Translated by Walter Kaufmann. New York: Random House, 1974.

————. "On Music and Words" (Fragment, 1871). Translated by Maximilian A. Muegge. In *The Complete Works of Friedrich Nietzsche*. Edited by Oscar Levy. Vol. 2. London: Foulis, 1911.

————. *The Portable Nietzsche*. Translated by Walter Kaufmann. New York: Penguin, 1968.

Norris, Christopher C. "Music and Pure Thought: Outline of a Study." *British Journal of Aesthetics* 15/1 (Winter 1975): 50–58.

Nussbaum, Martha C. " 'Finely Aware and Richly Responsible': Moral Attention and the Moral Task of Literature." *Journal of Philosophy* 82/10 (October 1985): 516–29.

————. *The Fragility of Goodness: Luck and Ethics in Greek Tragedy and Philosophy*. Cambridge: Cambridge University Press, 1986.

Ostransky, Leroy. *The Anatomy of Jazz*. Seattle: University of Washington Press, 1960.

Payzant, Geoffrey. "Hanslick, Sams, Gay, and 'Tönend Bewegte Formen.' " *Journal of Aesthetics and Art Criticism* 40/1 (Fall 1981): 41–48.

Perris, Arnold. *Music as Propaganda: Art to Persuade, Art to Control*. Westport, Conn.: Greenwood, 1985.

Pincoffs, Edmund L. *Quandaries and Virtues: Against Reductivism in Ethics*. Lawrence: University Press of Kansas, 1986.

Plato. *The Collected Dialogues*. Edited by Edith Hamilton and Huntington Cairns. Bollingen Series LXXI. Princeton: Princeton University Press, 1961.

Price, Kingsley. "What Is a Piece of Music?" *British Journal of Aesthetics* 22/9 (Fall 1982): 331–35.

Qureshi, Regula Burckhardt. "Qawwali: Making the Music Happen in the Sufi Assembly." *Asian Music* 18/2 (Spring/Summer 1987): 118–57.

Putman, Daniel A. "Music and the Metaphor of Touch." *Journal of Aesthetics and Art Criticism* 44/1 (Fall 1985): 59–66.

Radcliffe-Brown, A. R. *The Andaman Islanders*. Glencoe, Ill.: Free Press, 1948.

———. *Structure and Function in Primitive Society*. Glencoe, Ill.: Free Press, 1952.

Raffman, Diana. "Toward a Cognitive Theory of Musical Ineffability." *Review of Metaphysics* 61/4 (June 1988): 685–706.

Raffman, Rita Laplante. "Ludwig Wittgenstein's Concept of Family Resemblance and Contemporary Music." *Music and Man* 2/1–2 (1976): 117–23.

Randel, Don, ed. *The New Harvard Dictionary of Music*. Cambridge: Harvard University Press, 1986.

Reik, Theodor. *The Haunting Melody: Psychoanalytic Experiences in Life and Music*. New York: Da Capo, 1983.

Robinson, Jenefer. "Music as a Representational Art." In *What Is Music?* Edited by Philip Alperson. New York: Haven, 1988.

Rowell, Lewis. *Thinking about Music: An Introduction to the Philosophy of Music*. Amherst: University of Massachusetts Press, 1983.

———. "Thinking Time and Thinking about Time in Indian Music." *Communication and Cognition* 19/2 (1986): 229–40.

Sadie, Stanley, ed. *The New Grove Dictionary of Music and Musicians*. 20 vols. New York: Macmillan, 1980.

Savile, Anthony. *The Test of Time: An Essay in Philosophical Aesthetics*. Oxford: Clarendon Press, 1982.

Schaper, Eva. *Studies in Kant's Aesthetics*. Edinburgh: University Press of Scotland, 1979.

Schiller, Friedrich. *On the Aesthetic Education of Man, in a Series of Letters*. Translated by Reginald Snell. New York: Ungar, 1954.

Schönberg, Arnold. *Style and Idea*. New York: Philosophical Library, 1950.

Schonberg, Harold C. *The Lives of the Great Composers*. New York: Norton, 1970.

Schopenhauer, Arthur. *The World as Will and Representation*. 2 vols. Translated by E. F. J. Payne. Vol. I. New York: Dover, 1969.

Schueller, Herbert M. "Immanuel Kant and the Aesthetics of Music." *Journal of Aesthetics and Art Criticism* 14 (1955–56): 218–47.

Schutz, Alfred. "Making Music Together: A Study in Social Relationship." In *Symbolic Anthropology: A Reader in the Study of Symbols and Meanings*. Edited by Janet L. Dolgin, David S. Kemnitzer, and David M. Schneider. New York: Columbia University Press, 1977.

Scruton, Roger. *The Aesthetic Understanding: Essays in the Philosophy of Art and Culture.* Manchester: Carcanet, 1983.

——— . "Analytic Philosophy and the Meaning of Music." *Journal of Aesthetics and Art Criticism* 46, Special Issue (1987): 169–76.

——— . "Musical Understanding and Musical Culture." In *What Is Music?* Edited by Philip Alperson. New York: Haven, 1988.

——— . "Representation in Music." *Philosophy* 51/197 (July 1976): 273–87.

Seashore, Carl E. *Psychology of Music.* New York: Dover, 1938.

Sessions, Roger. *Questions about Music.* Cambridge: Harvard University Press, 1970.

Shepherd, John; Wirden, Phil; Vulliamy, Graham; and Wishart, Trevor. *Whose Music? A Sociology of Musical Languages.* New Brunswick: Transaction, 1977.

Singer, Peter. *The Expanding Circle: Ethics and Sociobiology.* New York: New American Library, 1981.

Slawek, Stephen M. "Popular *Kīrtan* in Benares: Some 'Great' Aspects of a Little Tradition." *Ethnomusicology* 32/2 (Spring/Summer 1988): 77–92.

Slonimsky, Nicolas. *Music Since 1900.* 4th ed. New York: Scribner, 1971.

Small, Christopher. *Music, Society, Education.* London: Calder, 1977.

Smith, F. J. "Music Theory and the History of Ideas." *Music and Man* 2/1–2 (1976): 125–49.

Sparshott, Francis. "Aesthetics of Music: Limits and Grounds." In *What Is Music?* Edited by Philip Alperson. New York: Haven, 1988.

Stravinsky, Igor, and Craft, Robert. *Memories and Commentaries.* Garden City, N.Y.: Doubleday, 1960.

Strunk, Oliver, ed. *Source Readings in Music History: Antiquity and the Middle Ages.* New York: Norton, 1965.

Subotnik, Rose Rosengard. "The Challenge of Contemporary Music." In *What Is Music?* Edited by Philip Alperson. New York: Haven, 1988.

Sudnow, David. *Ways of the Hand: The Organization of Improvised Conduct.* Cambridge: Harvard University Press, 1978.

Tallmadge, William H. "The Composer's Machine." *Journal of Aesthetics and Art Criticism* 19/3 (Spring 1961): 339–45.

Thampi, G. B. Mohna. " 'Rasa' as Aesthetic Experience." *Journal of Aesthetics and Art Criticism* 24/1 (Fall 1965): 76–80.

Thom, Paul. "The Corded Shell Strikes Back." *Grazer Philosophische Studien* 19 (1983): 93–108.

Thompson, R. F. *African Art and Motion.* Berkeley and Los Angeles: University of California Press, 1974.

Titon, Jeff Todd, ed. *Worlds of Music: An Introduction to the Music of the World's Peoples.* New York: Macmillan, 1984.

Trosset, Carol. "Welsh *Communitas* as Ideological Practice." *Ethos* 16/2 (June 1988): 66–79.

Tzu, Hsün. *Basic Writings*. Translated by Burton Watson. New York: Columbia University Press, 1964.

Wagner, Richard. "'Music of the Future.'" In *Three Wagner Essays*. Translated by Robert L. Jacobs. London: Eulenburg, 1979.

————. *Richard Wagner's Prose Works*. 8 vols. Translated and edited by William Ashton Ellis. Vol. 2. New York: Broude Brothers, 1893.

Walhout, Donald. "Discovery and Creation in Music." *Journal of Aesthetics and Art Criticism* 45/2 (Winter 1986): 193–95.

Walton, Kendall L. "What Is Abstract about the Art of Music?" *Journal of Aesthetics and Art Criticism* 46/3 (Spring 1988): 351–64.

Walton, Susan Pratt. *Mode in Javanese Music*. Monographs in International Studies, Southeast Asia Series, No. 79. Athens: Ohio University Press, 1987.

————. "Music of the Javanese Gamelan: Aesthetics and Mysticism." Paper delivered at the American Society for Aesthetics meeting, Vancouver, October 1988.

Webster, William E. "Music Is Not a 'Notational System.'" *Journal of Aesthetics and Art Criticism* 29/4 (Summer 1971): 489–97.

Weingartner, Rudolph H. "A Note on Kant's Artistic Interests." *Journal of Aesthetics and Art Criticism* 16 (1957–58): 261–62.

Werner, Eric. *Three Ages of Musical Thought: Essays on Ethics and Aesthetics*. New York: Da Capo, 1981.

Wier, Albert E., ed. *The Macmillan Encyclopedia of Music and Musicians*. New York: Macmillan, 1938.

Wollheim, Richard. *Art and Its Objects*. 2d ed. Cambridge: Cambridge University Press, 1980.

Wolterstorff, Nicholas. *Works and Worlds of Art*. Oxford: Clarendon Press, 1980.

Yu-Lan, Fung. *A History of Chinese Philosophy*. Translated by Derk Bodde. 2 vols. Princeton: Princeton University Press, 1953.

Zuckerkandl, Victor. *Sound and Symbol: Music and the External World*. Translated by Willard R. Trask. Bollingen Series XLIV. Princeton: Princeton University Press, 1956.

————. *Sound and Symbol*. Vol. II: *Man the Musician*. Translated by Norbert Guterman. Bollingen Series XLIV. Princeton: Princeton University Press, 1973.

: Index

absorption, 62, 148
acoustics, 14, 23–24
addiction, 185
Adorno, Theodor, 188
aesthetic: experience, 3, 5, 12, 15, 19–20, 21, 26–27, 44, 49–55, 56–57, 59–62, 63–64, 66, 67–80, 92–98, 100–101, 103–4, 107–8, 129, 131, 134–37, 138, 152, 157–58, 162–63, 189–90, 196, 204–5, 213n21, 224n63, 228n37, 232n9; stance, 49, 52, 55–57, 89, 97, 102, 107–8, 148, 159, 174. See also contemplation; disinterestedness; value
aesthetics, 2–4, 16–18, 20–21, 25–28, 47–80, 92–98, 116–17, 130, 134, 135–37, 139, 170, 190, 193, 195, 201–2, 204–5, 207n8
Affektenlehre, 25, 87, 106, 214n32
affirmation, 202
Africa, music of, 12, 14, 61, 71, 173–74, 178, 213n22
Afro-Pop, 2
aleatory music, 13–14, 109
amateurism, 9, 29, 172
ambivalence, 102
American Indians, 12, 14, 36, 154. See also Navajo; Sia
American music, 1, 8–9, 12, 17, 78, 150–51, 183, 185–88, 207n2, 231n37
analogical thinking, 9, 65, 66, 107. See also modeling, models
analysis, musical, 39, 45, 52, 58, 60, 69–70, 71–72, 74, 87, 104–5, 109–10, 117, 128, 133, 134–37,

170, 197–98. See also philosophy, field of
Anderson, James, 36, 211n53
Andrews, Julie, 33
animal sounds, 10, 11, 15, 147. See also birdsong; whalesong
animal spirits. See vital, spirits
anthropomorphism, 121–22, 154, 162, 226n16
Apel, Willi, 11
Apollonian, the, 183, 188–90
appreciation, 145, 160–63, 189. See also aesthetic, experience
Aristotle, 3, 58, 81–84, 87, 88, 121, 141, 142–45, 168, 169, 190, 192, 193, 217n4, 218nn7, 8
Armstrong, Louis, 179
art, 2, 11, 12, 47, 51, 52, 63, 67, 106–8, 124, 134, 152, 159, 177, 186–87, 192–93, 214n32, 216n55; agreeable, 63, 65; fine, 63, 66, 124, 149, 214n32; and hierarchy of arts, 66, 106–7, 214n32; and unity of arts theory, 89. See also literature; music; poetry; visual arts
articulation, 31, 43, 85, 86
artwork, 20, 22, 68. See also works, musical
assimilation, 175–77. See also minority groups; race relations
association, 6, 78, 94, 112–13, 117–19, 120–22, 136, 148, 177, 223n22
atomism, 68–69, 72, 77, 122, 132–33
Attali, Jacques, 171, 174, 230n27
attention, 48, 62, 77, 79–80, 91, 97, 107, 133, 147–48, 149, 193, 196–

attention (*continued*)
97, 198, 199–200, 225n3, 230n22
attitude, 8, 81, 222n15. *See also* emotion; outlook
Auber, D. F. E., 69
audience, 19, 83, 86, 123, 129, 138, 152, 153, 158–59, 171, 172
audience affiliation, 81, 129, 152–53
Augustine, Saint, 84–85, 142, 183
aural tradition (oral tradition), 43
autonomism, 4, 27–28, 139, 145–49
autonomy, 170–71
avant-garde music, 13, 109
awareness. *See* consciousness; self-awareness
awe, 126, 128, 149

Bach, C. P. E., 89, 90
Bach, Johann Sebastian, 10, 101, 148, 161, 208n9, 230n22
background/foreground, 77, 196
background music, 4, 10, 13, 63, 139, 150, 153, 227n22
balance, 5, 8, 168–69, 192, 194, 196–97, 200. *See also* harmony
Baptists, 183
Baraka, Amiri (LeRoi Jones), 178, 179, 180
Baroque period, 16–17, 22–25, 27, 218n6. *See also* seventeenth century; eighteenth century; Enlightenment
Basongye (tribe), 12
Batteaux, Charles, 88–89, 219n21
Beatles, 10
beauty, 26, 49–55, 58–59, 61–62, 67, 69, 71, 86, 94, 126, 128, 140, 157, 162–63, 202–3, 233nn19, 22; dependent, 52, 65; energizing, 189–90; free, 52, 63–65; melting, 189–90; musical, 93–94; sense of, 200–3, 233n19. *See also* aesthetic,

experience; response to music; symbol
Beethoven, Ludwig van, 10, 14, 38, 58, 69, 78, 95, 101, 113, 130, 208n9, 213n18, 230n22, 233n19
behavior, musical, 130–31
Bentham, Jeremy, 160
Berliner, Paul, 213n22
Berlioz, Hector, 95, 230n22
Berry, Chuck, 44
Binkley, Timothy, 217n60, 222n13
biology. *See* physiological effects, of music
birdsong, 10, 11, 15
Blackfoot, 14
Blacking, John, 10, 19, 34, 164, 207n8
Bley, Carla, 78
Bloch, Ernst, 230n27
Bloom, Allan, 1, 150, 186–87, 207n2
body, 1, 96, 103–4, 107, 117, 120, 129, 140–58, 160, 166, 173, 182, 187, 214n30, 221n37, 222nn14, 15. *See also* physiological effects, of music
Brahms, Johannes, 10
Broeckx, Jan, 13–14, 41, 58
Budd, Malcolm, 97–98, 102–5, 107, 219n20
Bugs Bunny, 112, 145
Bullough, Edward, 107–8
Burke, Kenneth, 47–58
Bush, Kate, 15
Byrne, David, 173

cadence, 24, 58
Cage, John, 10
Callen, Donald, 148
Calvin, John, 183
cantometrics, 172–73. *See also* Lomax, Alan
cantus firmus, 179–80
caring, 154–56, 171, 186, 192, 201–2

Carla Bley Band, 78
Carmichael, Stokely, 175–76
category, 78, 136. *See also* concept
Cazden, Norman, 165
celebration, 138–39, 151, 185–86, 195
Cendrar, Blaise, 179
censorship, 82
charm, 53, 54, 66, 68–69
Chaudhury, Pravas Jivan, 217n1
China, 1, 140, 160, 168, 182, 229n9. *See also* Confucius
choice, 6–8, 9, 141, 191–93, 233n16
chord, 68; changes, 43; identity, 23; inversion, 23; progression, 22–24, 170; root of, 23–24. *See also* harmony; intervals, musical; jazz, chart of
Christianity, 21, 84–85, 169, 183, 189
Cicero, 88
Clark, Kenneth, 47
classical: era, 58; music (Western), 1, 8, 13, 16, 23, 27, 45, 170, 171, 174, 188, 196, 202, 209n18, 227n18. *See also* eighteenth century; Enlightenment
closure, 13, 58, 109, 193
cognition, 50–51, 53–55, 149–50. *See also* intellect
cognitivism, 61, 102, 106, 119–28, 222n13
Coleman, Ornette, 180
Coltrane, John, 33, 178, 179, 181–82
common sense, 55, 75
communicability, 52, 53–55, 61
communication, 52, 54, 61, 77, 95, 132–34, 136, 150–51, 154, 157, 172–73, 222n15. *See also* discourse; emotion, communication of; language
community. *See* social; society
compensation, psychic, 189

competition, 155, 156–58. *See also* defensiveness
complexity, 6, 79–80, 82, 83, 169, 192–93. *See also* simplicity
composer, 22, 35–40, 55, 77, 89–92, 95, 119, 123, 131, 153–54, 172, 227n20
composition, 9, 20, 22, 25, 35–40, 41, 87. *See also* work, musical
computer music, 15, 33
concept, 49, 60, 61, 66, 67, 74, 189–99, 212n16, 216n55; determinate, 50–55, 75, 213n21; indeterminate, 213n21
concern. *See* caring
concert: hall, 16–17; rock, 150. *See also* ensemble
conformity, 12, 82
Confucius, 1, 140, 160, 168, 182, 229n9
Congo, 12
consciousness, 38–39, 86, 118–19, 155, 198. *See also* intellect; unconscious
conscious recognitions, 71–76, 77, 78, 104–5, 110, 210n43, 216n55
consonance, 22–23, 98, 165; imperfect, 22; perfect, 22. *See also* dissonance
contemplation, 12, 49, 50–57, 59–62, 67, 69, 76, 102, 104, 142–43, 148, 210n45. *See also* reflection
convention, 41, 43, 83, 87, 111, 120–21, 124–25, 223n29
Cooke, Deryck, 103, 222n15
cooperation, 173–82
counterpoint, 7, 22, 169, 173, 230n22
Cox, Renée, 39–40
creatability, 36–37
creationism, 35–40
creativity. *See* originality
cultivation. *See* education

Culver, Charles, 14
cyclical order, 164–70, 189, 191–97, 204–5

Dahlhaus, Carl, 27, 62, 75–76, 103, 210n35, 212n6, 214n33, 218n6, 219n20
dance, 14, 83, 86, 143, 146, 148, 149, 152, 183, 226n17; Andamanese, 152; inner, 146, 148, 169, 170
Davies, Stephen, 41, 130–31, 133, 148, 224n63
decision. See choice; moral
defensiveness, 147, 155, 156–58, 162, 163, 194
Descartes, René, 85–88
desire. See emotion; interest; sexuality
detachment. See disinterestedness
detail, 8, 104, 106, 133, 193, 199–203
deviation, structural, 111, 114, 115, 232n13
Dewey, John, 2, 107, 123–25, 177, 182, 222n19
Dionysian, the, 143, 183, 184–88
discourse, 51, 134, 137; about music, 45, 59, 69, 70, 71, 75, 209n18; technical, 45, 58, 69, 70, 71, 110, 134–37. See also emotion, talking about
discoverism, 28, 30–35, 37, 41, 44
disinterestedness, 6, 8, 49, 55–57, 89, 97, 102, 107–8, 148, 159, 174
Disney, Walt, 113
dissonance, 22–23, 60, 98, 144, 165, 169, 178, 228n5
distance, psychic. See disinterestedness
distraction, 16, 19, 56, 63, 79. See also attention
drama, 91. See also literature
Dreyfuss, Hubert, 192
Dvorak, Antonin, 101
dynamic, 37, 62, 104, 167, 204–5;

character of music, 32, 48, 62, 64, 67, 72, 82, 92–93, 99, 100–101, 103–6, 113, 121, 129–30, 131–32, 147, 221n6; forces, 33–34. See also emotion, dynamic character of

early music movement, 31–32. See also instruments, musical
ecstasy, 185–86. See also Dionysian
education: moral, 1, 66, 83, 109–10, 140–43, 185–86, 231n37; musical, 1, 59–60, 61, 70–72, 73–76, 77, 106–7, 110, 114, 140–41
ego, 158, 228n37
egoism, 155, 160
eighteenth century, 25, 58, 73, 84, 87–89, 90, 106, 219n21. See also Baroque period; Enlightenment
elements of music, 68–69, 106, 113, 172, 217n4, 222n14
elitism, 70–74, 77. See also snobbishness
Ellis, Catherine, 34
embellishment. See ornaments
emotion, 4, 6, 49, 72, 80–137, 199, 215nn42, 45; arousal theory of music and, 83, 84–88, 94, 108–19, 128–29, 214n32, 218nn7, 8, 219n20, 222nn14, 22; association with, 25, 82–83, 85–86, 87–88, 93, 112–14, 117, 120–22, 148–49, 223n29; in behavior, 121, 130–31, 132; -characteristics, 130–31, 133–34, 224n63; communication of, 73, 89–91, 92, 122, 123–26, 130–34, 219n21, 222n15; connection with music of, 5–6, 11, 12, 25–26, 48, 56–57, 61, 68–70, 76, 80–137, 141–42, 217nn1, 4, 218nn5, 7, 8, 219nn20, 21, 220n24, 224n63; definite, 8, 26, 70, 82, 92–93, 101, 105, 109, 126–27, 131–34; dynamic character of, 82, 101, 107, 121,

129–30, 132; elevated, 118–19; everyday, 91, 101, 107, 109, 121, 126–28; expansive, 103, 152, 161; expression theory of music and, 89–92, 94–96, 119–28, 220n24, 222n15, 224n63; feeling, as opposed to emotion, 104; feelings, as *Affektenlehre,* 87; imitation theory of music and, 82–84, 88–89, 91, 92–94, 100–108, 128, 131, 223n29; mirroring of, 128–31, 134; mood, as opposed to, 42, 129, 130, 151, 190; morphology of, 101–6; object of, 86, 93, 104, 110, 130; talking about, 69–70, 88, 131–37; vicarious, 128, 130–31; vocabulary of, 69–70, 92, 93, 99, 101, 110, 127, 131–34. *See also* association; discourse; expression; imitation; language; receptivity

emotional sensitivity, 5

empathy, 5, 108, 122, 123, 125–26, 127–28, 130–31, 132–34, 156–63, 174, 188

empirical evidence, 73, 108, 111–12

encounter, 9, 33–34, 153–54. *See also* social, interaction

energy, 47, 120. *See also* vital, drive

engagement, with music, 19, 33, 57, 135–37, 143, 148, 174, 225n3. *See also* participation

enharmonic equivalents, 24

Enlightenment, 73, 89–91. *See also* Baroque period; eighteenth century

ensemble, 11, 115–16, 153, 172–74, 178–82

environment. *See* world, external

Epperson, Gordon, 76

ethics: capacities of value for, 139–40, 156–63; definition of, 7–8; philosophical, 6–8, 191–205, 232n5

ethnomusicology, 4, 6, 10–16, 34–35, 115–16, 117, 170–71, 177, 207n8

ethos, 8, 90

etiquette, 203, 204. *See also* convention; norms, social

etymology, 11

Euler, Leonard, 53–54, 65

excitement, 171. *See also* sexuality

expectation, 18, 31, 57, 110–11, 129–31, 167, 223n30. *See also* preparatory set

experience, 16, 21, 56–57, 73, 103, 114, 196, 200, 203, 207n8. *See also* aesthetic, experience

expertise, 71–72, 73. *See also* education

expression, 11, 114, 119–28, 131, 134, 154, 180–82, 222n15, 224n63. *See also* emotion

expressionism, 89–92, 119, 220n24

expressive, musically, 120–21, 122–26

expressiveness, 42, 90, 119–28, 131, 148. *See also* "human touch"

fade-out, 58

failure, 169, 197–99

"family resemblance," 31, 76

Farah, Wanda Therese, 230n22

Feld, Steven, 14–15, 77–79, 135–36, 164, 207n8, 211n65, 215n52

Ferguson, Donald, 139, 165–66

film music, 13

Fingarette, Herbert, 233n21

foreground. *See* background/foreground

form, 4, 6, 20, 25–28, 44–46, 47–80, 100–106, 108, 111, 164–90, 197, 212n2, 214n32; logical, 100–101; perfection of, 100–101; significant, 100–102. *See also* logic (in music)

formalism, 4–8, 20–21, 25–28, 30, 34, 44–46, 47–80, 107–8, 110, 207n8, 210n45

Four Moments. *See* Kant, Immanuel, Four Moments of

freedom, 52, 63, 65–66, 96–97, 141,
  179, 191. *See also* Kant, Immanuel,
  moral theory of
free play, 50–52, 54–57, 59–62, 63,
  67, 75, 76, 79
frequency, 64, 65
Freud, Sigmund, 158
friendship, 156–63
frivolity, 189–90. *See also* play
fulfillment. *See* pleasure; resolution
fusion, 9

Gabriel, Peter, 159
genius, 91
genre, 86
Gestalt, 72
Gestalt psychology, 109
Giddins, Gary, 179
glissando, 42
God, 161, 162, 182, 188. *See also*
  religious
Goebbels, Joseph Paul, 183
Goehr, Lydia, 208n9, 212n16
Goethe, J. W. von, 184
Gold Coast, 14. *See also* Africa,
  music of
good, the. *See* morality
good will, 180–81, 197, 204–5
Goodman, Nelson, 3
Gore, Tipper, 1, 183, 231n37
Goswamy, B. N., 138
Gould, Glenn, 29
grace, 1, 170, 204–5. *See also* move-
  ment
gratification. *See* pleasure; resolution
greatness. *See* value
Greek, ancient, 21, 82–84, 88, 106,
  140, 194; music, 83–84, 106,
  218n6; notation, 21
Gregorian chant, 13, 21
Gregory I, Pope, 21
Grout, Donald Jay, 213n18, 218n6,
  220n25

Gurney, Edmund, 219n20

Habermas, Jürgen, 192
habit, 8, 186, 200
Halévy, J. F. F., 69
Hanslick, Eduard, 4–5, 20, 26–27, 44,
  46, 48, 65, 67–80, 81, 90, 92–98,
  99, 101, 106, 107, 113, 130, 131–
  37, 141–43, 148, 155, 163, 183,
  209n31, 210n35, 212n2, 213n19,
  215nn39, 42, 45, 217n59, 218n5,
  220n24, 221nn37, 6, 225n66,
  227n20; influence of, 5, 48, 67, 81,
  92, 99, 101; and *On the Musically
  Beautiful*, 20, 67–70, 76, 92, 97
happiness, 7–8, 167, 184, 196, 202
harmony, 7, 31, 59, 66, 144, 205;
  chordal, 22–24, 170, 178; of human
  powers, 4, 5–6, 50–52, 54–55, 59–
  62, 80, 125, 141–45, 147, 149, 155,
  157, 174; in singing, 23; social, 7,
  8, 151–54, 170, 173–82. *See also*
  chord; social
Hartshorne, Charles, 15
Haydn, Franz Joseph, 15, 208n9,
  213n19
hearing, 11, 16, 20, 30, 32–35, 67. *See
  also* senses; sound
hearings (multiple), 72, 199–200
heavenly metal, 17
heavy metal, 17
Heine, Heinrich, 89
Heraclitus, 199
Herde, J. G., 89
Herrigel, Eugen, 169, 184
heterophony, 114–15. *See also* voice
hierarchy of the arts. *See* art
history, 40, 44–45, 58, 64–65, 67,
  139; of association of music and
  emotion, 5, 82–98; intellectual, 73
Hitler, Adolf, 183, 188
Holiday, Billie, 180
Howard, Vernon, 121, 224n51

Huber, Kurt, 221n6
"humanly organized sound," 9, 10, 15, 139
"human touch," 42. *See also* expressiveness
Hume, David, 49, 134
hymns, 12, 23

I Ching, 168. *See also* China; Confucius
ideal: moral, 49; musical, 42, 66. *See also* performance, ideals of
idealism, musical. *See* Platonism, musical
idealization, 19–20, 41–42, 162, 163, 219n21
ideas, 38–40, 66, 67, 68, 173; aesthetic, 66, 67; musical, 26, 31, 67, 74, 92–93, 153–54
identification, 128–31, 156, 161, 179–80
ideology, 186–87, 189–90
imagination, 160–63, 164–90, 201–2, 204; Kantian, 50–52, 54–55, 59–62, 66, 67; role of, in interpreting music, 6, 16, 19, 31, 48, 67, 77, 79, 93, 94, 164–90, 196. *See also* free play
imitation, 15, 82–84, 85, 88–89, 91, 92–94, 100–108, 131, 180, 219n21, 230n22
improvisation, 3, 13, 21–22, 41, 42, 43, 96, 178–80, 195
India: music of, 8, 60, 146, 195, 215n2; music theory of, 6, 146, 168, 217n1
individuality, 7, 85–86, 87, 109–10, 170–71, 173, 178–82, 189–90, 200–203
individualization, 118–19, 200–203. *See also* maturity; self
inflection. *See* articulation
Ingarden, Roman, 28, 208, 233n14

inner life, 89–91, 106, 130, 144, 146, 163, 221n6
instrumental music, 14, 52, 63, 64–65, 67, 88, 90, 120–21, 146, 210n38, 214n32, 218n6, 219n21
instruments, musical, 12, 14, 24, 27–28, 31–32, 42, 53, 56, 63, 86
integration. *See* harmony; race relations
intellect, role of, in music, 4–6, 32–33, 49–62, 64, 67, 69–72, 73–76, 84–85, 96–97, 102–3, 109–10, 117–18, 119–28, 141–42, 163, 210n45, 232n9
intellectualism, 4, 26–27, 43, 56, 62, 67, 69–70, 71–72, 73–74, 75–76, 122, 141
intelligible world. *See* noumenal world
interest, 49, 109, 160. *See also* disinterestedness
"interpretive moves," 77–79
intersubjectivity, 5, 9, 17–18, 49–52, 54–55, 56, 64, 68, 71–72, 73–76, 81, 85–86, 87–88, 92, 105, 133–37, 151–54, 158, 214nn30, 32, 218n8, 228n37
intervals, musical, 12, 22–25, 60, 82, 87, 103, 165, 222n15
intimacy, 145, 158, 162
intuition, 177, 192, 204; manifold of, 50, 57; sensible, 65
Iran, music of, 14–15
Islam, 14, 25–26, 183, 231n36. *See also* Qawwali; Sufi
isomorphism, 100–106, 107, 113, 120–22. *See also* pattern
Ivey, William, 227n22

Japan, music of, 15
Java, music of, 71, 115–16, 216. *See also* melody, inner
jazz, 12, 13, 27, 42, 43, 135, 169,

jazz (*continued*)
175–82; chart of, 43; solo in, 7,
169, 177–82; progressive, 175–82
Jefferson Starship, 186
Jones, LeRoi (Bakara, Amiri), 178,
179, 180
Joplin, Janis, 101
Joplin, Scott, 101
Josquin des Pres, 78, 159
joy, 81, 103, 130, 160–63, 167,
222n14, 225n65
Judaism, 183

Kaluli, music of, 15, 71, 135–36,
215n52
Kant, Immanuel, 4–5, 25–26, 46,
48–67, 68, 72–80, 86, 106–7, 141,
143, 147, 148, 155, 159, 160, 169–
70, 192, 195, 212n16, 213n21,
214nn30, 32, 33, 215n39, 216n55,
228n37; aesthetic theory of, 4,
25–26, 49–67, 68, 72–80, 159,
212n16, 213n21, 214n32; *Critique
of Judgment*, 49–67; *Critique of
Pure Reason*, 50, 214n33; difficulty
of, with music, 4, 25–26, 63–67;
favorite drinking song of, 64; Four
Moments of, 49–62; influence of,
on Hanslick, 75, 215n39; moral
theory of, 64, 65–67, 141, 143, 147,
155, 160, 169–70, 195
Keil, Charles, 43, 178
key, 24–25, 68, 78, 170. *See also*
mode; tonality
Khan, Ali Akbar, 172
Khrushchev, Nikita, 1, 207n3
Kierkegaard, Søren, 200–201,
233nn16, 17
King, Dr. Martin Luther, Jr., 176
Kivy, Peter, 28, 37–39, 43, 99, 119–
28, 211n53, 222n14, 224n47
Kohlberg, Lawrence, 192
Koran, 14, 183
Kundera, Milan, 200–203, 233n19

Langer, Susanne K., 99–108, 121–22,
165, 217n60, 220n24, 221n6
language, 29, 54, 100–102, 214n32;
inadequacy of, 66, 100–102, 136,
213n22; music and, 51, 69–70, 95,
100–102, 107, 132, 136–37; music
as, 12, 77, 92; music as natural
form of, 88, 92, 219n21, 222n15
Laws, 218n5
Leach, Edmund, 170
Lee, Spike, 226n17
leitmotifs, 25
Lenneberg, Hans, 222n14
Levinson, Jerrold, 21, 31, 36–37,
40–41
Lippman, Edward, 87, 209n34
Liszt, Franz, 95
literature, 64, 66, 159, 192–93. *See
also* poetry; texts
location, 78, 79, 136. *See also* performance, situation
logic (in music), 33, 68, 95, 100–101
Lomax, Alan, 34, 172–73
love, 201–2, 233n22

McClary, Susan, 171, 229n15
MacIntyre, Alasdair, 192
machines, 10, 15, 42, 120. *See also*
computer music; technology
magic, 96, 117, 153, 163, 186. *See also*
religious; ritual
major, 12, 103. *See also* key
Marceau, Marcel, 204
Margolis, Joseph, 223n37
Martin, Linda, 231n37
Marxism, 216
masculinity, 171, 187. *See also* sexuality
mathematics, 46, 53–54, 64, 65,
84–85, 214n33
Mattheson, Johann, 222n14
maturity, 118–19, 179, 180–82,
192, 200
meaning, musical, 16–17, 26, 33–

34, 38, 40, 68, 77–79, 100–108, 109–11, 117–19, 125, 131, 213n22; emotional accounts, 26, 70, 100–106; Hanslick's account of, 26–27, 213n19, 215nn42, 45. *See also* emotion; language

medieval period, 84–85, 112. *See also* history

melody, 84–85, 86, 114–16, 147, 198, 217n4; contour of, 21, 120–22; inner, 71, 115–16. *See also cantus firmus;* Java, music of

memory, 86, 121, 201–2, 233n17. *See also* poetic memory

Mendelssohn, Felix, 69

Menuhin, Yehudi, 172

Merriam, Alan, 12, 14, 151–52, 154, 225n1

Mersenne, Marin, 85

metaphor, 15, 34, 48, 58–59, 70, 76, 135–37, 164–90, 201. *See also* discourse; language

Meyer, Leonard B., 99, 108–19, 121–22, 129, 135, 165, 181, 213n17, 223nn29, 30, 37

Michael, George, 187

Michaelis, C. F., 75

Michelangelo, 36

Middle Ages. *See* medieval period

Mill, John Stuart, 155, 166–67

mind. *See* consciousness; idea; inner life; intellect, role of; spirituality; unconscious

minor, 12, 78, 103, 121. *See also* key

minority groups, 7, 174–82

mode, 82–83, 195, 217n4. *See also* scale

modeling, models, 6–7, 8, 18, 62, 191–205, 233n21

modulation, 24–25

mood. *See* attitude; emotion

moral: danger of music, 14, 84–85, 97, 141–42, 158, 167–68, 182–90, 194, 226n17, 231n37; dilemma, 6–

8, 191–94, 200; effects of music, 4, 67, 82–84, 96–97, 106–8, 140–90, 220n30; law, 8, 49, 64, 186, 203. *See also* choice

morality, 4, 49, 64, 65–67, 96–97. *See also* norms, social

motion. *See* dynamic

motivation, 5, 165–66, 176

Moussorgsky, Modest, 113, 230n22

Mozart, Wolfgang Amadeus, 79, 133, 161–62

Muses, 15

music: as category term, 4, 8–9, 16, 101; definition of, 4, 8–9, 10–20; "in itself," 4, 10–46; and musics, 9, 11, 12, 71, 172–74. *See also* behavior, musical

nationalism, 79, 220n25

natural kinds, 12–13

nature, 66, 91, 141

Navajo, 12, 14, 36

navigation, 168–70, 197, 232n9

necessity, 26, 49, 54–55, 68–69, 76, 92, 94–95, 203, 233n19. *See also* value

Neoplatonism, 85

Nero, 183

Nettl, Bruno, 11–16, 34, 174

Newcomb, Anthony, 224nn51, 54

Nietzsche, Friedrich, 143, 158, 170, 183, 186, 227n20, 233n22

Nigeria, 174. *See also* Africa, music of

nineteenth century. *See* Romantic era

noise. *See* sound, nonmusical

non-Western music, 71, 73, 78, 114–17, 172–74

norm-kind, 29, 36

norms, social, 12, 203–5. *See also* morality

notation, 3, 21–22, 40–44, 68–69, 77, 87, 104, 172. *See also* score

noumenal world, 65–66. *See also* supersensible

novelty, 196
Nussbaum, Martha C., 192, 194–95

objectification of music, 4, 20–28
objectivity, 18, 50, 68, 71, 73–76, 87,
    88, 92–94, 98, 113, 135, 153–54,
    219n21
Olatunji, Michael Babatunde, 173–74
ontology of music, 20–21, 28–46,
    199, 210n41
openness. *See* receptivity
oral tradition (aural tradition), 43
organic criteria of successful art, 53,
    57–59, 62, 69, 76
organization: of life, 133, 164–70,
    190, 204; of music, 20, 22–25,
    56, 112–13, 117. *See also* social,
    organization
originality, 37–38
ornaments, 23, 42, 84–85. *See also*
    passing tones
Osborne, Harold, 217n4
Ostransky, Leroy, 179, 181
outlook, 140–41. *See also* attitude

Pachelbel, 4
Papua New Guinea, 15, 71, 136. *See
    also* Kaluli, music of
Parker, Charlie, 180
participation, of listener, 12, 61, 173
particularity, 6, 8, 51, 128, 199–203,
    232n15. *See also* detail
passing tones, 23
passion. *See* emotion; sexuality
passivity, 150
pathological enjoyment, 26, 69–70,
    74, 78, 141, 143, 145, 148, 231n37.
    See also pleasure
pattern, 6–7, 10, 33, 37, 48, 60–
    61, 77–79, 87, 100–106, 111–12,
    164–90, 196–97. *See also* form
Payzant, Geoffrey, 75, 92, 215n39
peace, sense of, 159. *See also* emotion
pedantry, 197–99

Peirce, C. S., 28
perception, 27, 32–35, 53–54, 65, 76,
    104, 153–54, 210n45, 221n6. *See
    also* sensation
performance, 3, 9, 11, 19, 20–21, 28–
    32, 41–42, 95–96, 101, 127, 135,
    142–43, 153, 172, 179–80, 195,
    199–200, 203, 225n65; ideals of,
    31–32; live, 150, 158; situation
    (setting), 3, 16–18, 25, 81, 129–30,
    153–54, 172–74
performer, 3, 22, 31, 95–96, 135, 173,
    178, 180
personhood. *See* individuality; self
Phaedrus, 15
phenomenal world, 66
phenomenology, 28, 153–54, 207n8
philosophy, field of, 2–7, 16–18, 26,
    29, 67, 69, 81, 85, 92, 137, 166–67,
    195–205, 232n5. *See also* ethics,
    philosophical
phrase, musical, 24, 33
physiological effects, of music, 1, 4, 5,
    56, 58–59, 87, 96, 103–4, 107, 129,
    139, 140–56, 157, 158, 214n30,
    221n37, 222n15
Pincoffs, Edmund L., 191
Pindar, 194
Plato, 1, 15, 25–26, 28, 45–46, 67,
    81–84, 85, 104, 106, 140, 141,
    143–44, 182, 205, 217n4
Platonism, musical, 4, 20–21, 28–46,
    47, 210nn38, 45
play, 78–79. *See also* free play
pleasure, 6, 11, 43, 49–57, 61–62, 63,
    65, 67, 69–70, 71, 75, 82–83, 98,
    142–44, 152–53, 156–58, 160–63,
    165, 167, 174, 179, 181, 185–88,
    188–90, 195, 225n3; and pain, 63,
    98, 118–19, 167. *See also* aesthetic,
    experience
poetic memory, 201–2
Poetics, 87, 121. *See also* Aristotle
poetics, 87, 201–2

poetry, 27–28, 66–67, 83, 88, 187, 218n6. *See also* literature; texts

Politics, 82, 87, 218. *See also* Aristotle

polyphony, 15, 115. *See also* counterpoint; melody; voice, human

polythetic, 153–54

popular music, 1, 8, 9, 12, 13, 15, 17, 23, 27, 183, 185–88

Post, Emily, 203

precision, 3, 26, 42, 68–69, 71, 105–6, 134, 136, 215n45

preparatory set, 129–31. *See also* expectation

Price, Kingsley, 29

"primitive" music, 116–17

printing, musical, 22

propaganda, 188–90

psychiatry, 56–57

psychological effects, of music, 139, 140–56

purposiveness without a purpose, 49, 53–54, 57–59

Pygmy, 173. *See also* Africa, music of

Qawwali, 231nn36, 39. *See also* Sufi

Quakers, 183

quandary ethics, 191. *See also* ethics, philosophical

quarter-tones, 60. *See also* intervals, musical

Qureshi, Regula, 231n36

race relations, 7, 175–82. *See also* assimilation; minority groups

Radcliffe-Brown, A. R., 152, 170

Raffman, Diana, 213n22

rāga, 195

Rameau, Jean-Philippe, 23–24

Randel, Don, 11

receptivity, 5, 9, 20, 60, 69, 125–26, 130, 147, 157, 173, 194–95, 226n17

recorded music, 2, 9, 15, 29, 41, 72, 150–53, 158, 162–63, 190, 199, 227n22. *See also* technology

recreation, 82, 172. *See also* relaxation

Reed, Lou, 10, 159

reflection, 4, 6, 8, 19, 54, 62, 66, 78, 118–19, 177–82, 186–90, 191–205. *See also* contemplation

Reich, Steve, 58

relaxation, 142–43, 146, 167, 168, 173. *See also* resolution

religious, 34–35, 112, 160, 162, 186; function, of music, 4, 12, 16–17, 84–85, 138–39, 148, 151, 174, 182, 231n36; music, 13, 14, 21, 78, 148, 231n36. *See also* Gregorian chant; hymns

Renaissance, 22, 31, 87–89, 103

representation, 12, 92–94, 100–108, 221n37, 224n63, 226n16; in art, 52, 60, 100–108, 216n55; Kantian, 50–51, 54

Republic, 82, 83, 217n4. *See also* Plato

resolution, 7, 23, 33, 57, 58, 98, 107, 108–12, 116, 119, 146, 164–70, 175–82, 193–96, 200, 204. *See also* relaxation; tendencies; tension

response, to music, 6, 10, 11, 12, 18–19, 48, 59, 81–137, 138, 140–56, 204, 218n6, 222n15, 224n63, 228n5

revelation, 139–40, 170–82. *See also* truth

reverence, 161–62. *See also* awe; religious

rhetoric, 87, 96, 117

rhythm, 82–83, 87, 103, 120, 178, 186, 195, 214n33, 222n15

risk, 6, 181, 194–95. *See also* vulnerability

ritual, 117, 151, 152. *See also* magic; religious

Robinson, Jenefer, 224n54, 226n16

rock 'n' roll, 1, 8, 12, 183, 185–88, 207n2, 231n37; ideology of, 186–87; magazines, 12; videos, 188, 231n43

Rolling Stones, 10
Romantic era, 58, 73, 81, 90–91, 112
Romanticism, 37, 73, 90–91
Rousseau, Jean-Jacques, 27, 219nn20, 21
Rowell, Lewis, 10, 19, 20, 146, 227n18, 232n11
Roxy Music, 186
Ruben and the Jets, 186. See also Zappa, Frank

Salieri, Antonio, 159, 161
Sartre, Jean-Paul, 166, 191
satisfaction. See pleasure; resolution
scale, 24, 195, 217n4. See also mode; rāga
Schiller, Friedrich, 156–57, 189–90, 227n20
Schönberg, Arnold, 38
Schopenhauer, Arthur, 147, 155, 198–99, 220n28, 228n37
Schubart, Daniel, 89
Schubert, Franz, 148
Schueller, Herbert, 64, 67, 214
Schutz, Alfred, 153–54, 207n8
scientific aesthetics, 26, 68–69, 71–72, 73, 76, 79, 92, 217n59, 221n37
score, 3, 4, 11, 13, 20–21, 27, 28, 40–44, 45, 68–69, 77, 104, 199, 210n38, 222n22. See also notation; work, musical
Scruton, Roger, 10, 19, 146, 148, 171–72, 209n18, 216n53
Segrave, Kerry, 231n37
self, 5; choice of, 200–201; dissolution of, 119, 186; individual, 49, 64, 85, 87, 89–91, 96, 150–51; as intelligible, 89–90
self-abandonment, 185; -assertion, 150; -awareness, 118–19, 144–56, 184–85; -conception, 145–50; -control, 184–88; -esteem, 149–50, 187; -examination, 172–

74; -identity, 187; -indulgence, 145; -sufficiency, 194–95; -transcendence, 186
sensation, 26, 54, 61, 63, 66, 103, 154. See also perception
senses, 16, 33, 50, 53–54, 56–57, 67. See also hearing
sensuous character of music, 25–26, 49, 53, 55–57, 61, 64–70, 84–85, 182–83, 210n45, 214n30
sentiment. See emotion
separatism, 175–77
serialism, 104
seriousness, 189–90. See also frivolity
Sessions, Roger, 32–33
seventeenth century, 87–88, 106. See also Baroque period; Enlightenment
Sex Pistols, 10
sexuality, 1, 85, 171, 173–74, 182–83, 184–88, 207n2, 233n17
Shaffer, Peter, 159, 161
Shankar, Ravi, 169
sharing. See intersubjectivity; social
Shepherd, John, 170
Sia (tribe), 154
silence, 10
Simon and Garfunkel, 159
simplicity, 82, 84, 183, 193. See also complexity
sin. See moral, danger of music
sincerity, 233n21
singing, song, 12, 14–15, 35, 64, 83–85, 120–21, 144–45, 146–48, 161, 172, 219n21; inner, 148, 161, 227n20. See also spirituality; Sufi; voice, human
sixteenth century, 22, 31, 87–89, 103. See also Renaissance
snobbishness, 69–70, 148
social, 49, 149–56; cohesion, 4, 17–18, 151–54, 188–89; consensus, 115–16; ethics as, 8; interaction, 7,

8; music, as social phenomenon, 5, 9, 18, 46, 61, 63, 72–76, 78, 79, 86, 122, 129, 135–37, 150–63, 171–74; organization, 4, 6, 34–35, 171–82; roles, 159–60, 174. *See also* organization

society, 150–51, 154, 155, 170–74, 216n53

sociology of music, 117

Socrates, 15, 83–84

sound, 9, 10–11, 14–15, 19, 32–35, 107, 146–47; nonmusical, 14–15. *See also* "humanly organized sound"

Sparshott, Francis, 3, 12, 79, 146–47, 149–50, 216n53

Spencer, Herbert, 219n20

spirituality, 1, 2, 6, 18, 79–80, 82–84, 89–91, 145, 148, 184–88, 190

Spohr, Ludwig, 69

staff, musical, 21–22. *See also* notation

status of music, 14, 63–67, 68, 69–70

Stravinsky, Igor, 147, 226n17, 230n22

style, 18, 31, 35, 43, 69, 71, 81, 111, 114, 129–30, 170–74, 223n29

subject, cognitive, 50, 86. *See also* self, individual

subjective, 6, 9, 71, 74, 85, 89, 153–54; character of aesthetic experience, 49, 50, 53, 54, 64, 68, 78; universal, 50–52, 54–55, 64, 68, 70, 89. *See also* Kant, Immanuel

Subotnik, Rose Rosengard, 170–71

Sufi, 231. *See also* Qawwali

supersensible, 65–66. *See also* noumenal world

"swing," 31, 42, 43

symbol, 6, 9, 12, 68, 77–78, 79, 93–94, 98, 100–106, 108, 121, 124, 140, 143, 144; beauty as symbol of morality, 59, 65–66; discursive, 100; music as, 6; presentational, 100; unconsummated, 101, 105. *See also* Kant, Immanuel

syntactical relationships, 118, 222n22

"table-music," 63

tāla, 195

talent, musical, 12, 73, 161, 220n30

tape-music, 13

technology, 2, 9, 150–53. *See also* recorded music

teleology, 23, 53, 56, 109, 117, 181, 232n11

temperament, 24–25

temporal coloring, 203

temporality, 6–7, 62, 64, 75, 102, 146, 152–54, 164–70, 185–86, 189, 191–97, 205, 214n33

tendencies, 33–34, 57, 108–12, 116–17, 165. *See also* dynamic, forces; resolution; tension

tension, 6–7, 58, 98, 107, 119, 121, 144, 146, 164–70, 175–82, 193–96, 200, 204

texts: associated with music, 1, 17, 27–28, 67, 83, 84–85, 88, 90, 91, 120–21, 185–88, 218n6, 231n37; emotional, 83. *See also* literature; poetry

Thampi, G. B. Mohna, 229n9

timbre, 31, 43, 53, 56, 63, 68–69, 86

time, 62, 146, 152–54, 164–70, 185–86, 191–97, 214n33; change over course of, 43, 146; endurance through, 13, 21, 29–30, 31, 35–40, 41; image of, 102, 165; moment, musical, 128, 199–203; suspension of, 232n11

timing, 42, 185–86

tonality, 91, 103, 170

"tonally moving forms," 26, 220n24, 232n9. *See also* form; formalism; Hanslick, Eduard

Tormey, Alan, 119

Townshend, Pete, 101
tragic suffering, 118–19
training. *See* education
transcription, 43. *See also* score
transposition, 24
truth, 39, 115–16, 139
tuning, 42; problems in, 24, 31. *See also* temperament
Tun-yi, Chou, 140
twentieth century, 58, 91–92
type/token distinction, 28. *See also* Peirce, C. S.
Tzu, Hsün, 160, 228n36

uncertainty, 57, 109, 118–19, 181
unconscious, 25, 50, 78–79, 141, 184
understanding, 5, 19–20, 32–35, 45, 48, 119, 197, 198, 199, 213n22; Kantian, 50–52, 54–55, 59–62, 67, 102; musical, 10, 16, 59–62, 67, 75, 77, 110, 196, 209n18, 232n11. *See also* free play
uniqueness. *See* particularity
universal: human characteristics, 12, 73–74, 90, 214n33; human themes, 179–80
universality, 6, 49–55, 73, 87–88, 89–90, 159, 174, 179–80, 197, 198–203, 214n33, 220nn24, 25
universals, 29

value, 4, 34–35, 61, 154, 200–205; intrinsic, 61, 102; in music, 5, 48, 58–59, 71, 73, 78, 94–95, 108, 118–19, 154, 165, 170–74, 180–81, 195, 213n17, 215n52, 227n18; of music, 17–18, 19, 154, 174–82, 199
violence, 147, 184
virtue ethics, 191–92. *See also* ethics, philosophical
visual arts, 63, 66, 91
vital, 11, 195–96; drive, 43–44, 56, 86, 87; spirits, 25, 86, 87, 103. *See also* dynamic, character of music
vocal music. *See* singing, song
voice, human, 85, 120, 146–47. *See also* melody; singing, song
vulnerability, 163, 194–95. *See also* risk

Wagner, Richard, 25, 37, 73, 90–91, 125, 183, 219n20, 220n30
Walhout, Donald, 36, 211n53
Walkman, 17–18, 150–51
Walton, Kendall, 224nn54, 60
Walton, Susan Pratt, 115–16
Weingartner, Rudolf, 64
well-being, 155, 190
whalesong, 10, 15
White, Leslie, 154
Who, The, 101
Wile E. Coyote, 159
Wittgenstein, Ludwig, 31
Wollheim, Richard, 28
Wolterstorff, Nicholas, 28, 35, 41, 43, 210n41, 211n53
Woodstock, 150. *See also* concert, rock
words, and music. *See* discourse; language; literature; poetry; texts
work, musical, 3, 13, 18, 20–46, 57–59, 111, 124, 125, 202–3, 212n16, 223n29
world, external, 33–34, 91, 149, 151, 154, 159, 171, 174, 228n35

yoga, 168
Yu-Lan, Fung, 229n9

Zappa, Frank, 1, 12, 186, 187
Zen, 169
Zimbabwe, 61. *See also* Africa, music of
Zuckerkandl, Victor, 33–34, 37, 154, 167–68, 198, 207n8